PERKY PUPPETS

With A Purpose

A Complete Guide To Puppetry & Ventriloquism In Christian Ministry

MARY ROSE PEARSON

Gospel Publishing House
Springfield, Missouri

02-0677

© 1992 by Gospel Publishing House, Springfield, Missouri 65802-1894.

Cover and book design by Jonesy Studios.

Library of Congress Cataloging-in-Publication Data

Pearson, Mary Rose, 1921-
    Perky puppets with a purpose : a complete guide to puppetry and
ventriloquism in Christian ministry / Mary Rose Pearson.
        p.   cm.
    Includes bibliographical references and index.
    ISBN 0-88243-677-5
    1. Puppet theater in Christian education.   2. Puppet making.
3. Ventriloquism in Christian education.   4. Church work with
children.   I. Title.
BV1535.9.P8P43   1992
246'.7—dc20
                                                            91-42507

Printed in the United States of America

Table of Contents

Foreword

"Countless churches, groups and individuals have discovered that a handful of foam rubber, fake fur and cloth can become a ministry tool with eternal results" (*Puppets: Ministry Magic* by Dale and Liz VonSeggen, p. 5).

Puppetry and ventriloquism have long been part of my ministry to children. That handful of foam rubber, fake fur, and cloth has made the gospel come to life for countless boys, girls, teens, and adults. I have taught workshops on puppetry technique and the making of puppets. I have used puppets and ventriloquism to minister effectively in camps, crusades, churches, and schools.

Perky Puppets with a Purpose is written in a style that is both informative and fun. Mary Rose Pearson presents on the written page an expertise that only years of faithful study and puppet ministry could produce. She blends well a heart for children's ministry, theory of Christian puppetry, and a practitioner's experience. Her continuous encouragement toward excellence in puppet ministry should challenge every serious puppeteer.

Whether a beginner in ventriloquism and puppetry, or a seasoned trouper, you will find this book to be both practical and refreshing. Ideas, and the tools to see them become reality, abound in these pages. My only regret in the reading of this is that such a book was not available in 1975 when I began using puppets in ministry.

In ventriloquism, voicing, characterization, scripting, and basic skills are well covered. As a practicing ventriloquist, I found this portion of the book fresh and informative. The exercises that the author presents are useful to any student of this art.

The puppeteer in me devoured each instruction, each script, and each design laid out for the construction of puppet and stage. The patterns and instructions are easily followed and implemented.

Mary Rose Pearson's grasp of the basics of puppetry and its application in ministry is commendable. Pay particular attention to the portion that deals with the use of puppets in church ministry. This is as balanced an approach to puppets and spiritual things as I have ever read.

With this book, you are embarking on a journey in ministry using puppets and ventriloquism. Once read, this book will become a valued resource in your children's ministry library, consulted again and again as your ministry with puppets progresses.

Open these pages and get your hands into a ministry that will change your life and the lives of those you serve.

DICK GRUBER
CHILDREN'S MINISTRIES CONSULTANT

Preface

Do you want to light up the eyes of a child? Bring out a puppet. I have taught children for fifty years in church-related work, twenty-six of these in full-time evangelism. I have put on thousands of stage puppet plays and ventriloquial dialogues, and I've found there is nothing that matches puppetry for attracting children to the church services, for gaining and holding their attention, and for illustrating gospel truths. If properly presented, puppets are just as appealing to today's children as they were twenty-five years ago when I first began using them.

Many church workers who would like to use puppets are at a loss to know how to begin. They need fundamental instructions in the use of puppets and in how to obtain or make them. Others who are already using puppets want fresh ideas. Anyone involved with puppetry constantly needs new dialogues and plays.

There are also those who are interested in learning the art of ventriloquism.

Perky Puppets with a Purpose is designed to meet all of these desires, giving basic instruction for the beginning puppeteer and ideas and suggestions for the more advanced. Part One is full of suggestions and instructions for improving your puppetry skills. Part Two contains patterns and instructions for making both hard-head and mouth puppets. The dialogues in Part Three may be used by a ventriloquist alone, by two people (an interviewer outside a stage and a puppeteer who holds one or two puppets in a stage), or by one person operating one or two puppets and using prerecorded dialogue or live voices.

May this book be used of the Lord to help you to take up—or improve—puppetry skills in teaching God's Word to His glory and honor.

PART ONE
Puppetry

CHAPTER 1
The Wonderful World of Puppetry

Mrs. Pearson, I like yer pupit shos. They are good. Will you writ me back, please? From Josh

Mrs. Pearson, I like your puppets very much! I like your song, to. I read my Bible to times. Your big pupets are relly funy. Michael

These notes from two youngsters are typical of many I've received in my twenty-five years of using puppets in child evangelism. Although I communicate the gospel message by various other means (for example, object lessons, flannelgraph, flashcards, stories, songs), it is always the puppets that the children mention in their comments. I feel this is significant, a good proof that puppetry should have a place in my ministry, perhaps in yours too.

The Value of Puppets

Puppets are a great aid for teaching children. They are being used more and more in both secular and Christian education. I've found nothing to equal them in their appeal. Those little actors entertain. But at the same time they can teach lessons, create a desire to follow the teachings of Jesus in daily living, and help to bring about right changes in behavior.

My husband and I have traveled in evangelistic work for many years. While he ministers to teens and adults, I hold services for children. When I began to use puppets, I had planned to bring them out only occasionally in my program. But the children were greatly disappointed if the puppets didn't appear each service. So I started planning all my lessons to include them. They have proven to be a wonderful means for presenting God's Word by making the teachings more effective and enjoyable.

Puppets impersonate people. Even talking animal puppets mimic human personalities and qualities. So the actions and conversations of the puppets reveal our characteristics and traits. That is why children identify with them and learn from them; they see themselves. When I want to show the results of sinning, for instance, I portray a puppet doing something wrong and then getting into trouble for it.

Puppet dialogues do the same thing in a Bible lesson that a preacher's illustrations do in a sermon. (A "dialogue" is a routine with a planned sequence of conversation.) They clarify or emphasize a truth. By hearing and seeing puppets, children pay better attention to the lesson. They learn more rapidly and remember the lesson longer. Puppets can clinch a teaching in a child's mind. While children may only half listen to what a teacher says, they become fully attentive and interested when a puppet appears. Children have often told me they remember certain puppets or puppet dialogues I used in their church a year or more previously, and occasionally they say what they learned. Michael, in his note at the beginning of this chapter, said he had read his Bible two times. One of my puppet shows had emphasized daily Bible reading.

A **DIALOGUE** IS A ROUTINE WITH A PLANNED SEQUENCE OF CONVERSATION.

A **PUPPET PLAY** IS A STAGE DRAMATIZATION.

A **SPONTANEOUS CONVERSATION** IS A SHORT MONOLOGUE BY A PUPPET OR A CONVERSATION WITH A PUPPET THAT HAS NO SET SCRIPT.

Bashful children will sometimes respond to puppets when they won't have anything to do with the teacher. I have seen crying children get quiet when puppets appear. Those who are too shy to participate in any other way will often join in songs or other activities led by a puppet.

There are times when children themselves can be the puppeteers. This is an excellent means of holding their interest, increasing their knowledge, and developing their talents. Even young children can operate simple puppets.

Today's children are surrounded by visuals in the secular world; they hardly know how to pay attention without them. Furthermore, most of them have been raised on TV and are accustomed to being entertained. While church teachers can't compete with the sophistication of TV, they do need to provide appealing, attention-getting visual aids for attracting children to church and holding their interest in the lesson. Puppets help keep attention, make deep impressions, cause stories and truths to become real, and increase attendance.

One more thing about the value of puppets: They are great for adults, too. Although older people aren't normally interested in other visual aids used with children, most are intrigued by puppets. A ventriloquial dialogue, or sometimes even a puppet show, can be used when only adults are present. Most certainly a good puppet presentation can be well-accepted by an audience of mixed ages. Often adults have told me, "I think I enjoyed your program even more than the children did!"

Definitions: Puppetry, Puppets, Ventriloquism, and Puppeteers

PUPPETRY

Puppetry, as defined in this book, is the use of puppets of any kind, including their use with ventriloquism.

I do both ventriloquial dialogues and puppet plays in my programs and find they each make a definite contribution to my teaching. (A "puppet play" is a stage dramatization.) Puppetry has greatly helped me in attracting children to my meetings, in teaching them God's Word, and in bringing many to a saving knowledge of the Lord Jesus Christ. Perhaps I could have done as much without my little friends, but I doubt it. I wholeheartedly recommend puppetry as an excellent means of reaching and teaching children.

PUPPETS

One dictionary defines a puppet as a "small-scale figure (as of a person or animal) usually with a cloth body and hollow head that fits over and is moved by the hand." That is, to qualify as a puppet, the figure must be animated by the human hand—not automated by mechanisms. Indeed, it is this human motivation that seems to produce a breathing, thinking, speaking person from that cloth body and hollow head.

"Is it alive!" startled children have asked upon seeing me perform with one of my ventriloquist dummies ("vent" figures for short and which I consider puppets).

Stage puppets come in one of three classes, depending on how they are operated: (1) by strings, (2) by rods, or (3) directly by the hand. String puppets (marionettes) are not used much in churches, neither are rod puppets. They usually take large stages or platforms for their manipulation, and they are difficult to operate. Of the three, the hand puppet is the most popular in Christian education.

Besides such variations as shadow and finger puppets, hand puppets usually come in two types: (1) the completely cloth puppet that features a movable mouth (in a more sophisticated form most often seen on *Sesame Street*) and (2) the hardhead puppet that features head, body, and arm movements, but generally no mouth movement (commonly shown on *Mr. Rogers*). In England, the hardhead puppet is called a glove puppet. But in America the glove puppet is the movable-mouth puppet. To avoid confusion in this book, I will use the terms "hardhead puppet" and "mouth puppet."

I use both kinds of puppets, and I find advantages and disadvantages with each one. Hardhead puppets are best for action stories because two of your fingers are free to move their hands, grasping objects and touching things. They can also interact with other puppets in various ways. Although they move in conjunction with the words, their actions do not have to be synchronized with each syllable. These puppets can be made to look more like real people than the mouth puppets can. Also, it is easier to change their costumes during a show.

Mouth puppets, however, are more popular and prevalent today, perhaps because of their extensive use on TV. They are good in skits that use mostly conversation. These puppets are somewhat harder to operate, in that their mouth movements must be synchronized with the words. They can't grasp objects or do hand and arm movements since it takes all your fingers to move their mouths. So they have limited use in stories with much action.

The arms of mouth puppets can be moved if rods (stiff wires) are inserted in them, but this means that you can operate only one puppet at a time, with one hand in the mouth and the other hand operating the rod. You can manipulate the rod so that the puppet can wave, lead songs, cover its eyes or its mouth with its hands, shade its eyes to look far away, hug, shake hands with another puppet. With the rod attached to each of the puppet's hands, one hand can be moved at a time or both, with much practice. Moving two hands can allow the puppet to clap its hands. To hold two rods at once, hold them with your bottom three fingers and use your thumb and index finger to bring the hands together (see Figure 1). Keep the movements as natural as possible. Don't let a

PUPPETRY IS THE USE OF PUPPETS OF ANY KIND.

A **PUPPETEER** IS ONE WHO MANIPULATES PUPPETS AND WHO IS CONCEALED FROM THE AUDIENCE'S VIEW.

AN **INVERVIEWER** STANDS OUTSIDE THE STAGE AND ENGAGES THE PUPPETS BEHIND THE STAGE IN A DIALOGUE.

VENTRILOQUISM IS "SPEAKING IN SUCH A MANNER THAT THE VOICE APPEARS TO COME FROM SOME SOURCE OTHER THAN THE VOCAL ORGANS OF THE SPEAKER."

A **VENTRILOQUIST** CARRIES ON A CONVERSATION WITH A PUPPET, SPEAKING FOR IT WITHOUT FACIAL MOVEMENTS.

A **PUPPET** IS A SMALL-SCALE FIGURE WITH A CLOTH BODY AND A HOLLOW HEAD, ANIMATED BY THE HUMAN HAND.

A **VENT FIGURE** IS A PROFESSIONALLY-MADE DUMMY USED BY A VENTRILOQUIST.

A **MOUTH PUPPET** HAS A CLOTH BODY AND A MOVABLE MOUTH. THE WHOLE HAND IS USED TO MANIPULATE THE MOUTH.

A **HARDHEAD PUPPET** HAS A HARD HEAD AND FABRIC BODY. TWO FINGERS ARE FREE TO MOVE THE HANDS.

puppet's arms assume a stiff position and stay that way, and don't have fidgety, unnecessary movements that have no meaning.

A puppet need not look like a human being or an animal. Any inanimate object can be used for a desired emphasis. A talking toy could teach fair play; a dishtowel could encourage household chores. The Talking Bible, 'Lijah Light Bulb, and the offering envelopes explained in this book are examples.

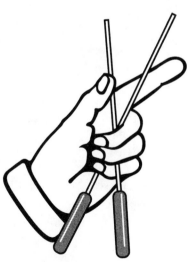

FIGURE 1: HOLDING TWO RODS

Although a professional dummy (bought at a great price) is generally thought of in connection with ventriloquism, almost any puppet with a movable mouth may be used. So a mouth puppet, if not too large, can also be used by a ventriloquist.

VENTRILOQUISM

One dictionary says ventriloquism is "the act, art, or practice of speaking in such a manner that the voice appears to come from some source other than the vocal organs of the speaker." Often people refer to this as throwing your voice, which is incorrect. An impression is created that it is; ventriloquism is an illusion.

With ventriloquism the audience sees two figures—a ventriloquist and his vent figure. Then a voice is heard which is not the same as that of the ventriloquist. Because the ventriloquist's mouth is not moving—and the figure's is—an illusion takes place: The onlookers think the sound is coming from the figure, when actually it is still coming from the ventriloquist's throat. This illusion happens because the human ear is a very poor judge of direction. We can't pinpoint the exact source of a sound by our ears alone; so our eyes are used to verify what our ears hear. If the ventriloquist has done a good job of making the figure seem real, the illusion is complete. It appears that the dummy has spoken.

Ventriloquism cleverly combines both hearing and sight. If you are seen moving your lips without producing a sound, you are a mime. But if you can produce sound without moving your lips, you are a ventriloquist. All you need is a mouth-like source (Señor Wences used only his bewigged hand, with thumb and forefinger movements) and the illusion is complete.

PUPPETEER

A puppeteer is one who manipulates puppets. Although strictly speaking a ventriloquist falls under this classification, I will use the term "puppeteer" to refer to those who operate puppets while concealed from the audience's view. "Ventriloquist" will be used for those who carry on a conversation with a puppet, speaking for it without facial movements. "Interviewer" will be used for the person who stands outside the stage and engages the puppets behind the stage in a dialogue. Almost anyone can become a puppeteer, and people of most ages can perform.

Teenagers and children often indicate they would like to become puppeteers. Eager teens can make excellent workers in a puppet ministry. Even if they do not actually put on the shows, they can help with making puppets, painting scenery, recording shows, etc. There are times when children can be puppeteers, but this should be allowed only under special circumstances. Most children do not have loud enough voices to be heard well nor the knowledge needed to keep a puppet show lively and interesting. When children do participate, their performance should be rehearsed with adult supervision. The exception to this would be the times when you have a spontaneous conversation

(A "spontaneous conversation" is a short monologue by a puppet or a conversation with a puppet that has no set script) in class, such as reviewing the lesson by letting the children act it out with the puppets.

Never let children play with the puppets. They could lose them, soil them, or damage them in some other way, hindering your use of them. Besides, the children will be more interested in the puppets if they have not become commonplace by much handling.

To do a good job a puppeteer must take the work seriously and spend time mastering the techniques. Certainly those who do church puppetry should not perform in a careless manner. To be a good Christian puppeteer takes time, effort, and a devotion to the cause of Christ. This should not scare off a beginner or bring despair to an already overworked teacher attempting to do some puppetry. There are ways to use puppets with very little time and effort. But I challenge you to be the best puppeteer you can with your talents, abilities, and amount of time available

Much work goes into the presentation of a good puppet show: an adequate, well-lighted stage with proper scenery; attractive, lively puppets; and an appropriate and enjoyable play that is easily heard and seen by the whole audience.

Getting ready for a show could involve the work of several people, but often is performed by one person— the puppeteer. The scenery, script, and puppets are the puppeteer's materials, just as canvas, brushes, and paints are the painter's. Once the stage, scenery, and puppets are made, however, they can last for years; and then a puppeteer need only concentrate on the productions themselves.

The manner in which the show is performed is the most important part of puppetry. Puppeteers Larry Engler and Carol Fijan, in their book *Making Puppets Come Alive*, say this: "The graphic and craft aspects of puppetry, while important, are only one element of a successful puppet performance. A beautiful set of puppets and a technically excellent stage are not enough to produce a successful puppet show unless they are used and brought to life by skilled performers" (p. 14).

We should be prepared to give the best performance possible, whether it is holding one small puppet and using a curtain as a makeshift stage, conversing with a ventriloquial figure, or putting on a complete play. As church workers, we are stewards of the gospel and are entrusted with precious souls. We are required to be faithful (1 Corinthians 4:1).

CHAPTER 2
You Can Become A Ventriloquist

"You mean I could be a ventriloquist? Isn't it necessary to have a specially-shaped mouth or some kind of mechanism to throw my voice?"

"Wouldn't I have to go to school to learn how to do it?"

"Don't you have to be born with a special talent?"

"Do you hold a device in your mouth?"

These are questions I often hear from people who are interested in becoming ventriloquists but who feel such an ability is not possible for them. If you are such a person, there is good news: You can become a ventriloquist. Anyone with normal speaking abilities can do it. No unique vocal mechanism is needed. College training is not a prerequisite. No special devices for the mouth are used.

Are you interested in ventriloquism? Congratulations! Perhaps the Lord is directing your interest in this art form that you might use it for His honor and glory and for the salvation of souls. Certainly there is a place for this medium, if rightly used, in presenting the gospel message. It is an effective, attention-getting means of sharing God's Word. Almost everyone, regardless of age, loves to see and hear a vent figure. As they watch and listen they receive a Bible teaching that they may remember better than they would a speech delivered on the same subject.

Advantages of Ventriloquism

Ventriloquism is a medium of communication that undeniably captures the attention and interest of all ages. It can put a new zest into teaching and can attract better attendance. It entertains while getting a message across.

To me the greatest advantage of all in using ventriloquism with children is that they identify with the vent figure, more so than with a stage puppet. It is a friend who has feelings and reactions much like their own. You can "teach" it that the lie it just told is a sin, and the children will learn something about their own lying. When you correct it for being selfish, the children can be taught about fair play. When your vent figure expresses some fear (such as being alone in the dark) your young audience can learn about trusting the Lord in times when they are afraid.

Since anything we do for the Lord should be done to the best of our ability, I hope that you will approach this subject with the determination to master it and to perform it in such a way as to bring glory to the Lord at all times.

Secrets of Ventriloquism

For years I'd heard of others who were gospel ventriloquists and was curious about how ventriloquism was done. But I'd never seriously considered using it in my work until after I'd been in full-time child evangelism for six years. I'd already been using stage puppets for four years and knew the tremendous attraction they were to the children and what excellent teaching could be done with puppets.

One day I had the flu and could not attend our campaign services. Lying in bed in the home of a church member, I looked in a nearby magazine rack for something to read and picked up a magazine. I saw an advertisement about ventriloquial figures. I copied the address and lay there thinking about beginning to use ventriloquism in my programs. The more I thought about it, the more I was impressed I was.

I didn't do any more about it at that time, though, because I couldn't afford an expensive professional dummy. Then someone told me the Sears and Roebuck Catalog had both a cheap vent figure and a record that explained ventriloquism. My problem was solved (but I'm not sure Sears could do the same for you these days). With the record and my new vent figure, Sunshine, I began learning how to be a ventriloquist. Two months later Sunshine was helping me give the gospel to children. I have always been glad I added this ability to my talents, and I'm confident of the Lord's leadership in this matter.

SECRETS OF VENTRILOQUISM

KNOWING THE PROPER WAY TO CONTROL LIP MOVEMENT

CONVINCING YOURSELF THAT YOUR VENT FIGURE IS A REAL PERSONALITY

SPENDING MUCH TIME IN PRACTICE

I know from experience that becoming a ventriloquist is not a complicated, difficult achievement. I learned the basics of it from a record and then began performing. Through the years I've studied books on the subject that went into greater detail, but added little to the knowledge and abilities I'd already acquired from the record and from my own practice.

What is the secret to becoming a good ventriloquist? I think there are three: (1) knowing the proper way to control lip movement, (2) convincing yourself that your vent figure is a real personality, and (3) spending much time in practice. All are vital. But the first two won't do you much good without the third. Robert H. Hill, in his excellent book *You Can Be a Ventriloquist*, says, "You see, there is only one real secret in ventriloquism, and that is *practice*" (p. 12).

The principles of ventriloquism are quite simple and can be learned quickly. They will be dealt with in the rest of this chapter and the next three. Making them work for you will depend greatly on how much time and effort you put into applying them. Being a good gospel ventriloquist takes dedication and a determination to continue until the art is mastered.

Understanding the Mechanics of Ventriloquism

Your voice, of course, plays a vital part in your performance in ventriloquism. So you first need to notice how you speak in normal conversation. Do you slur your words? Do you speak in a monotone? Do you drawl? Do you talk so fast that you stumble over words? Do people often have to ask you to repeat what you say?

You may need to make some improvements so that your every word is clear, crisp, and distinct before you try to speak as a ventriloquist.

The sounds you hear when you're talking are not the same sounds your listeners hear. They are catching your voice through the air in waves. What you hear is from inside your head, created from the vibrations of the bones. Have you ever heard your voice on a tape recorder? You were probably very surprised the first time you heard it. Usually people react with, "Do I sound like that?" Since you can't be an impartial judge of your own voice, stand before some friends or family members and read or speak. Ask them if they easily understand you.

Use a tape recorder for self-evaluation of your speech. Be critical and try to put yourself in your listener's place. Do you speak plainly enough for the average person to understand? If not, practice to improve. Don't forget, you must speak more loudly when in front of an audience, even with a microphone.

Understanding the mechanism that allows you to talk will help you learn how to speak ventriloquially. You don't need any technical stuff—just a few basic facts. (See Figure 2: Voice Mechanism.)

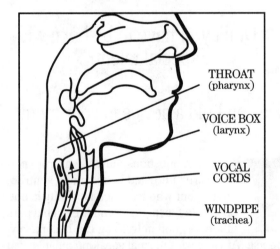

THROAT
(pharynx)

VOICE BOX
(larynx)

VOCAL
CORDS

WINDPIPE
(trachea)

FIGURE 2: VOICE MECHANISM

Inside the throat is the larynx, sometimes called the "voice box." It sits on top of your windpipe (trachea) much like a factory whistle on top of a steam stack. It is connected to the throat (pharynx) above and the windpipe below. Our every breath passes through the larynx, which is made up of a cartilage framework, shaped like a box, containing the two vocal cords, two muscles positioned horizontally between the voice box and the windpipe.

When a person talks or sings, air from the lungs rushes through the voice box, setting up vibrations. In breathing, our vocal cords are relaxed in the shape of a *V*. But in speaking, the cords are tightened, narrowing the V-like opening. Air is forced from the lungs through the larynx, along the throat, into the nasal passages and sinuses, to the mouth, and out as spoken words. As the air passes through the vocal cords, they are stretched and moved by the air. Speech sounds are also affected by the gums, tongue, teeth, and the roof of the mouth.

There are four parts to phonation, the making of human speech, which cause each person's voice to be unique. They are pitch, loudness, quality, and duration.

"Pitch" is highness or lowness of sound. The sound produced by your voice may be high-pitched, producing a high voice, or low-pitched, producing a low voice. Tightening your vocal cords produces a higher pitched sound. Women's vocal cords are shorter, so they usually have voices with a higher pitch than those of men. Boys and girls have nearly the same pitch in their voices. Boys' voice boxes grow larger as they mature, bringing about a lowering of the voice.

"Loudness" involves the intensity or volume of sound. To speak louder you must force more air between your vocal cords, which will produce more vibrations and cause the voice to be stronger. You need more breath to speak louder.

"Quality" comes from resonance—the reverberation, or little echoes, that follows the principal tone as it travels. Before the air leaves the windpipe, the sounds begin to reverberate in the chest, giving depth. The throat, the nose, and the sinus cavities are much like little amplifiers, raising the sound level by as much as twenty times. Resonating mainly from the chest usually results in a pleasing voice. Resonating mainly from other parts of your "sound system" results in a less than pleasing voice, for example, through the nose produces a twang.

"Duration" has to do with the length of time involved with the sounds we make. Speech that keeps its listeners' attention will be neither too fast nor too slow. If you speak too fast, your listeners may not be able to understand you. This is especially true when you are using your ventriloquial voice. If you speak too slowly, your audience will get bored. A good speaking rate varies from 120 to 160 words per minute. Pausing, occasionally speeding up or slowing down—pacing—keeps a speech interesting.

Record your voice on tape for evaluating its speed. Decide ahead of time what you will say, but don't read or memorize your speech. Most people read faster than they speak. Count the number of words spoken in several minutes and average them to discover if you need to improve the rate of your speech.

The mechanism that allows us to speak is a wonderful gift from God. He has made our voice well-organized and so much a part of us that we use our vocal cords, muscles, and lungs in all sorts of combinations without thinking about it. It will help, though, in learning ventriloquism to keep in mind these fundamentals involved in speech (and what can be changed about them).

Breathing Control for Ventriloquism

Since breathing is a very important part of our speaking mechanism, a ventriloquist needs to learn to breathe correctly. The proper way of speaking is to make good use of the diaphragm, which is the large, dome-shaped muscle that separates the chest from the abdomen. When we breathe deeply, the diaphragm moves downward, becoming flat and expanding the rib cage. This gives room for more air to enter the lungs. When we exhale, the diaphragm becomes dome-shaped again.

When you are having an ordinary conversation, your lungs can relax while the other person speaks. But when speaking ventriloquially, you speak both for yourself and your vent figure; so you need lots of air. This is not at all difficult, if you breathe correctly. You must be sure to breathe from your diaphragm and not your upper chest.

Take a couple of little tests to see if your breathing is from the right place.

🐾 Put your right hand flat on your chest about eight inches from your chin. Put your left hand flat against the bottom of your rib cage. With your mouth closed, breathe in gently through your nose, hold your breath a few seconds, and then exhale through your nose. If your right hand moved in toward your chest when you exhaled, you are breathing from your upper chest.

🐾 Sit up straight and relaxed in front of a mirror and breathe deeply. Watch your shoulders and your stomach. Notice them when you exhale. If your shoulders move up and down with your breath, you are not breathing from your diaphragm. If your stomach moves in and out, you are utilizing your air the way you should for correct speaking.

To help you breathe from your diaphragm and to strengthen its muscles, do the following exercises daily until you can speak with proper breath control. Hints for these exercises: head up; chest in; diaphragm tightened. Practice five or ten minutes, twice a day.

🐾 "Take a short sip of breath, and count aloud on a long single exhalation, as fast as you can. The first time, try for forty by tens: one, two, three, four, five, six, seven, eight, nine, ten, one, two, three, four, five, six, seven, eight, nine, twenty, etc." (*Speech Can Change Your Life*, by Dorothy Sarnoff, p. 40). Repeat this exercise daily, noticing that each time you can count a little farther, until you reach about 130.

"Inhale gently and raise your arms over your head. Hold your breath and slowly count '1-2-3-4-5.' Bring your arms down, and as you exhale whisper the sound 'aah'. . . . Hold the 'aah' for five beats. Breathe normally for a while and then repeat the exercise" (*Ventriloquism: Magic with Your Voice*, by George Schindler, p. 21). Each day thereafter try to increase the beats until you can reach fifteen to twenty. Also change the "aah" sound to "oo," "ee," and "oh."

🐦 "Take a deep breath and recite the alphabet slowly until you run out of breath. (Average students usually are able to say the alphabet one and a half times before running out of breath, if slowly and evenly said)" (*The Secrets of Ventriloquism*, by William Ogle, p. 16)

Are you a good candidate for ventriloquism? If you want to do it and are willing to put in the necessary time in practice you are. If you need to make some speech or breathing corrections, as just directed, work on these before you get into the next chapter. But don't get discouraged if you feel you can't do as well as someone else. If you can use this medium in your service for the Lord, and if you have prayed about it and are confident of the Lord's leadership, by all means proceed. You may be greatly surprised at how good a ventriloquist you can become.

What matters most is spreading the message of the gospel by whatever means we can. Clinton Detweiler, director of Maher Ventriloquist Studios, says in *More Than Just Words*, "The Holy Spirit has blessed many miserable presentations when they were given at the best of the vent's ability after prayerful preparation. DO pray and practice and prepare. DON'T expect a special blessing of the Holy Spirit to rescue you from your own laziness" (p. 49).

CHAPTER 3
The Art of Ventriloquism

Now you are ready for the phase of ventriloquism that probably interests you most—speaking without facial movements. The majority of the letters in the alphabet are very easy to pronounce without moving the lips. These make up what is called by ventriloquists the "simple alphabet." A few letters cannot be said in the normal manner without some movement. They have been named the "difficult alphabet." You must learn an alternate way of pronouncing these letters. This is done by letter substitution (which we will come to shortly).

The Position of the Mouth

Before using either of these alphabets, you must learn to position your mouth correctly. You want to become so accustomed to the mouth position that it will be automatic when you face an audience with your vent figure. Your lower jaw must be held still, but relaxed. Your mouth must be slightly open so that the sounds will be heard. Place yourself before a mirror and carefully observe as you do the following.

🐛 Rest your upper teeth very lightly on the lower lip. This is the position that is comfortable for me. However, some material suggests that you touch your teeth together lightly, not clenched. Other ventriloquists prefer parting the teeth about a quarter of an inch. I think it depends on the way your mouth is built. Try all three positions to see which way your jaws are most relaxed. In fact, some variation of these might be the best position for your mouth.

🐛 Say the following sounds as you try to determine which position is best for you: *ah, ay, ee, eye.*

🐛 Leave your tongue loose in your mouth. It should be allowed to travel freely inside, for it plays a valuable part in aiding you to pronounce your words. As you watch yourself in the mirror, move your tongue around in your mouth, touching the tip in various places, and

then drawing the tongue back toward your throat as far as possible. Keep your lips still.

🐛 Part your lips slightly in a natural position. Try smiling a little. You don't want a blank expression.

🐛 Keep your mouth as relaxed as possible. If you tighten up, you may get some unintentional movement, such as a quivering of your lips. This occasionally gave me trouble when I first began performing. It is the result of nervous tension. You can overcome the quivering by practice, by consciously relaxing your jaws, and by becoming more self-confident as you get used to doing your performances.

Putting all of the previous suggestions together, you should have the correct mouth position of the ventriloquist (which you should assume each time you practice the exercises in these lessons):

- jaws relaxed
- tongue loose
- lips slightly parted in a pleasant expression

The Simple Alphabet

Most of the letters in the alphabet require no movement of the lips for distinct articulation. In ventriloquial terms, such letters make up the simple, or easy, alphabet.

A C D E G H I J K L N O Q R S T U X Y Z

The vowels *o* and *u* may give you a little problem, but you do not need to move your lips in the shape of an *o* to say the letter. Practice saying it inside your mouth, with your tongue drawn back away from your teeth and lying at the bottom of your mouth. Pronounce the *u* by saying *ee-OO*, emphasizing the last syllable. It will sound like *you*. *Y* when pronounced alone is *oo-eye*, quickly blended. Watch in the mirror, assume the proper mouth position, and repeat each letter in the simple alphabet five times. Practice them until you can say them easily without a tense jaw or moving lips.

SIMPLE-WORDS LIST

Next, practice the following list of simple words. They should be easy for you to pronounce without lip movement. If the words beginning with *qu* bother you, slur a *k* and an *oo* and then add the rest of the word. For example, *quit* is pronounced *koo-it*. Say the list in order; then backwards; then across. Always watch for facial movement. Concentrate on words that give you trouble.

SAY	THING	DO	ACT	KING
SEE	CAT	HEAR	RIDE	GET
GO	TELL	CLOCK	TICK-TOCK	CAKE
DONE	TOY	SHARE	READ	LIKE
GOOD	CAN	SHAKE	DIN	NUTTY
TOE	SHE	TALK	EXCITE	DIG
HIS	DULL	CALLED	THICK	SO
DON	HER	LEE	GUN	DUST
HOIST	ISLE	TASTE	NEW	RAT
LAY	CITY	NICE	LIE	GATE
STEAK	QUAY	HOLD	ZOO	ILL
ZANY	OATS	LET	QUIT	NURSE
OUT	WRITE	ROOST	THIS	WRING
QUOTE	HOT	TALL	SHALL	STEW

SIMPLE SENTENCES

Now try the sentences that are listed below, watching in the mirror for lip movement. None of these words contain difficult letters. Say the sentences slowly and distinctly at first. Gradually increase your speed without sacrificing the enunciation of any letter. Give extra attention to sentences that give you trouble.

➤ Say the things I say and do the things I do.

➤ Eat like a king.

➤ See the cat and the kittens.

➤ Ride in that car to hear the lecture.

➤ Go quickly and get a good seat.

➤ Tell John that the clock says, "Tick-tock."

➤ The cake is done.

➤ Cut it in six slices and eat one slice.

➤ Share the toys.

➤ Read two sentences. Excellent!

➤ I like to do all the good I can.

The Difficult Alphabet

Once you have mastered the simple alphabet and have become accustomed to talking without moving your lips, you are ready to learn the difficult alphabet. These are the letters that are impossible to pronounce in the normal manner without facial movement:

B F M P V W

Looking in the mirror, say these letters the way you usually do. Notice all the movement. They can't be used when speaking ventriloquially. What then? Do we leave out words that contain them? There wouldn't be much we could say, would there? Your goal in ventriloquism is to be able to say anything at all that you wish to say—but without facial movement. This is accomplished by finding among the simple letters ones that sound a great deal like the difficult letters. We will substitute them for the difficult ones.

Not all ventriloquists agree on which substitutes are best. I am listing the ones I feel are best both for sound and usage. If you find another that suits you better, by all means use it.

<u>FOR</u>	<u>SAY</u>
B	D
F	ETH
M	N
P	T
V	THE
W	DUDDLE-EE-OO

At this point you must begin to train your mind to adjust to this new speech. For many years you have been pronouncing letters a certain way, and your mind automatically tells you to speak that way when you begin to talk. Now for the times when you will be using ventriloquism, you will want your mind to tell you which substitute letters to use for the difficult letters.

While you are consciously replacing a difficult letter with a simple one, you must be thinking the difficult letter. In this way you will be training your mind to help you in this new speech pattern. In other words, when you must use *b*, say *d*, but think *b*. For *f* use *eth*, but think *f*. Of course this will be distracting at first. But to continue this method of practice is very important. Eventually you will find yourself automatically saying the substitutes while thinking the original letters.

The following explanations of the difficult letters are in the order of easier to more difficult.

THE LETTER W

The letter *w* is never used in words the way we pronounce it as a letter: *double-you*. As you said the difficult alphabet, you pronounced it *duddle-ee-oo*. (When you get to the letter *b*, you will learn how to make this *d* substitution sound more convincing as a *b*.) But the sound of *w* in words is different.

Looking in the mirror, repeat the following sentence in your normal manner.

➤ We watched the waiter with the water.

Did you notice that you pursed your lips when using *w*, much as you do when saying *oo*? This sound can be made without moving your lips. Keep your lips still and say *oo* down inside your mouth. Now use the *oo* sound in place of *w*, drawing out each syllable separately and slowly.

➤ Oo-ee oo-atched the oo-aiter oo-ith the oo-ater.

When you can do this without lip movement, begin to blend the syllables together quickly, and you will have a smooth *w* sound. When using *w* and *h* together, say an h sound first: *hoo-air = where*. Push a little extra air through your lips as you blend these together. Then practice the following words and sentences using *w*. (The letter *y* is included in the lists to give you practice with it. If you have any trouble with it, use a quick little *e* at the beginning of the word.)

WHO	WHAT	WHEN	WHERE	WHY
SWEET	WILL	SWEAT	WEIGH	YELLOW
AWAY	SWAY	SWING	WE	YAWN
WATER	YOU	YET	WHICH	YES

➤ I wonder where you will wander.

➤ Why will you yawn when I talk but not when you talk?

➤ Yes, we want sweet water.

➤ I wish you would wear your yellow sweater when you swing.

➤ Watch the water where the white swan swims.

THE LETTER F

In saying the difficult alphabet, you have been using *eth* for *f*. This is a soft *th* as in *thin*, not a hard *th* as in *the*. Your normal way of pronouncing *f* is to brush your lower lip against your upper teeth. This takes movement.

Breathe in a bit and touch the tip of your tongue slightly against the lower inside part of your upper teeth. Blow softly through your lips as you pronounce the *th*. On some words you will find that the *th* can be barely audible, for the blowing alone will give the *f* sound.

Watch your mouth as you say in your normal speaking, *fine face*. Now repeat the words substituting a soft *th* for *f*: *thine thace*.

Now practice the following word and sentence lists for *f* until you are comfortable with saying them ventriloquially.

FILL	FALSE	FULL	INFANT	FUNNY
PHONY	FLOWER	FIRE	FEATHER	FRIENDS
DEAFEN	INFEST	FLUFFY	FAR	FOOLISH
DEFER	FOR	FLAKEY	FIELD	FLEA

➤ Fill it to the full with those funny, fluffy feathers.

➤ Those phony friends falsely accused Flossie.

➤ Floyd, fly to Florida and fix the freely flowing faucet.

➤ Find the fruit for Fred and Felicia.

➤ Unfurl the flag in the front of the foyer.

THE LETTER V

The letter *v* is similar to *f*. You will want to touch your tongue to the inside of your upper teeth. But this time you must push harder, getting the hard *th* sound, as in *the*. You will feel a bit of vibration in your tongue as you do so. Watch yourself in the mirror for lip control, think *v* but pronounce a hard *th*, and practice the following word and sentence lists.

VIVID	VERIFY	VINE	LOVELY	EVIL
VAST	VIRTUOUS	VERSE	VACATION	EVENT
VERY	VILLAIN	EVERY	VENTRILOQUIST	CAVE
VENDER	VOICE	EVENING	VIVACIOUS	EVOKE

➤ Can you verify that the vender is virtuous, or is he a villain?

➤ He is a very versatile ventriloquist.

➤ I love the vivid colors of every lovely violet.

➤ Every verse in God's Word is true.

➤ The values of the various vacant houses vary.

THE LETTER *M*

Looking in your mirror, say this sentence in your normal speaking manner.

➤ My mama makes much money.

The letter *m* is made by touching your lips together in a little humming sound. To make this sound without moving your lips, you substitute *n*. Now say the sentence.

➤ Ny nonna nakes nuch noney.

Repeat it again, but this time notice where the tip of your tongue touches. It is toward the front of the roof of your mouth, isn't it? Now put your tongue farther forward, up against your front teeth as you say *n*. Hold your tongue against your teeth for a brief moment as you add a little hum. Think *m* and say *n* in the above manner a number of times.

Now you are ready to repeat the sentence ventriloquially.

➤ My mama makes much money.

See how important the tongue is? In the same manner, practice these word and sentence lists. Remember to think *m* while saying *n*.

MAKE	ME	MONEY	MOST	MAMA
MUCH	MOTH	MIGHTY	MUSIC	MISTER
MIRACLES	MEMORY	MANTLE	MOUSE	MOON
MURMUR	MAT	MINIMAL	MANAGEMENT	
VENTRILOQUISM				

➤ My mama made me many milk shakes.
➤ Meet me at my mansion to make much money.
➤ The mule's mouth is mighty muddy.
➤ The missionary noticed many monkeys in ten minutes.
➤ My minister mentioned Nehemiah, Micah, Malachi, Matthew, and Mark in his message.

THE LETTER *P*

The last two difficult letters, *p* and *b*, are the hardest to pronounce ventriloquially. You have already learned that *t* is the substitute letter for *p*. Say the following sentence in your normal speaking manner.

➤ Put the paper on the porch.

Notice that your lips pop together in a slight explo-

sive sound as you blow out some air. The simple letter that comes closest to that sound is *t*. Now, substituting *t* for *p*, say the sentence this way.

➤ Tut the tater on the torch.

This doesn't sound like a very good substitute, does it? But it comes closest to giving that little explosive sound, so for most people it's the best substitution. By practicing, you can make *t* work for *p*.

Repeat the following sentence in your normal manner, noticing where your tongue is placed.

➤ Take them to town tomorrow.

Your tongue taps the roof of your mouth. To make *t* sound like *p*, thrust your tongue forward, almost to the bottom part of your upper front teeth, saying *t*, but thinking *p*, and letting out a small breath of air. Repeat this as much as necessary. Now repeat this sentence, substituting *t* for *p*.

➤ Put the paper on the porch.

It sounds more like the real thing, doesn't it? If not, additional practice and observing a few rules (given later) will greatly help. Now practice the word and sentence lists which use *p*.

PUT	PEAR	PENNY	PICK	STEP
PAN	PEACH	PUPPET	PEPPER	PUNY
PICK	PEOPLE	PONY	APPEAR	PICKLE
APPLE	PIE	POOL	OPEN	POP

The sound combinations of *pr* and *pl* are difficult. Practicing this word list will help you learn how to make the sounds well.

For *pr*, lightly trill your *r*, and see if that doesn't help. For *pl* use *thl* instead of *tl*.

PRACTICE	PRICE	PRESENT	PROMISE	PLEASE
PLANT	PLACE	PLAY	PRETTY	PRESS

➤ Promise to peel plenty of apples and put them in that pan.
➤ The pretty pupil picked a puppet to play with.
➤ Plenty of people put purple paint in their pails.
➤ Pick—but don't pinch—the peaches, pears, and apricots.
➤ Peter Piper picked a peck of pickled peppers.

THE LETTER *B*

Like *p*, the letter *b* is pronounced by putting both lips together. The substitute letter for *b* is *d*, but here again you will need to have the help of your tongue to make it plausible. Say the following sentence in your normal speaking manner while watching yourself in the mirror.

➤ The big boy bawled like a baby.

Now, watching the mirror, say it this way.

➤ The dig doy dawled like a dady.

The second sentence wasn't much like the first, was it? But say it several times until you can do so without moving your lips at all. Notice that the tip of your tongue is touching the roof of your mouth for *d*.

Now try for some improvement. Thrust your tongue hard against your upper front teeth while thinking *b* and saying *d*.

➤ The big boy bawled like a baby.

What an improvement! If it's not, keep working on it until it is. Then get in some good practice on your word and sentence lists for *b*.

BRING	BUNCH	BABBLE	BLUE	BROTHER
BACK	BIG	BANANA	BLACK	HAMBURGER
BOOKS	BETTER	BUY	BREAK	PEBBLE
BIBLE	BOAST	BIG	ABLE	BEAD

➤ Bring back the Bible and that bunch of books.
➤ I'd better buy a bigger bread box.
➤ Big boys broke the little boys' boats on the bus.
➤ Bobby, bash that black and blue bug.
➤ Betty Botter bought a bit of butter; but she said, "This butter's bitter!"
➤ Buy a better bonnet for the blue-eyed baby.

Mastering the Art of Ventriloquism

By this time you've learned how to pronounce each letter of the alphabet without lip movement, and you've been practicing words and sentences. I'm sure, though, that you are not entirely satisfied with the resulting sounds. Remember that the most important secret to becoming a good ventriloquist is practice. So don't be discouraged. Keep at it until letter substitution is so automatic that you won't even have to think about it.

Clinton Detweiler, of Maher Ventriloquist Studios, has had much experience in teaching the art of ventriloquism. In his book *Ventriloquism in a Nutshell*, he suggests that the reason most people fail to become ventriloquists after making a start is that they quit after they have mastered mechanical sound substitution. He encourages beginners to keep going, even though the substitute letters and sounds may seem awkward at first. Many people have mastered them, and you can too if you keep at it. Don't give up. Keep practicing.

From this point on, your own practice and experience will help you improve your speech. Although you will discover unique ways to help yourself, here are some general suggestions for improvement.

At first, avoid words that contain many difficult letter sounds. For instance, say God's Word instead of Bible, and daddy instead of father. This is only for a while, however—until you master your technique better. Never use synonyms as a crutch for any extended amount of time. You want to learn ventriloquism well enough to be able to say anything you want to say.

Be aware that in using substitute sounds, words will sound more strange when said by themselves than when used in sentences. So let your words flow right along, not pausing or stumbling over the substitute sounds. In the context of your speech, your substitutions will hardly be noticed.

Put emphasis into your vent figure's speech. Make it animated. The more lively and appealing your figure is, the less attention will be paid to your method of speaking for it.

If you think your vent figure's speech has not been clear at a certain point, repeat the words in your regular voice. For instance, the vent figure says, "I bought a Bible today." You say, "You bought a Bible? I'm very glad." Even though something of this nature may not be in your planned routine, you can ad-lib to repeat an unclear word or two and then go back to your text.

Speak clearly and distinctly at all times, whether speaking for yourself or your figure. This will help the audience get the gist of the conversation. Try to make every word of the conversation interesting and understandable.

Record your conversations with your vent figure on tape and listen critically to them. Where sounds are not distinct, work on them. Don't slur your words or mumble. Especially watch this when your vent figure is speaking. If necessary, let your vent figure speak a little more slowly than you do. Be sure every word is heard. If not, your message will not get across, and your audience, especially children, will become restless and bored.

Creating Your Vent Figure's Voice

You have learned how to talk without facial movement, but you are still not ready to perform with your vent figure. What voice will it have? It certainly can't speak with the same voice you do, or you couldn't create the illusion that two completely different personalities are conversing. You must find a voice that has enough contrast with your natural voice to make the two persons believable.

If you do not have a vent figure yet, get your voice first. That is, it is easier to develop a voice and then decide on a figure to match it than the other way around.

If you already have a figure, then you need to find a voice to fit it. Either way, you must know your vent figure's personality and characteristics before deciding on what voice to use. This will be discussed in the next chapter.

THE DISTANT VOICE AND THE MUFFLED VOICE

All the instructions given so far are for what is called in ventriloquism the "near" voice. This is when speech seems to be coming from a nearby vent figure.

For many people, their first encounter with ventriloquism was when someone seemed to make a voice come from a corner or some other faraway place. This is called the "distant" voice.

There are some ventriloquists who use a suitcase finish with their figure, when it is placed in a suitcase but protests from inside it that it doesn't want to be there.

This is the "muffled" voice, one which seems to be coming from inside or from behind some object.

The distant and muffled voices are similar to the near voice. But there is some difference in learning to produce the distant and muffled voices. In speaking for puppets, the near voice is all that is essential. If you are interested in the other voices, you can find instructions in almost any book that deals with ventriloquism. (See the Bibliography for resources.)

SINGING WITH YOUR VENT FIGURE

Whether you have a good singing voice or not, think seriously about adding singing to your routine. People seem to think it is harder for a ventriloquist to sing than to talk. But this is not really so. Just sing in a voice that is high or low, the same as you use when your vent figure talks, and use your letter substitutions for the difficult sounds. At first pick songs that don't have too many difficult words to pronounce. Of course, you'll need to know all the words of the song before you sing them.

To become a good gospel ventriloquist requires hard work and precious time. But it's worth it. After you've been using your vent figure with children for a while and they begin to talk and interact with it as though it were real, you'll find a genuine satisfaction in your work. And when someone gets saved following your lesson, you'll know a feeling of great reward. Besides, doing ventriloquism is fun! Do you know of any other profession where you can still play with children's toys and get away with it? This will keep you young in heart and mind.

CHAPTER 4
Making Puppets Come Alive

Whether you are a ventriloquist or a puppeteer, your success will depend mainly on how well you bring your puppets to life. In the hands of a skilled manipulator, almost anything can be made to seem real. On the other hand, no matter how elaborate a figure is, it will be drab and uninteresting to an audience if the illusion is not created that it's real.

A puppet's face is immobile, except for those with hand-controlled mouth, eye, or eyebrow movement. Even then, the expression usually stays the same. Some cloth puppets can be manipulated to appear to smile or pout. But for the most part, a puppet is not capable of any facial expression beyond its original one. So a puppet's reactions to different situations must come about through its body movements and the tone of voice used. This, of course, is up to you as the puppeteer or ventriloquist.

Because stage puppets and vent figures are, for the most part, brought to life in a similar manner, the instructions in this chapter will be equally fitting for the puppeteer or the ventriloquist. Where there are differences, they will be noted.

What Puppets Should You Use?

The late Fred Maher, founder of the Maher School of Ventriloquism, said, "The ventriloquist's dummy is to the ventriloquist what a musical instrument is to the musician. The musician plays his music through his instrument. The instrument through which the ventriloquist plays his wit and humor is his ventriloquial dummy.... The ventriloquist cannot bring forth hearty laughter nor properly display his technique through an inadequate ventriloquial figure" (*Ventriloquial Figures*, p. 3).

The very first consideration in making your puppets real, then, is to choose the right ones for your use. Every puppet you work with should be proper and adequate for the part it plays. This doesn't mean that you have to spend a lot of money for puppets. Buying all the figures you use in puppetry can prove to be very expen-

sive. But you can make excellent puppets yourself at little cost. If you are not able to sew or work well with your hands, perhaps you can find an artistic friend or someone in your church who would be glad to render this service for the Lord.

Whichever way you obtain your puppets, they should be sturdy enough to withstand much use and should be appealing and personable. When choosing a puppet, think about these areas.

Does the figure appeal to you?

What voice and personality would be suitable for that particular puppet?

Is the voice one that you can manage easily?

Will you be comfortable with the personality?

THE VENT FIGURE

Almost anything with a movable mouth is suitable for use with ventriloquism. Your purpose is to have a figure that will help you with the illusion that your voice has another source. So don't think it's necessary to buy a large vent figure in order to perform. I began twenty years ago with a twenty-four-inch boy figure I had made into a girl by adding a long-haired wig and a dress. The mouth was controlled by a string, but the head did not move. I had given her a new, more lifelike body, which was hollowed out in the back for a control stick that my husband had fixed for moving her head. I still use her and children love her. I now have many other figures, which range from five inches to over five feet.

If you want to buy a vent figure, here are several details you should consider:

🐾 Deal with a reputable company qualified to give you good workmanship.

🐾 Choose a figure that is hand-carved from basswood or pine, if possible. Less-expensive, molded figures are made of wood fiber or fiberglass. They are lightweight and will last a long time if well cared for.

❧ Choose a figure whose face is winsome, attractive, and lifelike. The moving parts should make the figure appear real. The mouth should open and shut smoothly. Additional features might include moving, winking eyes, lifting eyebrows, wiggling ears, protruding tongue. Remember, the more movements the figure has, the harder it is to manipulate. Also, this means more parts could need repair or replacement. One of the best-known dummies of all time, Charlie McCarthy, had no hand-controlled movements except the mouth. He came to life through the skills of Edgar Bergen without extra gadgets.

❧ Be sure the body is made with wire or wood with stuffing. Movement in one arm or leg is optional.

Buying a good vent figure will be expensive, but you should get many years of use and enjoyment from it. Follow the manufacturer's suggestions for the care of your figure. Develop your skills in using the figure, and it will become your faithful, loyal friend who can aid you greatly in presenting the messages and lessons you wish to convey.

There are much cheaper, manufactured vent figures that can be bought in toy stores or through department store catalogs. They are made of vinyl or plastic. Get the kind with a hollow back in which there is a control stick for moving the head.

THE MOUTH PUPPET

Puppets with movable mouths are popular with both ventriloquists and puppeteers. Almost anything—a human figure, an animal character, or an inanimate object—can come to life if given a movable mouth and a bit of help from its manipulator. Search through puppet catalogs and supply houses for just the right puppets for your needs. (See the Bibliography for sources.) Or you can make your own. Then you can have almost anything you want. Stretch your imagination and make some unusual mouth puppets. Start with the patterns and instructions in this book, for all-purpose as well as specialty puppets.

Mouth puppets are recommended for beginning ventriloquists. They are easy to work with as you develop your skills. You will need to make them with whole bodies for the most part. Some exceptions would be those that pop out of boxes or other objects and are not entirely exposed. For example, in this book instructions are given for making Jonah: connected to, and coming partly out of, the mouth of the fish that swallowed him (see Part 2, chapter 9).

Stage puppets are easier to handle if they do not have legs and lower bodies. Just be sure that the costume is long enough to be below the bottom ledge of the front of the stage, covering the puppeteer's arm. A puppet with legs can perch on the bottom ledge of the stage opening, hanging its feet over the side. Usually you will want larger puppets for ventriloquism than for stage use.

THE HARDHEAD PUPPET

Hardhead puppets are not suitable for ventriloquism but are excellent for the stage. I use hardhead puppets for most of my story dramatizations because they can move freely, pick up or hold props, and touch and interact with other puppets. If you mold them from papier-mache, you can make them look more like real people than the mouth puppets, and you can give them faces with expressions of gaiety, sadness, villainy, etc. In fact, you can design almost any creature you wish to have. (See the instructions for making hardhead puppets in Part 2, chapter 10.)

Developing a Character
GET TO KNOW YOUR PUPPET

Three secrets were given in chapter 2 for becoming a good ventriloquist. The second secret was that you must convince yourself that your vent figure is a real personality. You will never persuade your audience that there are two of you talking and acting unless you are conscious of two personalities. Whether you are a ventriloquist or a puppeteer your puppets must seem alive and real to you. This will be transmitted to the audience when you endow them with human qualities.

On the other hand, if you are thinking, *What in the world am I doing up here in front of everybody talking to a piece of wood or a bundle of cloth*, your show will surely be a failure. If you will ad-lib with your vent figure at home or even occasionally on stage, you will find yourself less restricted, and soon the vent figure's own separate personality will begin to emerge. When your puppet becomes so real to you that it will even surprise you with some reaction or remark, you know that it has indeed become a distinct personality, almost as though it has a mind of its own.

Each puppet must have its own special characteristics, just as human beings do. In deciding what kind of personality a puppet should have, make up a list of qualities and historical data about your vent figure.

How old is it?

What are its interests?

Is it intelligent or dull-witted?

Is it friendly or funny or awkward or cranky?

What does it like and dislike?

Who are the members of its "family"?

Is it from the country or the city?

The better you know your vent figure the better your act will be. Having decided on your puppet's personality, keep it in character. Of course, there will be times when it acts out of character just as human beings do.

CONSIDER SUITABILITY TO PURPOSE

In using puppetry in Christian service, the first factor in choosing a personality for your puppet would be that of suitability. The most important aspects are the teachings you want to get across, and your puppets must have characteristics that will enable you to present an effective lesson. This doesn't mean your puppets will be sweet and good all the time. Lessons can be learned from misbehavior and mistakes as well as from good behavior. But the puppets' personalities must have a potential for teaching situations.

THINK OF DIALOGUE POSSIBLITIES

Think of the possibilities for dialogues or plays when choosing a personality. Your most frequently used figures need to be versatile enough to give you many ideas for their actions and conversations. The ones I use most represent normal children. Other puppets, ones that have limited uses, are for special occasions or for teaching particular lessons. They help to provide variety. Sometimes I make a puppet and then decide how I can best use it. Other times I develop lessons and then make one or more puppets to help teach those lessons.

ENHANCE CHARACTER TRAITS

When you have chosen a puppet and decided what personality it should have, there are ways you can enhance its character traits.

Choose a name carefully; it is very important. It should fit the type of personality you are giving the puppet. Among my puppets are Sunshine, a sweet, happy, little girl; Sugar Bear, who can't stay away from sweets; Corn Pone D. Nutt, a country boy who is sometimes backwards and other times very witty; and Honey Dew, a southern girl who considers herself quite a lady. The names suggest some of their characteristics almost without any description.

Clothes also help identify the puppet's personality. Corn Pone wears blue jeans, a cowboy shirt, and a cowboy hat. Sunshine wears pretty, frilly dresses. Chil-

dren's clothing can often be fitted to your puppet. A thirty-two-inch puppet would take size ten months to two years. A thirty-six-inch puppet wears size four to six. Clothing does not need to be brand new. Good, clean clothing from a used clothing store or garage sales can greatly reduce the cost. But don't use clothing that wrinkles easily.

CONSIDERATIONS FOR STAGE PUPPETS

Not only should ventriloquial figures seem real and alive to you, stage puppets should also. Those who always play themselves will have their own individual personalities. Characters in a play will have temporary personalities that fit that particular dramatization.

As a puppeteer you should feel you are out on the stage yourself when the puppet you are holding is speaking or acting. When my son used to help me put on a play he said the real show went on behind stage, for I often showed on my face or in bodily movements what the puppet on stage was supposed to be doing. The puppet had become so real to me that I was performing its part off stage as well as on. Sometimes I catch myself grinning widely at the moment the puppet I hold on stage is supposed to be laughing.

The costumes of stage puppets used in dramatizations are very important for identifying the type of character being portrayed. For foreign or historical characters, get costume ideas from encyclopedias, *National Geographic* magazines, or other sources in your library. For biblical costumes, get ideas from illustrated Bible dictionaries or visual aid materials for teaching children. Costumes need not be elaborate to identify the character. After all, small details can't be seen from a distance. Only a few accessories or additions put on top of the basic costume will be necessary to change it to fit the occasion. Costume jewelry can be used for special accents. Patterns and instructions for clothes are in Part 2, chapters 8, 9, and 10.

Puppet Voices

Having decided on your puppet's personality, you can fit a voice to it. A voice tells a great deal about a puppet's personality, so keep it in character.

Will your puppet use good or poor English?

speak with an American dialect?

have a foreign accent?

show its age?

Be sure that a puppet's voice is as different from your own as possible. This is especially important in ventriloquism. The audience must believe that it is the voice of someone else.

One very important rule about voices: Regardless of what voice you use, be sure you are heard. Learn to project your voice, forcing the air out of your throat by tightening your diaphragm and giving it a little push.

PITCH

The first thing to consider in selecting a voice is whether its pitch should be low or high. Pitch, more than any other single element in voices, helps to distinguish who is speaking.

For stage puppets, varying the pitch of the voices helps the audience determine which puppet is speaking, so you will want as much contrast in pitch as possible.

For ventriloquism, if your voice is naturally low, you will want your vent figure to speak in a high voice; if your voice is naturally high, you will use a low voice for your vent figure. A man will probably want the vent figure's voice higher than his own. A man is well-suited for this, since he can usually speak in a falsetto voice. A woman might choose a voice either higher or lower than her own.

To discover the pitch you want to use, sing the scale (*do, re, me*, etc.) making as deep a tone as possible for *do* and going as high up as you can. Find the highest pitch that is comfortable for you. Somewhere near that pitch select a voice that comes easiest and most distinct without irritating your throat. You will have to speak for long periods of time, so you don't want to strain your voice and cause hoarseness. Tighten the throat muscles when you speak. This will raise the pitch of your voice. Perhaps this high voice is just what you want for your figure. If not, try a low tone, near your lowest pitch.

If neither a high nor a low voice suits you, find a pitch somewhere in between—just be sure it's at least a couple of tones higher or lower than your own natural voice. If you work with several puppets, you may have to use pitches both below and above your own.

PINCHED VOICE

A second way to change your voice is to use what is called the pinched voice. This is a nasal sound, radiating partially through the nose. To see what this is like, pinch your nose shut and try to talk. Then release your hold slightly and talk again. Now try to force the sound out in the same manner without holding your nose. Add pressure by tightening up your diaphragm.

SPEED

The third way to change your voice is in contrasting the speed of speech between you and your vent figure or between the various stage puppets. With ventriloquism, it would be better to speak more slowly for your vent figure than you do yourself. This will help the vent figure's voice to be understood better. For stage puppets, vary the speed of the different voices. However, at no time should you speak so slowly that you bore your audience or so fast that you make the speech hard to understand.

ACCENTS AND DIALECTS

The fourth way to change your voice is to speak with a foreign accent or a regional dialect for your puppet. Not everyone can do this well enough to be understood. Use this method only if you know how all the words should be pronounced, and if you can keep that particular method of speech constant. If done well, an accent is a very good contrast between voices.

VOICE INFLECTIONS

The fifth way to change your voice is to use different voice inflections for individual puppets in accordance with their personalities or characteristics. This is the best way of all to denote who and what a puppet is. Here are some examples:

🐀 A child. Children's voices are not necessarily higher than adults, but they have a thinner quality to the sound, and words are pronounced more immaturely. Pay attention to children's speech and attempt to mimic it. Speak in short phrases of two or three words, pausing slightly between phrases. To make a girl's voice different from a boy's, try a higher pitch. A girl's voice is the highest one I do (with the exception of a mouse's voice). The boy's voice can be in a medium range, just slightly higher or lower than your own. Try giving it a bit of a nasal tone. If two girl or two boy puppets are being used together with ventriloquism or on stage, one must speak more slowly, have an accent or dialect, use poor English, or have some other voice difference.

🐀 A woman or man. When speaking for a puppet of your own sex and age when you are behind a stage, try to change the voice at least a little so that your audience will be thinking of the puppet, not you.

It is very difficult for most women to sound like a man. Use a man to say the part, record a man's voice ahead of time, or change the script to use a woman instead of a man in the play. For an eccentric man, such as a villain, a woman could speak as low as possible and use a twang, the pinched voice. Likewise, an eccentric woman's voice could have a twang, but with a higher pitch than you use for the man.

In ventriloquism, if your figure is supposed to be your sex and near your age, you must be sure your vent figure's voice has some characteristics that differ from your own.

🐀 An old woman or man. Use a voice that is higher and thinner than your own, with a quaver.

⅏ Animals. These can be similar to the human voices already mentioned, being sure the voice fits the character. You wouldn't want a loud, gruff voice coming from a mouse or a tiny squeak from a bear. For a cat, try a fairly high, nasal sound, something like a *meow*. A duck could speak with a nasal sound, similar to its quack. (Don't try a Donald Duck imitation, which is barely understandable even when done by a professional.)

VOICE SWITCHING

You must learn to switch from your natural voice to your puppet's voice automatically. What you eventually want is to be able to change from one to the other in conversation without having to think about it. If you are speaking for more than one vent figure or stage puppet in a single dialogue or play, you must switch from one voice to the other. Make each change crisp and distinct; don't slide from one voice into another.

This may seem hard at first, but as with anything else, you develop the habit through practice. One good rule is to put a very short pause between the speeches, except of course when a sudden reaction or response is necessary. If each time you speak for a puppet you become that personality in your mind, you will find the change in speech will be almost automatic.

With all this in mind, practice your puppet voices and voice switching. Remember, herein lies the greatest secret of success: practice, practice, practice. The following exercises will help.

⅏ Refer again to the lists of words and sentences in chapter 3. Choose a puppet voice you want to use and say everything in that voice. Then alternate, doing one word in your own voice and the next in your puppet's voice; then say one sentence in your own voice and the next in your puppet's. If you will be using more than one puppet at a time, switch back and forth between puppet voices.

⅏ Pick up a book or newspaper and read new material, switching voices with each sentence.

⅏ Sing familiar hymns, alternating voices on each stanza.

⅏ Practice the dialogues given in the back of this book.

To see how you'll sound to others, record all your voices on a cassette tape, switching from one puppet voice to the other or to your own voice. Evaluate the recording, asking yourself these questions.

Can I easily tell the difference?

Am I bringing out the personality of each puppet by means of its voice?

Would the speeches be understood even by those on the last row of the room? (Remember, especially where children are present, there may be some extraneous noises.)

You should be ready now to put on an act to test your abilities with your different voices and with voice switching. Memorize "Now Is the Time" (a dialogue in this book) and perform it while watching yourself in a mirror. Then do it again before an audience of family or friends. If you're a ventriloquist, try to do your act with your vent figure without moving your lips.

If you're a puppeteer, use a second puppet to take the part of the interviewer in the dialogue. A stage isn't necessary, and you needn't worry about moving your lips.

In either case, your purpose is to check on the voices. Ask for evaluation from your audience.

Could they easily distinguish between the voices?

Were your words all clear and distinct?

Did a definite personality emerge from your puppet?

Puppet Movements

Your puppets now have personalities and voices. They are becoming your friends. As a beginner in puppetry, you are still very conscious of the speech of your puppet. To complete the illusion that your puppet is alive, you must be concerned with its actions as well as its voice. There must be plenty of lifelike mannerisms and movements. Your task now is to observe the way human beings move their bodies and then to imitate these movements with the manipulations of your puppets. However, this cannot be strictly achieved. Puppets aren't able to do all the gestures and movements that people can. But you can create an illusion of life by using the movements that are possible for the puppets within the limits of their individual construction. On the other hand, some of your puppets may be able to perform actions that you can't do. I have a puppet who flips over on its back and doubles itself up so that it's hiding its face beneath its legs. I certainly can't do that! Let your puppets perform with lively actions that fit them, and you'll have gone a long way in convincing your audience that they're real.

HOLDING YOUR PUPPETS

The Vent Figure

Come before your audience with your puppet sitting erect on your open left hand if you're right-handed or on your open right hand if you're left-handed. Your other hand should hold the control stick, with a finger or thumb in place on the ring or lever used to move the mouth.

There are several ways to hold a vent figure while performing. A man might put his foot on a chair or stool and hold the vent figure on his knee. Either a man or a woman could sit down and hold the puppet. I like to be standing so the audience can see better, so I hold the vent figure on one hand as I stand, or I place it on a small lectern beside me. (The latter way leaves one hand free.) One of my puppets is large enough to stand on a chair beside me, and my largest one stands on the floor.

The Mouth Puppet

If the puppet is full-bodied and is being used in ventriloquism, it will be seated in one of the positions described for the vent figure. It can also pop up from a bag or box. If used in the stage, it will be seen from the waist up, unless it sits on the lower ledge of the stage opening with its feet hanging over the side. Place four fingers on the top of its mouth and the thumb under the bottom part.

The Hardhead Puppet

If the hardhead puppet has a very small neck, place your index finger in the head, your middle finger in one arm, and your thumb in the other arm. Your last two fingers fold up in the chest area, which usually produces a slight bulge in the body. If the neck is large enough, the better way is to put your middle and index fingers in the head, your other two fingers in one arm, and your thumb in the other arm. Be sure that your palm faces toward the front of the puppet when you put it on. You don't want it to be facing backwards when it goes out. Once I walked a puppet out on stage with its back to the audience. I didn't know it until I heard the laughter.

MOUTH MOVEMENTS

Only the vent figure and the mouth puppet have mouth movements. (The hardhead puppet shows it's talking by body movements.) Synchronizing the mouth movements with the words being spoken is the most important part of any puppet movement. This is spoken of as "lip synchronization," or "lip sync." With a vent figure, pull down on the ring or lever control to open the mouth; release to close it. With a mouth puppet, pull the fingers and thumb apart to open the mouth, and bring them back together again to close it.

To get proper lip sync, open the mouth at the beginning of a syllable and close it after the syllable is finished. If you open the mouth before saying the word and then close it as you say the word it will appear that the puppet is *eating* its words. Use the following sentence as you open and close your puppet's mouth to illustrate the improper and proper ways to do it.

My name is Charlie.

Improper Way: Open mouth and close down as you say "My." Open back up and close, saying "name," etc.

Proper Way: Begin to say, "My," opening mouth widely as you do. Close mouth. Open again as you say "name." Close, etc. For the two-syllable word "Charlie," open the mouth only partway for "Char" and close it. Open it again quickly as you say "lie." Close it.

Your puppet's mouth must not just flap along rhythmically as you talk, with disregard to what is being said. Open and close it with the syllables. People vary their mouth openings, both as to amount and length of time. You will not want to open the puppet's mouth wide on every syllable. Accented syllables require big mouth movements, and unaccented, small. Some syllables may occur so fast in the speech that there is no mouth movement at all. On the syllables which have the greatest stress, you will probably hold the mouth open longer.

Never leave the mouth gaping when the puppet is not speaking.

Practice mouth openings in front of a mirror as you again perform the dialogue, "Now Is the Time."

Do the mouth openings look smooth and appropriate for what is being said?

Do you have good lip sync? (Keep practicing if the puppet looks like it is eating its words.)

BODY MOVEMENTS

The Vent Figure

As you work with your vent figure, you will find ways to move it that seem natural and lifelike. Much will depend on how many controls you have on the headstick (e.g., eye or tongue movements). Practice until you can work all levers smoothly and quickly. Don't overdo the mechanical operations of your puppet. It will appear jittery and unreal if it continually blinks its eyes or raises its eyebrows, and you won't be able to concentrate well on the dialogue. Keep all mechanical movements lifelike.

Your vent figure should not sit completely still very long at a time, even when you are saying your part of the dialogue. You should shift its position a bit from time to time, just as a human being would do. It must appear to be aware of the audience and to react to what you say. Turn the head, tilt the body, or move it closer to you or farther away. Most of this should be accomplished with your wrist movements and with your knee or the palm of your hand, depending on where the puppet is sitting.

The Mouth Puppet

Whole body movements are especially easy with mouth puppets. They can do almost any movement your wrist and arm will allow: twist, turn, bend, and jump up and down. If they have pliable mouths they can even appear to smile or frown. Arms and legs should not dangle lifelessly. Putting bendable wires in them will cause them to move some when the body moves (see chapter 8).

If I have a mouth puppet sitting on my palm, I can cause a leg to move by tapping on the underside of the puppet's thigh with my finger. You can cause your puppet to point or gesture if you put your hand on its elbow and move its arm as needed. The audience will hardly notice or care that you helped. Raise your whole arm up quickly to have the puppet jump up on its feet and lower it to go back to a sitting position.

The Hardhead Puppet

Hardhead puppets depend on body movements to show that they are speaking. Otherwise, the audience will be confused about which one is delivering the lines. (Other puppets on stage should remain practically still while one is talking.) You should exaggerate the movements. That is, the puppets should move far more than a person would when talking. But don't just wiggle a puppet or wave its arms all the time. Sometimes one hand can move up and down with the words, as though gesturing. Then the head can nod, and then the other hand can gesture.

Contrary to what most puppetry books advise, I prefer to have a ledge (called a "floor") inside my puppet stage. It reaches from one side of the stage to the other. It is six inches below the bottom ledge of the stage opening and is about a foot wide. This gives me room to lay out the puppets needed, to place props, and to rest my elbows while holding the puppets. It is very tiring to hold puppets up in the air for a long time. Placing your elbows on the floor assures that the puppets will be seen from the waist up, and the different puppets will be about equal in height.

The main objection to this arrangement is that the puppeteer is liable to lean the puppets forward instead of holding them straight up. There is no reason why you can't hold your arm up straight while resting your elbow if you pay attention to what you're doing.

If you work in a stage that doesn't have a floor, hold your puppets over your head or directly in front of your face while standing, sitting, or kneeling. Be careful to establish a puppet height with your audience in mind

and keep it constant, not dipping down and up, giving the impression that your puppet is stepping in potholes.

To move a hardhead puppet you will use your fingers, wrist, and arm.

🐾 The fingers move the head and arms. Use them to cause the puppet to nod and turn its head, point to itself and others, clap hands, wave, pat its stomach, pick up objects, hand props to others, and do many other tasks.

🐾 The wrist provides body movements, like bowing from the waist, turning to the side, and looking up or down.

🐾 The arm is used in making the puppet appear to walk, hop, run, or fall down.

Let your puppets enter from the sides of your stage backdrop. This is much more natural than to have them pop straight up from below. Keeping your arm straight up from the elbow, move toward the front of the stage so that the puppet appears to walk in. Move quickly when you want it to run, bend it slightly forward, and let its head bob up and down. A hopping puppet would take one jump at a time, done by lifting your elbow off the stage floor, moving it forward slightly, and back down on the floor with a bounce. A broad arm movement either forward or backward will make the puppet appear to fall.

EYE CONTACT

Regardless of the type they are, all puppets follow the same rules for where they should look. When facing the audience they should seem to have eye contact. The heads of some puppets will have to be bent downward a little so their eyes may be seen. Have someone sit where your audience will sit and direct you in the positioning of your puppets to give the right look.

When a puppet turns to look at another puppet or the ventriloquist, it should be turned only partially, so that the audience can still see its face. Otherwise, the people sitting on the sides will see only the back of the puppet's head. It is not necessary for it fully to give the impression that it is looking at someone. Occasionally turn the puppet's face toward the far right or left to give people sitting there a chance to see it better.

In completing the illusion that a vent figure is alive, the ventriloquist should pay attention to where he himself looks.

🐾 Turn toward the vent figure when it speaks, just as you would if a human being were talking to you.

🐾 When you begin to speak, look toward the audience. This will project your voice so every listener can hear.

🐦 Before you finish speaking, turn sharply and look at your figure (which should be looking at you).

🐦 When your vent figure speaks, have it turn slowly toward the audience, and you do the same.

This means that most of the time you are facing the audience while doing both voices. You don't need to follow these moves constantly. You and your figure can look over the room occasionally. But remember two rules:

1. Be sure you are heard by facing the audience the majority of the time.

2. Never turn the figure so far toward you that people see only the back of its head. They should see the mouth move.

As for how you should look, you will not want just a blank expression on your face, even though you will be keeping your lips still. Your facial expression is a vital part of creating the illusion of two separate characters. The look on your face must always be that of yourself. Never show on your face what would be on the face of your figure if it were alive. For instance, even though it may be speaking in an angry voice, your facial expression will be passive or show a reaction to its speech, such as surprise. You must react to what your vent figure says and does as though you had no idea what it would say and do.

Are your puppets now alive and anxious to go before an audience? Do you almost feel guilty if you don't feed them breakfast? Then you're about ready to get on with the show.

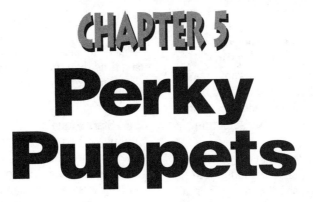

CHAPTER 5
Perky Puppets

Having developed your skill in puppetry, you are ready to consider public performances. You've been studying and practicing for one reason: to put on shows. There are two main ingredients that go into a good performance:

1. Adequate preparation

2. Skillful presentation

If you fail in either of these, your show will not be a success.

Adequate Preparation

Whether you perform as a puppeteer or a ventriloquist, you must prepare. Puppets don't talk and act on their own. You must know what they are going to do and why they are going to do it. Having perky puppets isn't enough for a presentation. You need to have a definite purpose for being there. Preparation takes some of your precious time and energy, but it's necessary.

OBTAINING DIALOGUES AND PLAYS

The first step in adequate preparation is to have a dialogue or play for your performance. No matter how small your crowd or how young the children, don't just take a puppet or two with you and hope that something will come into your mind to say. You should know what conversations and actions you want from your puppets. In only a few situations should you do anything impromptu. Sometimes when my lesson is finished and there is still a little time left, I let the children ask questions of one of my puppets and I ad-lib the answers. You may have moments when it's all right to improvise. But usually you should know what is going to be said and done. That's the only way you can be sure you'll have a worthwhile message. Even if the extent of your puppetry for the day is to have a puppet greet the children upon arriving or to help them learn a memory verse, you need to plan well. Otherwise, you'll lack variety and

purpose, and your audience's interest will wane.

Where can you get materials? This will be a continuing problem for anyone who makes much use of puppetry.

You can buy puppet dialogues and plays in Christian bookstores and from Christian publishers, especially those who publish curriculum materials. (See the Bibliography for some sources.) Not all scripts are worth buying. Check them for message content and for material suitable to your age group. You may not wish to use every word of the scripts you buy, especially if they are mostly conversation. They can be changed around to fit your own style and needs.

Your best source of material is your own writing. Only you know what suits you and your puppets best and what will appeal to your audience. Even if you don't feel qualified as a writer, you should be able to write some simple Bible stories or short conversations. Whether you buy material or write your own, consider the following guidelines.

🐾 Every good dialogue or puppet play will have a beginning, middle, and end, just as a short story. You should have an attention-getting opening, a middle section that has continuity and sustains interest, and a fitting climax for the end, resolving the conflicts or providing a solution to the questions presented. If you're using humor, save one of your best jokes for last.

🐾 Select a theme for your material and stick with it. It should in some way illustrate the lesson you 're presenting.

🐾 Keep each speech as short as possible. Your audience, especially the children, will lose interest when the puppets have lengthy conversations. Break up long speeches with questions from, or other interruptions by, another puppet or yourself.

🐾 Use humor when you can. This is generally expected from puppetry. Grace Harp, in *Handbook of Christian Puppetry*, says, "Whenever possible, it is a good idea to add some humor to a presentation, since humor is an effective means of gaining and keeping attention. Often children will learn better when humor is included in the teaching process" (p. 78). She goes on to explain, though, that there are times when you will want to present a drama or Bible lesson where humor would be out of place. Puppets are just as appealing when they dramatize a serious story as when they are doing something hilarious.

A ventriloquist routine should not be just a string of unrelated jokes and gags. Everything, including both humorous and serious elements, should tie together in keeping with your theme. Robert H. Hill, in *You Can Be a Ventriloquist*, says, "Think through the plot of the routine and the roles that will be played by you and your dummy. Put the various elements into their proper sequence. The routine should move through the subject and humorous elements and come to some sort of a logical conclusion" (p. 123).

🕭 Keep your audience in mind when writing. Many jokes appreciated by adults are not understood at all by children. Puns and twisting of word meanings are not good to use with young audiences. Listen to children as they tell jokes to give you an idea of what they think is funny. In a serious presentation, remember that young children think concretely and need illustrations and stories that explain such abstract biblical principles as faith and love.

🕭 Whether your material is a dialogue or a dramatization, remember that it must include actions as well as conversation. You must keep those puppets alive: Plan their moves. For example, for a stage play, plan and practice your puppets' entrances and exits as well as the raising and lowering of the curtain (if you use one).

🕭 The length of stage dramatizations should be from five to fifteen minutes. Longer presentations should be given in more than one part, continued from one service to the next. If you present a long play in one day provide a break halfway through.

🕭 A good length for a dialogue is from eight to ten minutes. There are times, of course, when a puppet pops in and out of a service for a very short time.

🕭 A stage play (dramatized story) should have conflict in it, which is the struggle of your leading character against opposition—either with others, the environment, or himself. Introduce the conflict early, develop it, and then resolve it. The development of the dialogue should have momentum, that which carries the conversations and actions forward.

🕭 Stage plays should be stories that appeal to the ages and sexes present.

🕭 Write plays that require no more puppets on stage at a time than there are hands available to hold them and space to accommodate them. For example, I work alone, so all my plays have only two puppets on stage at once.

🕭 Start compiling an idea file for writing dialogues and plays. Write down ideas on 3- x 5-inch index cards, one to a card. Glean what you can from joke books, children's story books, biographies of famous people, missionary stories, songbooks, and the Bible. Don't forget jokes you have heard, short illustrations from sermons or books, short stories from Sunday school papers and other sources, especially those that feature children, and ideas from your own experiences and those of family or friends.

🕭 When you are ready to write a dialogue or play, decide on your theme. Go to your idea file and get together all the jokes, illustrations, and stories that relate to the theme. Let your mind mull over the material, perhaps for several days, until you get the needed inspiration for your presentation. Then write your dialogue or play.

MEMORIZING DIALOGUES

Does the thought of performing before an audience unnerve you? Do you lack self-confidence? You may have learned the art of puppetry until you are very good at it, your puppets and accessories may be top-notch, and the material for your dialogue or play may be the best you can obtain, but if you don't know your material, you will fail in your attempt to put on a first-rate show. Of course you'll feel jittery the first few times you perform. Even veteran actors admit they have some nervousness before they go on stage. But nothing aids you more in gaining self-confidence than knowing exactly what you'll do and say.

You may choose to do a play live or prerecord it. Memorizing the words will give a smoother performance than trying to read a script and work the puppets at the same time. In doing ventriloquism, you must know both your own speeches and those of your partner. Some suggestions to help you memorize your material follow.

🕭 Get very familiar with the material. Read through the entire dialogue or play six or more times. You may want to record it and then listen to it. Note where the beginning, middle, and end occur. Note how one section relates to and leads into another. Especially observe what message is being conveyed.

🕭 Memorize one section at a time. Write down a few key words and use them to jog your memory as you repeat a section. Put the sections together, and, using only your key words, say the entire text. Repeat this several times until you can say the whole thing without your key words.

🎭 Practice the dialogue in front of a mirror using your puppet; then practice in front of your family or a friend.

RECORDING DIALOGUES

An alternative to memorizing a dialogue or play is to prerecord it on cassette. You do not need to memorize every single word of a recorded play, but you should know the material so well that you can synchronize the puppets' movements with the words on the tape. This is extremely important if you have mouth puppets, for their mouths move on almost every syllable. The tape won't wait, so you must know exactly when your puppets should enter and exit and perform their actions.

Advantages to prerecording your puppet dialogues and plays follow.

🎭 You can use the voices of people who can't be present when you do the shows.

🎭 You can make better use of sound effects.

🎭 You can record until all mistakes have been eliminated.

🎭 You can have musical backgrounds and interludes.

🎭 You can use a sound system, thus increasing the volume to suit the size of your audience. (When performing live, you can use a microphone, but it will pick up the extraneous noises you make in moving around behind the stage.)

The following are disadvantages to prerecording your puppet dialogues and plays.

🎭 Recording can be difficult and time-consuming.

🎭 In performing a show, you must be very familiar with the words and actions in order to synchronize them with the recording.

🎭 If anything causes a delay in your work with the puppets you could fall behind the recording.

If you plan to regularly record your shows you'll find these ideas helpful.

🎭 If you must use other people to help you record the sessions, schedule recording sessions every month or so. Then you can get several shows done at one time.

🎭 Find a room as free from outside noises and distractions as possible.

🎭 Decide who will do each voice.

🎭 If you use music in the background for special effects, designate a person to be responsible for it. It can be live—with someone playing, for example, the piano or the guitar—or prerecorded. Be sure any background music is not so loud that it overpowers the speaking parts. The mood and tempo of the music must fit the action on the stage.

🎭 Pauses may be necessary to show a lapse of time in the action or to give the puppeteers time to make changes in puppets or scenery. These can be covered by a musical interlude. Before you record, practice the actions that will be taking place behind scenes and time them. Then record music on the tape for that length of time. Keep your pauses as short as possible. I find that thirty seconds is usually enough time. A longer pause will allow the audience to grow restless.

🎭 You can purchase sound effects records or tapes, or borrow them from the library. Or you can make your own sound effects with the aid of simple objects or your own voice. Here are a few suggestions.

➤ Drop several pieces of silverware on a hard surface to imitate glass breaking.

➤ Rustle cellophane to make the sound of a crackling fire.

➤ Tap a stick on a tabletop for drum beats.

➤ Stamp your feet on the floor to imitate tramping.

➤ Click the four fingernails of one hand on a wood surface in rapid succession, from the little finger to the index finger, to get pounding horse's hoofs.

PRACTICING WITH OTHER PUPPETEERS

Practicing alone is necessary whether you will be performing alone or with other puppeteers. But if others are involved with your shows, you must practice with them too. You will have to make many decisions, including which puppets each person will hold, who will open and close the curtain, who will change the backdrops.

If it is at all possible, keep the puppets in a locked storage room or cabinet when they're not in use. Don't let them stay out where children can play with them. If several people will be using the same puppets, arrange for one person to be in charge. Be sure that the puppets are available when you plan to use them.

ASSEMBLING ACCESSORIES

For many stage shows and sometimes for ventriloquial acts, you will need props (as discussed in Part 2, chapter 7). These and other materials must be assembled before your show. Forgetting even the smallest item can upset your performance. I keep a detailed list of everything I need for each show and ventriloquial routine and check these lists before each performance to be sure I'm ready. The following are two sample lists.

PUPPET SHOW

Title: Trespass, the Terrible Ogre

Puppets Used:
Mary Ann (girl)
Trespass (evil man)
Sir Goodheart (knight)
Lady Reformer (old woman)
Queen Sweet Talk (woman)
Prince (young man)

Costumes:
ogre—black cape
knight—armor and helmet
old woman—shawl
queen—robe and crown
young man—robe, jeweled head scarf, red plastic tape scars on hands

Props:
small open Bible
two swords
stick

Backdrops:
outdoor scene

Recording:
tape R, side one, show one

VENT ROUTINE

Title: Nobody Loves Me
Puppet: Honey Dew
Props:
handkerchief
telephone
foot pedal for tape recorder
Recording:
tape X, side one (sound effects)

Keep these pointers in mind when setting up to perform a puppet show.

🐾 Arrive early at the place you will perform.

🐾 If you're doing ventriloquism, put your vent figure where it will not be seen by your audience but will be ready for use. If you're doing a stage show, arrange your puppets on the floor of the stage in the order of use, side by side, face up, with the costume openings facing you so you can easily slip your hand inside. (Some people prefer sewing rings to the hems of the puppets' costumes and hanging the puppets on cup hooks screwed to the bottom of the stage floor or prop shelf.)

🐾 Place props where they can easily be reached.

🐾 If you will be using more than one backdrop, put the first one to be used on the cuphooks on the stage backboard. Lay the other backdrops nearby, in the order of use.

🐾 Test your audio equipment for proper sound. Adjust the microphones to the proper height, within about ten inches of a speaker's mouth. Be sure they're turned on. A wireless microphone is excellent if you're moving around much.

There is no preparation that supersedes praying for the Holy Spirit's guidance and help. A brilliant performance is a spiritual failure if it's done merely through the force of human personality. And it is presumptuous to expect the Holy Spirit to work miracles if you have simply failed to adequately prepare. But having done the best you can, look to the Lord for the power and ability you need in His service.

Skillful Presentation

You are becoming a proficient puppeteer, your script is written and memorized, you have assembled all needed puppets and accessories, and you have arrived at your place of performance. Let the show begin.

TIPS FOR THE PUPPETEER

Although almost all angles for a skillful presentation have been covered already, there are a few additional tips on puppeteering.

🐾 You and your puppets should be dressed in clean, appropriate clothing. The way you're dressed has much to do with your poise and self-confidence. A properly-dressed teacher of children will gain their respect, set a good example, and may even help them be better disciplined. Keep your puppets and their clothes in tip-top shape if you want to look professional.

🐾 Leave your troubles at home and present a smiling face and effervescent personality.

Show genuine love and interest in individuals, especially children.

Speak clearly and distinctly with plenty of enthusiasm. Avoid speech tics, those annoying, repetitious words and phrases like "you know," "well," "like," "listen," and "I mean."

Be sure your audience can see everything well. Arrange for small children to sit near the front.

Be aware of the passage of time. Watch that you don't bore your audience or encroach on someone else's part in the program.

Be in control at all times. When unexpected things happen or you make a mistake, don't get flustered. Think of a fitting ad-lib to put your audience at ease. This will relieve tension as well.

If you don't know ventriloquism, you can still use some ventriloquial dialogues with a little modification. Two people can work together: An interviewer standing outside the stage can say the part that the ventriloquist would say, and a puppeteer speaking for the puppets can say the vent figure's part. Most of the dialogues in this book can be done in this manner. This means, of course, that you will have to practice with the other person.

Ventriloquial dialogues can be performed by two puppets in the stage with no one outside the stage. One puppet takes the part of the ventriloquist and the other does the vent figure's speech.

Use backdrops in the stage. They can be made to fit many plays or dialogues; for example, a river could be used for a play about Moses saved from death by the pharaoh's daughter. It could be changed during the performance to a scene inside the pharaoh's palace as the action moves inside. Put a front curtain on your stage that can be closed when you want to change scenes or props. (See Part 2, chapter 7, for details on backdrops and curtains.)

Whether there are one or more puppeteers behind the stage, someone must have a free hand to open or close the curtain at the proper time. When I know the curtain is to be operated, I plan to have only one puppet on stage (or none at all). And because I work the curtain with my left hand, the on-stage puppet must be on my right hand.

If the puppet shows are performed live, music can be used to cover awkward pauses in the performance. Have a music tape in your tape recorder and play it as needed. If no puppeteer has a free hand to push the start button, use a foot switch that can be plugged into the remote control jack adjacent to the mike jack of your recorder. Press the play button on your recorder ahead of time. During the show, if you want music, use your foot to push the foot pedal and hold. Release it quickly to stop the recorder. Practice will make this work smoothly. Foot switches can be purchased at audio equipment stores for a small cost.

A puppeteer can exchange the puppets on one hand while holding a puppet on stage with the other. Be sure the puppets are laid out on the floor of the stage so you can easily insert your hand. If there is a problem with getting the puppet on smoothly, use your other arm for leverage (down low so the action won't be seen). Or use your teeth to pull the puppet on.

No matter how well-prepared you are, there are times when something will go wrong in a puppet performance. In that case, you may have to stop the recording or the live performance temporarily to take care of the problem. Remain calm and in control. Remove the on-stage puppets, if necessary, and turn off the tape recorder. I usually call out something like: "Stay tuned to this channel. The puppets will return momentarily." Correct the trouble, rewind the tape a fraction, start the recorder, place the puppets in position, and continue.

TIPS FOR THE VENTRILOQUIST

Some tips for the ventriloquist follow.

Timing, knowing how and when to say each line in the dialogue, is important in a vent routine. Give the audience time to react to what is said, especially the jokes. Wait for laughter to subside before continuing. You must react to the figure's remarks, and laugh at its jokes. Be especially careful that the punch line of a joke is understood. If you don't get an expected laugh from a joke, proceed. Pause at times to get the right effect and give the words a chance to register with the audience.

A puppet can sometimes portray moods and thoughts better by actions than by words. For instance, have it duck down under your arm when embarrassed or slowly turn away from you and lower its head, but say nothing. Mouth puppets are very good for these kinds of actions.

Bringing your vent figure out for your show and removing it afterwards can sometimes be a problem. If the room where you will perform has wings or side rooms adjacent to the platform, your figure can rest there out of sight until needed. You can then bring it out seated on your hand and return it the same way. If there are no side rooms, consider these suggestions.

➤ If you have a puppet stage, screens, or other objects in the room, they may furnish a place to hide your figure.

➤ In a church auditorium, it is sometimes possible to place a puppet behind the choir rail or pulpit until it's needed.

➤ Have the figure seated on a chair on the platform until it's used. Return it to the chair to sit again. (When I must do this, I usually say, "Now sit quietly and listen to the lesson. Be a good example of obedience.")

➤ Bring your figure on stage in a suitcase. Return it to the suitcase at the conclusion. (Ventriloquists disagree on whether a suitcase finish, when the puppet protests that it doesn't want to be put inside, should be used. Sometimes the audience, especially small children, object to such treatment of their little friend. If it's necessary to put the vent figure in a suitcase on stage, try letting it beg to get in its case, because it's sleepy or wants to fix itself some food in there.) If little children see me carrying away a bag or suitcase, they sometimes ask if my vent figure is in there. I reply, "Yes. It's sleeping in its sleeping bag," or "She's in her little bed in the case." This usually satisfies them.

🙐 A ventriloquist should keep in mind how different ages respond to vent figures. These are my observations:

➤ Preschoolers, especially the younger ones, are often frightened when they first see a doll that can talk and move. When one of my granddaughters was two, she begged to see my puppets but hid in fright when one appeared, peeking out to get a glimpse but refusing to come near. When she was three, I sent her a miniature of her favorite puppet. Upon opening the package, she begged her parents to send it back to me. But with gentle coaxing, they helped her not to fear it, and soon it became her favorite toy. A quiet approach is better with small children. Let them get used to the vent figure a little at a time. Don't force them to come near. Preschoolers don't understand jokes. Simple conversations, singing, and short stories are best.

➤ Early-elementary-age children (six through eight) are enthralled with a vent figure and thoroughly enjoy almost anything it says or does. Be sure your jokes are geared for their age. They love to talk to a puppet and will dominate the show if you let them. If there is time, I let them talk with the vent figure when my program is done.

➤ Mid- to late-elementary-age children (ages nine through twelve) appreciate jokes more than younger children, but you must still learn the type of humor they enjoy the most. (Borrow children's joke books from the library and listen to the jokes told by this age level.) They consider a vent figure their buddy and will identify with it in its conversations and its experiences.

➤ Teens, particularly the younger ones, don't want to be embarrassed and may feel as though they are too old to enjoy puppets. If they are in a mixed group, they will present no problem, but in a group by themselves, they may seem to be completely bored with your performance, not responding to the humor at all. Actually, they do enjoy ventriloquism very much; they're just afraid to show it. Treat them as young adults. Don't talk down to them. Use material that matches their intelligence. Ignore their seeming indifference, and both you and they will have a good time.

➤ Adults are often interested in the art of ventriloquism as such. They love to see how well you can perform. Don't be intimidated by this. You probably know far more about ventriloquism than any of them do. Plan a dialogue that fits the occasion, practice it well, and go before them with as much confidence as you would with children.

CHAPTER 6
Puppets with a Purpose

In a Christian ministry, if puppets aren't used for the glory of God, they should not be used at all. "Whether you eat or drink or whatever you do, do it all for the glory of God" (1 Corinthians 10:31). All Christian puppeteers should be mindful of this verse every time a puppet is used.

The words of the puppets must be a part of the teaching of God's Word. Of course there will be occasions when the puppets will be used for activities not directly associated with the lesson, such as welcoming visitors, making announcements, or promoting contests. Puppets will occasionally be used purely for entertainment. But a Christian puppet ministry should always glorify God and be kept in line with His Word.

The Great Responsibility

"Assemble the people before me to hear my words so that they may learn to revere me as long as they live in the land and may teach them to their children" (Deuteronomy 4:10). God wants us to hear His words and worship Him all our days. But our responsibility doesn't end there. We are also to teach our children to hear His words and worship Him. Each generation has a responsibility for the next one. Psalm 145:4 says, "One generation will commend your works to another; they will tell of your mighty acts." Our prayer to the Lord, then, should be like Manoah's when he sought God's guidance in bringing up his son: "Teach us to bring up the boy" (Judges 13:8).

Anyone who has any part in the instruction of children at church should be aware of the great importance of our teaching and of the small amount of time in which to do it. There are 168 hours in a week. Where does a child spend these hours? For those old enough to go, school takes about 35 hours. Most of the rest of the time—up to 133 hours—are spent in the home, or at least under the supervision of parents. The church has children for a very small time in comparison—from 1 to 5 hours.

Who will teach God's Word to children? Will the school do it? Certainly the public school does not. Even the Christian school can't devote a great deal of time for this. Will the family do it? Unsaved parents can't teach God's Word to their children, and saved parents often can't or don't spend as much time as they should. It is likely that the majority of Bible teaching a child receives happens at church. The one hour the children sit before you in class may be their only Bible teaching of the week. Doesn't that make every minute valuable? This applies not only to the use of puppets but to every other phase of teaching as well.

Whether conscious of it or not, we influence each child who sits before us in church, teaching them by words, actions, and example. A soldier who lay dying on the battlefield told a chaplain, "Please send word to my Sunday school teacher that I thank her for faithfully teaching me God's Word and for leading me to Christ." A twelve-year-old Mexican girl began attending a church during my children's crusade. One night she received the Lord as Savior. On the last night of our services, she told the pastor's wife, "I hate to see Mrs. Pearson go. She's the only one that's ever showed me any love." Oh, may we always be aware of the great influence we have on the lives of the children whom God has placed in our care!

Another factor motivates me to guard the time and opportunities I have with children: They may not live to be grown. Young lives are taken by accident, disease, and suicide. I've learned of the deaths of fifteen children who once sat in my services; none lived to be older than twenty-one. One eleven-year-old boy who had been raised in a cult attended one of my classes. Thank the Lord, he trusted Jesus to save him that night. Three weeks later he was dead from spinal meningitis. So far as the church folks could ascertain, mine was the only gospel service he'd ever attended in his life.

What a responsibility Christian teachers of children have! How we need to guard every precious moment! Even the times of fun and entertainment should glorify the Lord and exercise the proper influence on the lives of children. We must not assume that we have plenty of time to teach them and lead them to Christ.

A Puppet's Relationship to God

There are differing opinions among Christian puppeteers about how to deal with a puppet's relationship to God. This issue raises a number of questions.

Should puppets be represented as Christians?

Would it be right to have a puppet pray?

Should puppets speak of going to heaven?

Should puppets be taught Christian values and be told to please God?

Puppets are not alive. We bring them to life by way of human hand and voice. Then we pretend that they can see, hear, think, and perform people-like actions. We carry out the illusion that they are not made of cloth or wood but of human flesh. But do we also make believe that they have living souls and can have a relationship with God?

When I first began to do ventriloquism, I reasoned that Sunshine, my vent figure, represented a real girl and should therefore be treated in all aspects like a person. I taught her about salvation and had her say she would trust Jesus as Savior, although I never had her pray before the class. As I added other vent figures to my acts, I treated the people puppets the same way, although animal puppets were never spoken to as having souls.

I wasn't quite comfortable, however, in acting as though the puppets could be saved. So I've changed my tactics. In most ways I still treat my puppets as though they're real people. I reprimand them for being bad and compliment them for being good. We talk of Bible characters and stories and even of Bible doctrines. But when we speak of anything that has to do with a personal relationship with God, my puppets talk of what people should do. In other words, I pretend they possess body, mind, and emotions, but not soul and spirit.

For instance, "What's That in Your Hand?" (Dialogue 2, Part 3) teaches Numbers 32:23. First, the puppet tries to hide a dollar bill in its hand, which the ventriloquist discovers. Then it is taught that children can't hide their sin from God. In the dialogue "Nobody Loves Me," a puppet says nobody loves her, but she finds that the ventriloquist, the audience, and other puppets do love her. The discussion then centers on the fact that all children are loved too, especially by God. "Volunteers for Jesus" deals with witnessing in a similar manner. Read these dialogues and note how spiritual matters are related to the puppets.

Since children identify with puppets and consider them their friends, this matter must be handled with sensitivity and carefulness. If you've done a good job of making the puppets seem real, children, especially younger ones, may be upset at the thought that their little friends can't be saved and go to heaven. It is sometimes difficult to know where illusion should stop and reality should begin. But I find you can make the transition in a way satisfying to children if, when you apply spiritual truths, you speak of people, with no mention of the puppet.

These are the guidelines I try to follow in regard to spiritual matters and puppets.

🐛 Ventriloquial figures may not be represented as having a relationship with God.

🐛 Stage puppets who always keep the same identity as puppets should be treated the same as vent figures. These would be puppets who speak with people and interact with the audience.

🐛 Stage puppets that play the parts of people in dramatizations of stories may act out anything that people can, including getting saved and praying. Stage puppets who always keep the same name and character but always play the part of a particular person fall into this category, for they are not playing themselves as puppets, but represent people.

🐛 Animal puppets in dialogues or stories should never be treated as though they have souls, are Christians, or are going to heaven.

🐛 A puppet should never be used in giving an invitation to Christ. Children might come forward just to be near the puppet. If possible, all puppets should be out of sight at invitation time.

Puppets as Teachers

Puppets are miniature teachers. Here are some rules I find practical in keeping them in line with the Bible and in doing what will bring glory to God.

PUPPETS' BAD BEHAVIOR

🐛 Puppets may do wrong. (How could they represent people if they were only good?) However, because children are imitators, the wrong actions should be pointed out and corrected. The puppet should confess bad behavior, make amends, change, or whatever is called for to show that God disapproves of sin, calls for repentance, and forgives.

🐛 Puppets who play the parts of villains or other bad characters should not be too lovable and attractive, so as to discourage imitation. They should be dealt with appropriately before the play ends, or they should change and become good.

🐛 No puppet should be a constant smart aleck. An

occasional joke is all right when done tastefully. But to frequently make snippy, snide remarks can set a bad example for children, giving the impression that it's okay to talk disrespectfully to their elders or to belittle other children. A pastor once told me that he'd like to have me do a ventriloquial act, but only if I didn't make him the butt of the jokes. He said every ventriloquist who had performed in his church had done it, and he felt it showed disrespect to the office he held. Another pastor told me that he felt like destroying the next vent figure that made a joke about his bald head. A little good-natured teasing is all right; but the feelings of the one who is teased should be considered.

🐾 No off-color jokes and stories should ever be told, on or off the platform.

🐾 Watch your language. These days children may often hear swearing on television. They may also be around adults who swear. As a result, one can hear children talking in the same way, including misusing the name of the Lord. Watch out for slang words that are really oaths in a shortened form. For instance, the dictionary says "golly" is a euphemism (an alternate word) for "God," and "gee" is a euphemistic contraction of "Jesus."

🐾 Puppets in the stage should not do long-winded speeches, trying to teach the lesson. Children get bored with this.

🐾 Some teaching is possible when doing ventriloquism, since at that time you face your audience along with your vent figure.

🐾 When teaching with a vent figure, stand before your audience, making good eye contact. The vent figure can make a statement to drive home a truth or illustrate a teaching. Then, facing the class again, you can explain the meaning of the puppet show and make spiritual applications as needed.

🐾 I believe it's best to teach the lesson first, when children are fresh and alert. Then give your main puppet presentation, followed by your application.

ANIMAL PUPPETS

Animal puppets are loved by children, they are rather simple to make, and they can be a source of many ideas for scripts. Some people object to having animals talk. But without speech, the use of animals will be greatly curtailed. All of puppetry is a kind of pretense. Why not pretend animals can talk? These are guidelines I follow in using animal puppets.

🐾 Animal puppets converse with the ventriloquist, the interviewer, or members of the audience.

🐾 In dramatic plays, I usually have animals make their natural sounds when people puppets are present.

They talk when alone on stage or to other animals. This is a personal preference, but there needn't be a strict rule about this.

🐾 Teaching can be more effective with animal puppets if you let them exhibit human emotions and characteristics.

🐾 When Bible stories are acted out, animal puppets should behave like animals. With the exception of Balaam's donkey and the serpent who spoke to Eve, animal puppets should not speak to human beings.

🐾 Be sure your animals don't contradict Bible truths or alter facts.

🐾 You could use animal puppets to tell Bible stories. For instance, a pig could tell about the prodigal son, or a lion could tell about Daniel in the lion's den. (See "You Can't Hide from God," Dialogue 17, Part 3, when the fish that swallowed Jonah tells his story.)

BIBLE STORIES

I've never used a puppet to play the part of Jesus. I don't think it would represent Him properly and magnify His glory. Seeing Jesus in the form of a puppet could give children a misconception of His Person. In allegories (stories in which people, things, and happenings have another meaning) I use puppets to represent Jesus, for example, when a prince leaves the king's palace to go into the realm and take the punishment a condemned prisoner should have.

🐾 Puppets can play the parts of people living in Jesus' time, and they can tell what happened in an incident where He was present. For instance, the man with the withered hand who was healed on the Sabbath could meet a friend who notices the hand is healed. Then follows the story of the healing.

🐾 Puppets can act out incidents in the life of Jesus when He is heard, but not seen. For example: The curtain opens on a home scene. A father arrives home from work, and his son excitedly tells that he saw Jesus that day. The father asks for the story, and the son tells how he and his mother heard that Jesus was nearby. He says they hurriedly packed a lunch and started out. The curtain is closed and opens on an outdoor Bible times scene. The mother and son walk along and talk about hoping to see Jesus. They look toward one corner of the back of the stage and the boy says, "Look at the crowd of people! Jesus must be there. Oh, I want to get up close to Him!" A disciple appears and tells them not to bother Jesus. Then a voice is heard saying, "Let the little children come to me" (Matthew 19:14.) Mother and son walk toward the back and exit, supposedly to see Jesus. The curtain closes and reopens on the home scene again. The son then tells the father what it was like to receive the blessing of Jesus.

🕭 A picture or silhouette of Jesus in the background of a scene could represent Jesus. An effective, solemn portrayal of the crucifixion could be done like that. The curtain could open on a city scene, representing Jerusalem. One puppet meets another and discusses some events of Jesus' capture and trial. He says Jesus is being crucified, and they decide to go and see for themselves. The curtain next opens to reveal the scene of the crucifixion. The backdrop has a mountain in the far distance on which three figures are silhouetted on three crosses. In the foreground of the picture is a crowd of people (flannelgraph figures or other pictures pinned or taped to the cloth). The two puppets enter and stand at the front part of the stage, turning partially toward the scene and talk of what they see. If desired, the words of Jesus from the cross can be given, lights can be dimmed to show the darkness, and the earthquake can be simulated by a slight rocking of the stage and puppets.

🕭 Keep dramatized Bible stories true to the Scriptures. The language can be up-to-date to be understood by children, but should not deviate from the true meaning. If characters or events not found in the Bible are added, keep them minor or be sure your audience knows they are fictional.

🕭 If a story is based on a Bible incident but involves characters not described in the Bible, I sometimes explain to the children that the people in this play are imaginary, but the events of the play are true. The puppets act out the events as stated in the Bible. For example, in the story of the death of the firstborn in Egypt, I use four characters: an Israelite father, mother, and son, and an Egyptian woman. The story of what happened to all of the Israelites and Egyptians is acted out through their experiences.

🕭 Younger children are not time and space conscious and can easily be confused by stories that put Bible events in contemporary settings or contemporary items in a biblical setting. Adults and teenagers can appreciate the humor of having Pharaoh look in the yellow pages for a locust exterminator, but children may think this actually happened. Make the Bible stories exciting and interesting, but factual.

🕭 Humor is good with puppets but is not always necessary. Often a small amount of humor can be worked into a serious dramatization. When humor is used, keep it clean and wholesome. Use jokes the children understand.

OTHER STORIES

Both true and fictional stories may be used with puppets. These guidelines may be helpful in using stories.

🕭 There should be a reason for telling the story: to teach a lesson or expand knowledge.

🕭 Stories should feature, or at least interest, children.

🕭 Choose stories with plenty of action.

🕭 Keep conversations short and lively.

🕭 It is usually best to *imply* the lesson in the story and *apply* the truths afterward.

🕭 Let children know which stories are true and which are not.

🕭 Use stories to teach good behavior (e.g., obeying parents and teachers, attending church, giving, Bible reading, and sharing).

🕭 Use stories to show that bad behavior is known by God and will sooner or later bring trouble.

One Theme Per Session

In planning a service, always keep in mind three basic educational goals.

1. Every lesson should impart knowledge of God's Word.

2. Every lesson should attempt to affect attitudes.

3. Every lesson should aim for a change of behavior.

You can't accomplish these goals with a hodge-podge of ideas and teachings in one session. You need one central theme, and you should use all teaching aids, including puppets, to teach, reinforce, and review that one theme. That is how learning takes place. It comes with repetition and review. Too many subjects at one time only confuse children and hinder the learning process.

Children need to have time to think about what you are teaching. They need time to reflect, to let the lesson sink in. That is why they must not have too many different ideas presented in one lesson. Dr. Ruth Beechick, in *Teaching Primaries*, says, "Fast moving cartoons and TV commercials, and even the earlier days of Sesame Street, ignore this need for reflection in learning, and in effect teach children not to learn from the stimuli around them. Such 'sensory overload' may be a cause of many perceptual learning difficulties which are in epidemic proportions today" (p. 81).

Know what your aim for a lesson is. What do you want to accomplish? All class activities should be in keeping with your aim and central theme, including songs, memory work, play activities, games, and puppets. All of these can illustrate, review, reinforce, and establish the teaching.

MAKING THE LESSON UNDERSTANDABLE TO CHILDREN

Can children be taught in abstract terms or can they understand only what is concrete? One dictionary says *concrete* means "belonging to immediate experience of actual things or events." *Abstract* means "to consider apart from application or association with a particular instance."

Most children from six to about twelve think concretely and find difficulty with abstractions. But important Christian doctrines and concepts are abstract, such things as faith, love, hope, grace, mercy, forgiveness. What are we to do with these vital teachings, if most of our children can't understand the use of abstract terms? Should we leave them alone? No. They are essential in teaching about salvation and Christian living. How do we solve the problem, then?

We simply follow Jesus' technique: He often told stories to illustrate abstract concepts, such as love, forgiveness, mercy. His stories as well as other stories in the Bible can help explain abstracts. For instance, to teach about faith, first give a definition of the word. Here is a good one: "Faith is taking God at His Word and acting upon it." Then tell the story of Abraham's call to leave his country and go to a strange land. He took God at His word and left, believing God to guide him and care for him. Or tell the story of Peter walking on the water. That was faith in action.

Contemporary stories can illustrate abstract principles. A father tells his blind child to walk to him, even though the child hears dogs barking furiously. The father tells the child the dogs are chained and can't hurt him. When does the child have real faith? When he says he believes the father about the dogs, or when he walks to his father?

Puppets are a great aid in helping explain the abstract by way of concrete illustrations. They can dramatize biblical, historical, and contemporary stories that explain abstract principles. And puppets that retain their identity as puppets can "experience" happenings that illustrate love, forgiveness, mercy, and so forth.

Ways to Use Puppets in the Classroom

Puppets can appear at almost any time in your service to aid in capturing attention and help you teach. Naturally, you would not use puppets in everything you do in one session. Variety and surprise keep a service lively and interesting. One Sunday you might use the puppets in one way, and the next Sunday in another way. Sometimes they might not appear at all. Avoid overexposure. You don't want them to become too commonplace. A few suggestions for using them in different ways follow.

Have a puppet welcome children as they arrive. This works well in small classes, especially with younger children.

The puppet can call each child by name and have a short conversation. But don't force the puppet on a very timid child.

Where many children come at once, such as when bus riders arrive, it is best not to have any puppets appear until the service starts. Then the puppet can welcome the whole group, perhaps calling out some names.

A puppet might introduce visitors and welcome them.

Have an alarm clock set to go off at the exact moment your service should start. When it rings, a bird puppet (maybe Erlene Early Bird) appears. She commends the children for being on time. She calls out the names of two or three children, and if they're present, they get a peck on the cheek or some other recognition for being present and on time. She introduces visitors and tries to make them feel welcome. She recognizes all the children who have brought their Bibles or learned their memory work. You may make a straw nest that contains jelly bean eggs that Erlene gives to children as a reward. (See chapter 9 for a bird pattern.)

Use puppets to promote contests. See Dialogue 34 and Dialogue 35, Part 3, for ideas.

Use puppets to give variety to the song service.

Let a puppet lead a song. Children may sing better for it than for your regular song leader.

When you think the words or message of a song aren't clear to the children, let a puppet do a routine where it mispronounces some words or puts a wrong meaning to them. In getting it straightened out, the children learn too.

A puppet can introduce a new song to the class by singing it first.

Use puppets for a special song.

Have puppets lip sync a prerecorded song. One puppeteer, using one or two puppets, can do solos or duets. Two puppeteers can do duets, trios, or quartets. The livelier the music, the better.

Have puppets "play" instrumental numbers together with a prerecorded song or live music behind stage.

For the mouth puppet, fasten a toy horn or saxophone to its hands with wire or rubber bands. The mouthpiece can be placed in its mouth and held in place by pressing down hard inside the mouth with your fingers to keep it closed. Hardhead puppets can hold instruments with their hands, but the closed mouth presents a problem. Punch a small hole in the mouth and tape a piece of toothpick to the end of the horn. Before the puppet goes on stage, place the toothpick in its mouth.

A stringed instrument can be held with each end of a ribbon fastened to the instrument. Hang the ribbon around the puppet's neck. Fasten one hand of the puppet to the neck of the instrument. A hardhead puppet can appear to be playing by moving the other hand across the strings. A mouth puppet can do this only if its hand is controlled by a rod.

A puppeteer can play a kazoo behind the stage while operating a puppet on stage. Use one hand for the kazoo and one for the puppet. Or if both hands are needed on stage, hold the kazoo between your teeth, or fasten it with tape to a harmonica holder that goes around your neck. Play the kazoo while the puppet "plays" another kazoo or a horn. (Kazoos and harmonica holders can be purchased in music stores.)

🎭 A puppet can make announcements. You can be sure that children will pay better attention to your announcements and will be more likely to remember them if puppets aid you in making them. (See Dialogue 30 and Dialogue 33, Part 3, for ideas.) Some suggestions for using puppets follow.

➤ A puppet tries to make the announcement but gets very confused. An interviewer helps get it right. In doing this, the announcement is repeated several times.

➤ The announcement is made to the children. A puppet later makes the announcement but gets it all confused. The children can correct its mistakes.

➤ The interviewer forgets to make the announcement or gets it mixed up. The puppet reminds him of the correct announcement.

➤ Several weeks in advance of an important event, the puppets can talk of a big secret that will be revealed some Sunday soon.

➤ Puppets can hold signs, notes, pictures, or objects related to the announcement.

🎭 Puppets can emphasize giving. They can forget to bring their money, hate to part with their money, or be very generous and happy about giving. They can ask questions about what the money will be used for and why people should give. (See Dialogue 29, Part 3, for attitudes about giving.)

🎭 Puppets can help children memorize. This is an excellent time to use puppets. They can repeat verses correctly or incorrectly, hold up signs, read the Bible or notes, play memory games, and give out awards to those who have completed their memory work. (See Dialogue 31, Part 3, for ideas for memorization.)

🎭 Puppets can read the Bible. Stage puppets can hold a prop that looks like a Bible. (See chapter 7.) A ventriloquist or interviewer can hold a Bible while a puppet "reads" it. Bible readings should be short. There should be no joking at Bible reading time, and emphasis should be on reverence for God's Word. I find children always listen with interest and respect when I use my Talking Bible for Bible reading. (See chapter 12 for a pattern and Dialogue 36, Part 3, for dialogues.)

🎭 Puppets can help with discipline. You might promise children that a puppet will come out to talk to them if they are good; but if they misbehave, it won't appear. Don't do this with your scheduled appearances of puppets, especially a presentation that you have planned to aid you in teaching, or you might have to forego a vital part of your lesson. But Chucky Church Mouse (or any special puppet) could come out when children have been good. Chucky could tell them he's been listening to them and wants to compliment them on their good behavior. But when the class has been noisy, he will not appear. The noise has sent him scampering away! (See chapter 10 for a mouse pattern.)

Most discipline problems occur when children are bored or are not truly interested in what is going on in class. With the proper use of puppets, you will have less unruly behavior.

🎭 Puppets can teach about missions. They can talk about missions and about people who don't know the gospel story. They can dramatize stories of missionaries and of their converts.

🎭 Puppets can promote participation. With strict supervision, children themselves can sometimes operate puppets. This could be a good way to review a lesson or act out some kind of behavior you've been learning about. A child who learns the memory work perfectly might be rewarded by being allowed to say it while operating the puppet.

Puppetry in Other Church Services

When you become a good puppeteer, you will find that you will be in demand to perform in other services of your church. These could include youth meetings, opening assemblies, banquets, evangelistic campaigns, worship services, ladies' or men's meetings, missionary meetings, and social get-togethers. Almost any type of service could be enhanced by a well-performed puppet presentation. Just remember to fit your program to the ages present and the type of service being held. (Some dialogues intended for adults or mixed ages may be found in Part 3, Dialogue 26 and Dialogue 29, for example.)

Puppetry Outside the Church

Puppets can be effectively used in ministries outside your church. This will often afford you an excellent opportunity for witnessing. Even in places where you will not be allowed to give direct Bible teaching (like public schools and libraries) you can still give moral lessons, teachings on such things as kindness and generosity, the harmfulness of tobacco, alcohol, and drugs. Through these outside appearances you may have an opportunity to invite people to your church. What follows is a partial list of places where you and your puppets might perform.

➤ Nursing homes or private homes where there are shut-ins

➤ Children's hospitals

➤ Christian schools and kindergartens

➤ Public schools

➤ Public libraries (in their children's programs)

➤ Shopping centers and malls

➤ TV programs

➤ Family reunions

➤ Clubs (senior citizens, scouts, etc.)

➤ Backyard or home Bible classes

➤ Open air meetings

➤ Church or bus ministry visitation

➤ Camps

I have used ventriloquism and stage puppets in all of these kinds of situations. When you have practiced and performed for a while, you will find yourself having the same opportunities. It is exciting—your puppet ministry is expanding.

PART TWO

Props and Patterns

CHAPTER 7
Construction & Use of Stages & Props

A puppet stage may be velvet curtains and hardwood, a few pieces of cardboard taped together, or a sheet hung across a doorway. Everything that conceals the puppets can be considered a stage. There are stages that hold only the puppets and ones that completely hide the puppeteers. Stages can be portable or permanent fixtures. This chapter will give directions for making a sturdy stage that can be portable or permanent, a lightweight stage that can be carried in one hand, makeshift stages for various occasions, and props.

A Sturdy Stage

The most popular puppet stage is a booth of three sides, with the proscenium (stage opening) in the upper front of the middle partition. Some stages are designed so the puppeteers stand erect behind the stage. Others are made for the puppeteers to be kneeling or sitting inside with their hands raised over their heads. The following features make this stage different from those found in many churches.

Front Curtain. The stage has a front curtain that may be raised or lowered. It can be worked quickly and easily with one hand. When it is raised it is entirely out of the way. When it is closed it allows the puppeteer to change scenery, props, or puppets. When it is lowered for a few moments, a passage of time in the story can be indicated.

Backdrops. The stage uses backdrops. Backdrops are made from fabric and are placed a foot behind the proscenium on a backboard. While the backdrops may be plain, scenery drawn on them will add much to the effectiveness of the story, for it will depict the setting for each situation. Making scenery on backdrops may be time-consuming, but the backdrops will last for years if they are taken care of. I still use some that are over twenty years old.

Floor. The stage has a shelf (called a "floor") inside the puppet stage. It reaches from one side of the stage to the other. It is six inches below the bottom edge of the stage opening and is about a foot wide. This gives room for the puppeteer to lay out the puppets needed, to place props, and to rest his elbows while holding the puppets.

If you don't plan to move your stage often you can make it from heavier material than that for a stage that needs to be portable. However, I often hear puppeteers complain about stages being too heavy to move easily, so consider weight when choosing wood. Depending on your needs, choose 1/4-, 3/8-, or 1/2-inch plywood, which comes in 4- by 8-foot sheets. The thinner plywood may need to have a framework of 1- by 2-inch boards.

THE BOOTH AND STAGE FLOOR
(See Figure 3: Making the Booth.)

MATERIALS NEEDED

2 sheets of 4- by 8-foot plywood

6 three-inch hinges

A 1- by 2-foot board, 4 feet long (longer if you want the side panels of the booth at a wider than 90 degree angle to the middle panel; cut the ends of the floor at the appropriate angle if you do this.)

Nails, or hooks and eyebolts

INSTRUCTIONS

1. From one sheet of plywood cut two 2- by 6-foot side panels.
2. From the other sheet of plywood cut one 4- by 6-foot middle panel.
3. From the 4- by 6-foot panel cut out a 3- by 1 1/2-foot proscenium 6 inches from the top and sides.
4. Attach the 2 side panels to the middle panel, one on each side, with 3-inch hinges. You will then be able to collapse the stage for easy storage or portability. (If you put the hinges on the inside, be aware that the side panels will not fold completely flat unless you remove the hooks for the stage floor.)

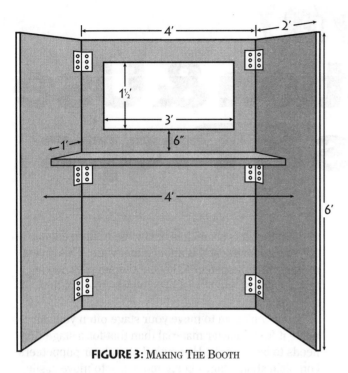

FIGURE 3: MAKING THE BOOTH

5. If your stage is a permanent fixture, nail the 4-foot board (floor) 6 inches below the bottom of the proscenium on the inside of the stage. If the stage is collapsible, screw hooks into the plywood 6 inches below the proscenium and screw eyebolts into the edge of the board. Hook the floor board in place.

THE FRONT CURTAIN

MATERIALS NEEDED

Thick cloth, such as heavy velour: 1 piece 4- by 4-feet and 1 piece 3- by 42-inches

Fringe or other decoration

4 pieces of ribbon or seam tape, each 24 inches long

A 1- by 2-inch board, 52 inches long

A 42-inch dowel or broomstick

4 pieces of 6-foot-long fishing line

INSTRUCTIONS

(See Figure 4: Making the Front Curtain.)

1. In the 4- by 4-foot piece of cloth, sew a 3-inch hem along both sides of the cloth and a 3 1/2-inch hem along the top. Put a narrow hem and fringe or other decoration along the bottom.

2. With a long machine stitch, sew four rows for gathers from the bottom edge to just below the top hem, 2 on each side and 2 about 14 inches in from each side. Fasten the threads securely at the top, and

gather the fabric from below so the curtain measures 24 inches from top to bottom.

3. Pin 24-inch-long ribbons or seam tape to the inside of the cloth along each of the gathers to reinforce the stitching. Machine stitch along the tape or ribbons twice to secure the gathers. You should now have three scallops along the bottom edge.

4. Pin the 3- by 42-inch piece of cloth in place near the bottom edge of the inside of the curtain. Machine stitch the piece along the top and the bottom, folding under a hem, leaving the ends open for the 42-inch dowel to be inserted. Insert the dowel.

5. Cut slots near the ends of the 52- by 1- by 2-inch board to hang the curtain on the side stage walls.

6. In the hem at the top of the curtain insert the 52- by 1- by 2-inch board. This is to fit onto your stage directly behind the proscenium.

7. Thread one of the fishing line lengths into a needle with a large eye. At the bottom of the curtain on the inside, just above the bottom rod, push the needle through the cloth. Pull a few inches of line through and push the needle back in the cloth just below the rod. Remove the needle and securely tie the end of the line to the line itself, so the rod is secured.

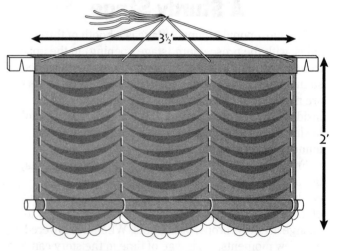

FIGURE 4: MAKING THE FRONT CURTAIN

8. Now thread the needle with the other end of the line. Push the needle through the cloth on the inside near the rod. With very long stitches on the inside and shorter stitches on the outside, continue to stitch toward the top of the curtain. Go over the top rod from the outside and leave the line dangling temporarily.

9. Repeat the two preceding steps along each of the other three gathers. (Explanation for finishing off the lines will be under the backboard instructions.)

THE BACKBOARD

MATERIALS NEEDED

A 1- by 6-inch board, 52-inches long

6 hooks

A small metal or plastic ring

INSTRUCTIONS

(See Figure 5: Making the Backboard.)

1. Cut slots in the board so it will fit over the top of the side panels.

2. Screw three hooks on the front of the backboard about 1 inch from the bottom edge with the open ends up. Put one in the center, and the other two 19 inches from the center on each side. They will hold the backdrops.

3. To make guides for raising and lowering the curtain, screw a hook on the top edge of the board 26 inches from the end, which should be the middle. Turn the hook so that it opens on the right (when facing the stage from the inside). Screw another hook on the top edge of the board 2 inches from the left edge (when facing the stage from the inside). Turn the hook so that it opens on the left.

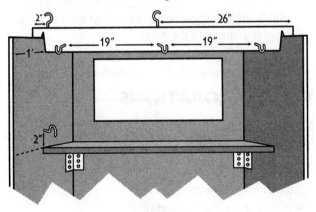

FIGURE 5: MAKING THE BACKBOARD

4. Screw a hook on the left stage wall straight down from the hook on the top edge of the board, about 2 inches above the floor (shelf) of the stage. Turn the hook so that it opens toward the floor.

5. Take all four fishing line ends and bring them together around the middle hook, over to the left hook, and down to the hook near the stage floor. Pull them down until the curtain is fully raised. Cut the lines so that when they are tied to the ring and put on the hook they will hold the curtain up. Tie the ring to the ends of the lines. Release the ring and the curtain should fall. If it doesn't fall as far as it should, put some weights on the bottom.

BACKDROPS

The backdrops can be placed on the backboard hooks and quickly removed for a change of scenery during a show.

MATERIALS NEEDED

As many 39- by 25-inch pieces of unbleached muslin as you will make backdrops. (The fabric should be a weight you can see through, but the audience can't. To check the thinness of your cloth, hold it in front of your eyes as you face a window. You should be able to see objects on the other side. To check its thickness, stand in front of a dark background, facing a light, and hold the cloth in front of your face. Ask someone if you can be seen.)

3 small rings for each backdrop

Black liquid embroidery pen or black crayon or black felt pen

Crayons or watercolors or pastel chalks

INSTRUCTIONS

(See Figure 6: Backdrop Ideas.)

1. Fold the edges over 1/4 inch on all sides for a hem, and press. Fold the edges over again 1/4 inch and stitch the hem. The finished size should be 38 by 24 inches.

2. Sew three small rings to the top of the backdrop, one in the middle and the other two at the corners, matching the hooks on the backboard.

3. Draw scenery on your backdrops or, if preferred, use pastel-colored cloth. The scenery adds greatly to the atmosphere and gives a setting for the action. First, draw the outlines of the scenes with a black liquid embroidery pen, crayon, or felt pen that won't bleed on the cloth. Then color the scenes with crayons, water colors, or pastel chalk. When the backdrop is completed, spray it with fixative to preserve the colors.

4. Be sure your scenery is not so elaborate and detailed that it detracts from the puppets. It should be simple, merely suggesting the setting. When choosing colors, remember that your puppets must not merge into the background. There should be contrast—darker, brighter colors on the puppet costumes and lighter, more subtle shades on the scenery.

5. Take good care of your backdrops. Fold them neatly and put then in a good storage place. If the storage place allows, avoid creases from the folds by rolling the backdrops around cardboard cylinders. Slip rubber bands around each end to hold them in place.

Mountain Scene

City Street in Biblical Times

River or Lake

Inside Home

City Street in Modern Times

Pathway

FIGURE 6: BACKDROP IDEAS

STAGE LIGHTING

Illumination of the stage is very important when you are doing stage dramatizations since puppets and props are small. The strongest lighting should be on the puppets' faces. Where possible, I have all lights in the room turned off, with just the stage lights on during the performance. If you don't use lighting, be sure room lighting and windows are in front of the stage, not behind it, so the puppeteers won't be seen.

MATERIALS NEEDED

Two or three 100-watt lightbulbs

A blue lightbulb

Push-button floor switches

3-sided box made of nonflammable material

Metal strips for attaching box to backboard

String of white Christmas tree lightbulbs

INSTRUCTIONS

1. Fasten two or three 100-watt bulbs to the backboard. Shade the bulbs to focus them on the puppets in the stage below. Add a blue bulb for dimmer lighting when needed. Run wires from the bulbs to push-button floor switches mounted on a panel on the floor. These can be foot-operated while the puppeteer's hands are busy.

2. If you don't get proper lighting with lights over the middle of the stage, set up a lighting system at the front to illuminate the stage.

3. Place a string of white Christmas tree bulbs along the front of the stage floor for footlights.

STAGE DECORATIONS

Make your stage as attractive as possible. Use your imagination for endless possibilities.

MATERIALS NEEDED

Paint in bright colors

Self-adhesive plastic covering

Pictures of children or animals

Glue

Decals

INSTRUCTIONS

1. Paint the stage in bright colors.

2. Cover the stage with self-adhesive plastic

3. Glue figures of children or animals to the stage.

4. Attach decals to the stage.

5. Decorate the proscenium with scalloped wood nailed around its edges or with curtain valances on the top and bottom. (I have the latter on my stage, along with gathered drapes, which cover the sides and are attached by Velcro hook and loop fasteners.)

A Lightweight Portable Stage

For times when I need to set up in a hurry for a puppet presentation, I have a lightweight portable stage I can carry in a bag in one hand. It is especially good for one-time appearances with small audiences. Since it does not have a stage floor, I use a chair or small table, placed inside the stage or nearby, on which to put my puppets and props.

This portable stage will fold easily. With a cloth bag to fit over the parts, it can be carried in one hand.

The stage top may be used alone on a tabletop. The puppeteer will need to be seated behind the table. Cover the table with a cloth to hide the puppeteer.

THE STAGE TOP

MATERIALS NEEDED

1 dressmaker cutting board, 40 by 72 inches, referred to in the instructions as Panel 1. (If you can't find this size, a smaller size will do, but you will need to adjust all measurements.)

3 dowels: 2 at 30 inches long, 1 at 40 inches long

12 spring clothespins

Enough self-adhesive plastic to cover the outside of the cutting board

3 small hooks

INSTRUCTIONS

(See Figure 7: Making the Portable Stage.)

1. Cut 6 inches off the top of Panel 1, reducing the height to 34 inches.

2. Cut a 22- by 20-inch proscenium in section 3 of Panel 1, six inches from the top. The sides of the opening will be about 1 1/2 inches from the folds in the cutting board.

3. Cover the entire outside of Panel 1 with self-adhesive plastic, folding it to the inside over every edge.

4. Cut six holes in Panel 1, large enough to insert the dowels. Two holes should be made three inches from the top edge of sections 2 and 4, two inches from the folds of section 3. Two holes should be even with the bottom of the proscenium (25 inches below the top holes) on sections 2 and 4, two inches from the folds of section 3. Two holes should be three inches from the top on sections 1 and 5, two inches from the folds of sections 2 and 4. Put tape around the holes to keep them from enlarging.

5. From the inside of the stage, insert the ends of the dowels through the holes. Put the two 30-inch dowels in the holes in sections 2 and 4; put the 40-inch dowel in the holes in sections 1 and 5.

6. To hold the stage firmly in place, pin two clothespins on each stick, one on each side of the stage wall.

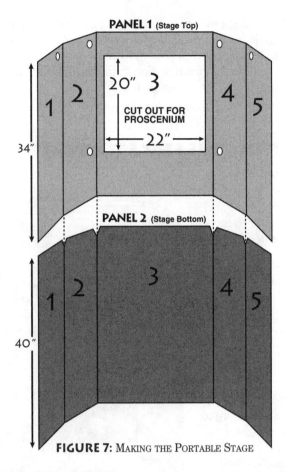

FIGURE 7: MAKING THE PORTABLE STAGE

BACKDROPS

See the instructions under "Backdrops" for the sturdy stage. The finished size for these backdrops should be 36 by 24 inches. If you change backdrops with this stage it will be seen by your audience, since it doesn't have a front curtain to hide the changes.

To hold the backdrops in place, screw 3 hooks on the dowel between sections 1 and 5: one in the middle and the others 18 inches on each side of the middle hook. (See Figure 8: Putting the Stage Together.)

THE STAGE BOTTOM

MATERIALS NEEDED

1 dressmaker cutting board, 40 by 72 inches, referred to in the instructions as Panel 2. (If you can't find this size, a smaller size will do, but you will need to adjust all measurements.)

Enough self-adhesive plastic to cover the outside of the cutting board

8 craft sticks

INSTRUCTIONS

(See Figure 7: Making the Portable Stage.)

1. Cover the entire outside of Panel 2 with self-adhesive plastic, folding it to the inside over every edge.

2. Make four 1-inch cuts at the top of Panel 2. One cut should be on the fold between sections 2 and 3; one on the fold between sections 3 and 4; one on section 1, three inches from section 2; and one on section 5, three inches from section 4.

3. Reinforce the cutting board by gluing craft sticks on the sides of the cuts.

PUTTING THE STAGE TOGETHER

MATERIALS NEEDED

Panel 1 and Panel 2
Decals or pictures
for decoration

INSTRUCTIONS

(See Figure 8: Putting the Stage Together.)

1. Place Panel 1 on top of Panel 2, fitting them together with the cuts.

2. Decorations can be added, such as decals or pictures glued on the stage walls and scallops added around the proscenium.

FIGURE 8:
PUTTING THE STAGE TOGETHER

A Pipe and Curtain Stage

Another puppet stage you might want to consider is the PVC pipe and curtain stage. It is a popular stage because of its versatility and ease in storage for travel. It also is able to hold more puppeteers than the previously described stages.

You can make a pipe stage to fit your puppeteering needs. It can be 2-tiered, 3-tiered, or 2-tiered with a backdrop. Make the first level around 4 feet from the floor, high enough to conceal kneeling puppeteers. The second level should be close to 6 feet from the floor to hide standing puppeteers. For the width of your stage, allow 2 feet per puppeteer; for example, if you have 3 people at one level your stage will need to be at least 6 feet wide.

The pipe stage is built with 1 1/2-inch plastic plumbing pipe. If you don't glue the pipes together, you will be able to dismantle the stage and store the pieces out of the way.

Use a velour or heavy polyester fabric for the curtain. Sew a casing on one edge to slip the pipe through before assembling the stage.

For detailed instructions on making pipe stages, see the Bibliography.

Makeshift Stages

Sometimes you may not be able to use a regular stage. There are many ways to improvise stages with whatever is available at the moment. Almost anything will do, so long as the puppets are seen and the puppeteers are not. Some suggestions follow.

🐦 Stretch a sheet across the top half of a doorway on the puppeteer's side, with the bottom a little above waist-level. Stretch a second sheet across the bottom half of the doorway on the audience's side, and extending about six inches above the bottom of the first sheet. The puppets are operated in between.

🐦 Place two chairs side by side and cover their backs with a sheet or blanket. The puppeteer kneels behind the chairs and holds the puppets above the chair level.

🐦 Place a card table on its side, with the legs open. The puppeteer kneels behind the table and holds the puppets above table level.

🐦 The puppeteer stands behind an upright piano and holds the puppets above the piano top.

🐦 Put a flannelboard on an easel and cover it with a sheet that reaches to the ground. The puppeteer stands behind the easel and holds the puppet above the top of the easel.

🐦 Make a temporary stage from a large cardboard carton.

🐦 When the audience is outside, a puppeteer can kneel down inside at a window or behind a porch rail or a hedge, over which a sheet or carpet is thrown. Or the puppeteer can stand behind a clothesline over which a blanket is draped. Puppets appear above any of these.

Obtaining and Using Props

Portable articles used in plays or other performances are called *properties*, or *props*. All items are in miniature, of course, to fit the size of the puppets. They may be a bit larger proportionately so that the audience may see them better. Sometimes the props can be picked up and held by the hardhead puppets. Since their hands can move freely, puppets can even exchange props on stage. Props can also be fastened to the puppet's hand by use of double-sided tape or Velcro hook and loop fasteners. An elastic loop sewn into the hand of a puppet can have a stick or other small object inserted into it. If a puppeteer has one free hand, he can hold a prop himself but by concealing his hand make it appear that the puppet is doing so.

Before the presentation, props should be placed on the stage floor so that they can be picked up easily during the show or carried on stage from behind the scenes.

Keep your eyes open for small objects like the following that can be used for props.

🐾 Sample or miniature items.

🐾 Small toys.

🐾 Discards from home, such as medicine bottles, small boxes, pieces of cloth.

🐾 For puppet jewelry, use bits of costume jewelry. For vases, cover small medicine or other bottles with beads and glass jewels.

Make your own props. Following are instructions.

A BED

MATERIALS NEEDED

Four 8- by 10-inch pieces of wood

One 10- by 10-inch piece of wood

Two 6- by 8 1/2-inch pieces of fabric (any kind) for the bed pad

Two 8 1/2- by 4 1/2-inch pieces of fabric for the pillow

One 20- by 10-inch piece of fabric for the bedspread

Polyester fiberfill for the bed pad and pillow

Velcro hook and loop fasteners

INSTRUCTIONS   (See Figure 9: Making a Bed.)

1. Glue and nail the pieces of wood to make a 5-sided box, 10 by 10 by 8 inches.

2. Set the box on its side so that the open end is visible. Cut a 3- by 6-inch slot 1 1/2 inches from a corner.

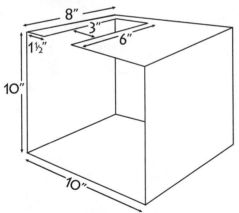

FIGURE 9: MAKING A BED

3. For the bed pad slipcover, sew the two 6- by 8 1/2-inch pieces of cloth, wrong sides together, on 3 sides, making a 1/4-inch seam. Turn the slipcover right side out. The finished size should be 5 1/2 by 10 inches.

4. Lightly stuff the slipcover with polyester fiber. Slip-stitch the open end, turning it under 1/4 inch.

5. Place the slipcover on top of the box, even with the bottom end of the bed. Fasten it with tape to hold it in place.

6. For the pillow, sew the 8 1/2- by 4 1/2-inch pieces of cloth, wrong sides together, on 3 sides, making a 1/4-inch seam. Turn the pillow cover right side out. The finished size should be 8 by 4 inches.

7. Glue 2 pieces of Velcro hook and loop fasteners to the bottom edge of the pillow, and 2 to the box where the pillow will be attached.

8. Drape a piece of cloth over the bed for a bedspread. Pin it to the pillow on the closed side, but leave it folded back at the slot.

9. The puppet enters the bed from the open side. Keep him straight up for sitting in bed, and lay him back on the pillow for lying down. Angle the bed in the stage so that the open side is not seen by the audience.

10. With the pad and pillow removed, the box can be used as a table or as a stand to hold other props. Just put the open side on the bottom and the slotted side toward the back.

AN OPEN BOOK

MATERIALS NEEDED

Three pieces of 2 1/2- by 5-inch lightweight cardboard

A piece of 2 1/2- by 5-inch black felt for a Bible (Use a different color, of course, according to the kind of book you want to feature.)

A 3-inch dowel

INSTRUCTIONS

1. Fold each piece of cardboard in half, making a crease in the middle.

2. Put all three pieces together and staple them on the crease to hold the book together.

3. Cover the outside of the book with the felt.

4. To make a handle for the puppet to hold the book, glue the dowel on the crease on the inside of the book with 1 inch in the crease and 2 inches extending below the book. The hardhead puppet can hold the book in his two hands, with the puppeteer's fingers on the outside of the book and thumb inside. Or you can sew an elastic loop in the hand of any puppet and insert the dowel in the loop.

A SUITCASE

MATERIALS NEEDED

A small hinged, velvet box that jewelry sometimes comes in

A piece of heavy string about 4 inches long

INSTRUCTIONS

1. Open the box and insert the ends of the string, leaving the loop outside the box for a handle.
2. Glue around the edges of the box and close the box. Let the glue dry.

SIGNS

MATERIALS NEEDED

Posterboard

Markers or paint

A 6-inch dowel for each sign to be carried by a puppet

INSTRUCTIONS

1. Cut the posterboard into pieces large enough to be seen by the audience.

2. Print your message on the sign using large, clear letters.

3. Glue or tape the dowel to the back of the poster, leaving a handle about 4 inches long.

CROWNS

MATERIALS NEEDED

A strip of cardboard slightly larger than the circumference of the puppet's head

Beads, glass jewels

INSTRUCTIONS

1. Cut along one side of the cardboard to make the crown's points.
2. Glue or staple the ends together, fitting the crown on the puppet's head.
3. Glue beads and glass jewels on the outside of the crown.

CHAPTER 8
Making Person Mouth Puppets

Almost all the puppets made from the instructions in this chapter can be used either behind a stage with a puppeteer or directly before an audience with a ventriloquist.

If a puppet will never be seen below the waist, making legs is not necessary. If the puppet is legless, the puppeteer's hand is inserted at the bottom of the puppet; if a puppet has a whole body, the hand is inserted midway in the back.

Patterns are given for three sizes of person puppets. The small person puppet has limited use (it is used to make Jonah, see p. 76, and Betchacan Bee, see p. 73). The medium person puppet is the most common and can be used either for ventriloquism or behind the stage. The large person puppet is best for ventriloquism, but may be used without legs behind large stages. Details are given for making the medium puppet. Making the large and small puppets are similar, so only the differences are noted for making them.

❧ Fabrics needed: Use strong, flexible fabric for puppet bodies. You may use double knits, medium-weight velour, or fake fur. Don't use see-through fabric. Felt won't hold up well. Use durable, wrinkle-free fabric for clothing. Specific quantities of fabrics needed will be given with the instructions.

❧ Circles, squares, and letters are used on the pattern pieces when specific matching points are necessary.

❧ Words in the instructions are defined as follows:
  Narrow hem: Turn under the raw edge 1/4 inch and machine stitch.
  Slip stitch: Take a small stitch through the folded edge, picking up a thread of fabric directly underneath.
  Topstitch: Stitch on the right side of fabric.
  Gather: Stitch where indicated using long machine stitches.
  Reinforce: Machine stitch along the seam, using small stitches to strengthen the seam.

Medium Person Puppet

Finished length: 28 inches with legs;
16 inches without legs

PUPPET BODY

MATERIALS NEEDED

Puppet pattern pieces 1A, 1B, 1C (optional), 1D, 1E from chapter 13

1/2 yard of 60-inch wide or 7/8 yard of 45-inch wide fabric for the puppet body

One 6- by 7-inch piece of cotton or other thin fabric for lining the mouth

For the mouth itself, one 6- by 7-inch piece of medium-weight, durable fabric (e.g., double-knit, velour) in a color contrasting with the puppet body fabric

One 5- by 7-inch piece of sturdy, medium-weight cardboard, such as the back of a writing tablet

Thread that matches the puppet body fabric

Four 18-inch lengths and two 14-inch lengths of stiff but bendable galvanized steel wire (16 or 18 guage) from a hardware store or floral wire from a craft store

Pins
Scissors

INSTRUCTIONS

1. Enlarge the pattern pieces. (See "Enlarging Patterns," p. 61).

2. Lay out all pattern pieces needed for the puppet on your fabric.

   a. Cut 1 of piece 1A (body). (Note that the slit at G in the mouth should not be cut now; it will be clipped to fit when the mouth is put in.) Reverse the pattern and cut another one.

   b. Cut 4 of piece 1B (arm), reversing 2.

   c. If you are adding legs to your puppet, cut 4 of piece 1C (leg), reversing 2.

Head and Body

1. Bring the circles of the dart together and stitch the dart along the stitch lines in each head piece. Press the dart flat.

2. Pin together the two body pieces, right sides together, lining up notches and points.

3. Stitch together the body from point A to point D, around the top of the head. (If you will be adding legs, stitch from point A to point B and from point C to point D, leaving an opening between points B and C. Narrow hem edges from point B to point C.)

4. Stitch together the body from point E to point F.

5. Put in the mouth. (See "Making the Mouth," p. 63.)

6. Add a foam lining to the puppet head and body. (See "Lining Puppets with Foam," p. 62.)

Arms and Hands

1. Pin together 2 pieces of 1C (arm), right sides together, and machine stitch from point H to point J, going around the fingers.

2. Stitch from point K to point I.

3. Repeat the 2 preceding steps with the other arm.

4. Clip the curves of the fingers and turn the arms right side out, poking the fingers through.

5. Put wires in the fingers and arms. (See "Putting Wires in Arms and Legs," p. 63.) Use 18-inch lengths of wire for the fingers, 14-inch wires for the arms.

6. After you have inserted stuffing in the opening between points J and K, slip stitch the opening, turning under a hem.

7. Slip stitch the opening from point H to point I, turning under a hem.

8. On each side of 1A (body), cut the arm slit between points H and I.

9. With the body wrong side out, insert the arms into the arm slits from the right side of the puppet's body (which is on the inside now), matching points H and I on the body and on the arms, thumbs facing forward. Pin the arms in place.

10. Machine stitch the arms in the body.

11. Turn the body right side out.

12. If you are not adding legs, hem the bottom of the body, turning the cloth to the inside over the foam and lining. If you are adding legs, bring points F and D together and pin them. The legs will be inserted on either side of the pin.

Legs and Feet

1. Pin together 2 pieces of 1C (leg), right sides together, and stitch around the edge, leaving the top of the leg and the space between points L and M open.

2. Repeat the preceding step with the other leg.

3. Clip the curves and turn the legs right side out.

4. Put wires in the legs. (See "Putting Wires in Arms and Legs," p. 63.) Use 18-inch lengths of wire for the legs.

5. After you have inserted stuffing in the opening between points L and M, slip stitch the opening, turning under a hem.

6. Insert the legs about 1/2 inch into the bottom of the puppet body, one on either side of the pin, feet facing forward, and pin them in place, turning under the raw edges at the bottom of the body.

7. Topstitch the legs to the body, about 1/2 inch from the bottom of the body, stitching through all the pieces of the fabric. Reinforce the seam.

8. Add stuffing to give the top of the head and the bottom of the body more shape and stability. (See "Stuffing Puppets," p. 62.)

FACIAL FEATURES

Facial features—hair, nose, ears, eyes—give the puppet personality. Use variety and ingenuity to make each puppet an individual character.

HAIR

There are several options for hair for your puppets. Halloween, acrylic, or human-hair wigs may be cut to size and sewn to the puppets' heads. Or you can make hairpieces for your puppets from yarn or fake fur. Craft fur makes very pretty hair, but it becomes disheveled easily. It can be brushed, and hair spray helps hold it in place. Fake fur-like fabrics, like those used for animal or monster bodies, work well (short or medium hairs stay in place better than long, but long hairs look better for girl puppets). See "Working with Fur," p. 64, for tips on working with fur. Yarn comes in many colors, adapts to any head size, and can be braided, cut short, piled on top of the head, etc. Basic instructions for making yarn and fur hairpieces follow. Many variations may be done.

Yarn Hair

MATERIALS NEEDED

Yarn

Pieces of cardboard (sizes specified in the instructions)

Pieces of fabric (same as that used for the puppet body; sizes specified in instructions)

Ribbon for braids and ponytails

Scissors

INSTRUCTIONS
Girl's Braided Hair (See Figure 10: Yarn Hair.)

1. To make bangs, cut a 1 1/2- by 5-inch strip from the same fabric as the puppet body and lay about 30 loops of yarn across the strip, with 2 inches of the loops hanging down past the strip and the top loops just above the top edge of the strip.

2. Stitch the yarn to the strip and then cut through the bottom loops.

3. Center the strip on the puppet's head, about 1 3/4 inches in front of the darts.

4. Hand stitch the strip to the head. Don't trim the bangs now.

5. To make the rest of the hair, wrap yarn about 65 times lengthwise around a 6- by 16-inch piece of cardboard.

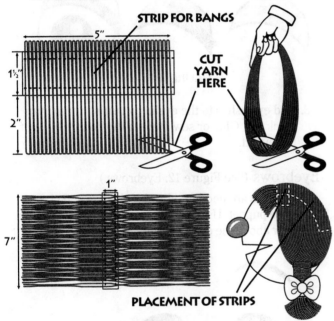

FIGURE 10: YARN HAIR

6. Carefully remove the yarn from the cardboard and holding the loop with one hand, cut through the yarn at the bottom.

7. Cut a 1- by 7-inch strip from the same fabric as the puppet body. Evenly spread the center (the place you were holding while you cut the loop) of the yarn over the strip of fabric and stitch the yarn in place.

8. Hand stitch the fabric to the center of the head, starting near the bangs and following the seam to the back of the head.

9. To make braids, smooth the yarn in place on each side of the head, divide the yarn in three parts, and braid. About 1 inch from the ends, tie the braids

with an extra piece of yarn, winding it around the braid several times. Cover the piece of yarn with a ribbon bow.

10. To make ponytails, tie bows at the hairline and let the yarn hang loose.

11. Cut the bangs to suit.

Boy's or Girl's Short Hair

1. Cut a 1- by 3 1/2-inch strip from the same fabric as the puppet body.

2. Cut an 8- by 6-inch piece of cardboard for a boy, a 10- by 6-inch piece of cardboard for a girl, and wrap the yarn around the cardboard lengthwise 70 times.

3. Carefully remove the yarn from the cardboard and, holding the loop with one hand, cut through the yarn at the bottom.

4. Evenly spread the center (the place you were holding while you cut the loop) of the yarn over the strip of fabric and stitch the yarn in place.

5. For a side part, sew the yarn to the strip 2 inches off-center.

6. For boy's hair, cut a 3/4- by 7-inch strip from the same fabric as the puppet body. Stitch it to the bottom of the hairpiece, with ends overlapping slightly. Hand stitch the strip to the head near the neck.

7. Frame the face with hair as desired. Tack yarn to the head where needed.

Fur Hair
MATERIALS NEEDED

Craft fur (usually comes in 9- by 12-inch pieces; use fur with extra long hairs for girl puppets)

Scissors

INSTRUCTIONS
Boy's Hair Style One

1. Cut a 4 1/2- x 12-inch strip of fur and pin the center of the bottom edge of the fur to the center back of the head. Pin the fur behind the ears, folding under to fit around the ears. Bring the two sides together at the top center of the head for a part, folding the fur under to make it fit.

2. Arrange the fur around the face as desired.

3. Hand stitch the fur to the head.

Boy's Hair Style Two

1. Cut a 7 1/2-inch circle of fur and pin one edge of the fur at the bottom of the head in the back. Pin the fur around each side and behind the ears.

2. Fold under the fur edges where they come together, making a part.

3. Trim the excess fur in the front.

4. Hand stitch the fur to the head.

Girl's Hair

1. Pin the center of the 9-inch side of a 9- by 12-inch piece of fur to the forehead. Continue pinning the fur around the face, folding under each turn and pleating as needed to fit, until reaching the area below where the ear would be. Tack the fur to the head at that point and hand stitch it where it has been pinned.

2. In the back, cut the long piece up the middle from the nape of the neck. Separate the pieces and tack them at the side. Using a hair brush, style as desired. You may put a tie around each to make pigtails.

Bald-headed Man

1. Add enough stuffing in the head for it to be sufficiently smooth. (See "Stuffing Puppets," p. 62.)

2. Pin a 3- by 7-inch strip of fur from behind one ear to the other around the back of the head.

3. Hand stitch the fur to the head.

EYES

Craft wiggle eyes (20 to 30 mm) give more life to a puppet because they move and give the appearance of eye contact. You can buy kinds that are either glued or sewn on. For more variety you can make your own out of felt or buttons. Experiment with sizes and colors.

MATERIALS NEEDED

Scraps of black and white (or other colors of) felt

Large flat black or white buttons

Thick craft glue

INSTRUCTIONS

Felt Eyes

1. Draw a circle on black felt and one on white felt by tracing around a fifty-cent piece or a similar-sized circle. Cut out both circles. Then trim the white felt circle slightly.

2. Draw a circle on black felt by tracing around a nickle and cut it out.

3. Glue the small black circle on the white circle and the (trimmed) white circle on the large black circle.

4. Putting a little dot of white felt or paint on each black circle will make the eye more lifelike.

5. Follow these same instructions for the other eye.

Button Eyes

1. Sew buttons backwards on the puppet's head.

2. Glue felt pieces on the button for the white of the eye and the iris.

Eyelids (See Figure 11: Eyelids.)

1. Eyelids can help achieve some unusual effects. Before placing the eye on the head, trace around the top third of the eye on the back side of the material. Enlarge the eyelid by 1/8 inch for felt or 1/4 inch for fabric to allow for the amount to be turned under before gluing or sewing in place. Draw a slightly curved line across the bottom. Cut out 2 of these pieces from felt or fabric of the puppet, and fit it over the eye. Trim it if it's too big.

FIGURE 11: EYELIDS

2. Add eyelashes to the eyelid by cutting them from black felt. Glue or sew them to the bottom edge of the eyelid.

Eyebrows (See Figure 12: Eyebrows.)

Eyebrows are good for showing the age and character of the puppet. Use yarn or fake fur. Glue or sew the eyebrow above the eyes.

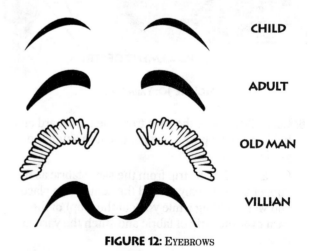

CHILD

ADULT

OLD MAN

VILLIAN

FIGURE 12: EYEBROWS

Eye Placement

1. Eyes should be placed halfway between the top of the forehead and the chin. Normally-shaped eyes should be about the width of an eye apart. Round eyes, unless very large, can be a little more than an eye-width apart.

2. To position the eyes, cut two pieces of paper the exact size of the eye. Choose the spots where the eyes should go and pin the paper eyes to the puppet. Hold the puppet in front of a mirror to check for the eyes' proper position. If it is correct, push pins straight into the head, ringing the outside of the paper eyes. Remove the papers and glue the eyes inside the circle of pins.

3. If the puppet fabric is made of fur, trim the fur so the eyes will fit flat to the head.

4. Use a thick craft glue. Apply an even coat to the back of the eye and to the spot on the face where it goes. Allow the glue to set up for a minute or two and press the eye in place, holding it a few seconds.

NOSES

MATERIALS NEEDED

Chenille pom-poms or ball fringe (various sizes and colors) or fabric and stuffing

Glue

INSTRUCTIONS

Round Nose

1. Cut a 2-inch circle from fabric and gather 1/4 inch from the edge. Pull the threads slightly. Stuff with polyester fiber.

2. Pull up the thread tightly and hand stitch the nose to the face.

Human Nose

1. Double the size of pattern #1 in Figure 13: Noses. Make it larger or smaller as desired. Cut 2.

2. Put pieces together, right sides together, and pin.

3. Stitch 1/4-inch seam around the edges, leaving the straight edge open.

FIGURE 13: NOSES

4. Turn the nose right side out and stuff it with polyester fiber.

5. Hand stitch the nose to the face about 3/4 inch on either side of the center seam, and 1/2 inch above the mouth, folding in the edges as you go.

Bulb Nose:

1. Double the size of pattern #2 in Figure 13: Noses. Make it larger or smaller as desired. Cut 2.

2. Put pieces together, right sides together, and pin.

3. Stitch 1/4-inch seam around the edges, leaving the straight edge open.

4. Turn the nose right side out and stuff it with polyester fiber.

5. Hand stitch the nose to the face about 3/4 inch on either side of the center seam, and 1/2 inch above the mouth, folding in the edges as you go.

EARS

(See Figure 14: Aligning the Ears.)

Most female puppets won't need ears, since their hair covers the ear area.

MATERIALS NEEDED

A 10- by 10-inch piece of fabric of the same fabric as the puppet body

INSTRUCTIONS

1. To make two ears, cut two 3-inch circles (bigger or smaller according to the size of the puppet).

2. Cut each circle in half and pin the halves together and stitch with 1/4-inch seam. Leave a small opening on the side.

FIGURE 14: ALIGNING THE EARS

3. Turn the ear right side out and stuff it lightly.

4. Hand stitch the ear to the side of the head with the flat side facing front. Turn under the flat edges as you go. The top of the ear should be on a line between the eye and the eyebrow.

PUPPET CLOTHING

Patterns are given for clothing for the medium puppet. If clothing is desired for the small puppet, adjust the patterns to fit. The large puppet can wear children's clothes. Add shoes, hats, jewelry, as desired.

MATERIALS NEEDED

Pattern piece 1F from chapter 13

An 18- by 26-inch piece of fabric for pants

A 22- by 24-inch piece of fabric for the shirt

A 30- by 7-inch piece of fabric for the skirt

INSTRUCTIONS

Pants (See Figure 15: Making Pants.)

1. Enlarge the pattern piece. (See "Enlarging Patterns," p. 61.)

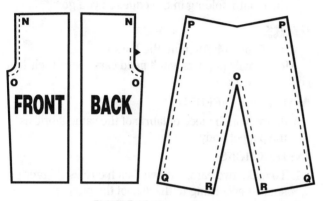

FIGURE 15: MAKING PANTS

2. Cut out 4 of piece 1F, reversing 2.

3. Right sides together, pin 2 of 1F, matching notches to make the front, and 2 to make the back.

4. On the front, machine stitch from point N to point O.

5. On the back, machine stitch from the notch to point O.

6. Open the front and back pieces and pin them, right sides together. Machine stitch from point P to point Q on both legs.

7. Machine stitch the inside legs of the pants from point R on one leg up through point O and down to point R on the other leg.

8. Narrow hem the leg openings.

9. Narrow hem the opening from the notch to point N.

10. Turn the pants right side out and put them on the puppet. Turn under the waist edge and hand stitch the waist to the puppet body.

Shirt

1. Enlarge pattern pieces 1G (shirt) and 1H (shirt sleeve). (See "Enlarging Patterns," p. 61.)

2. Cut out 2 of each piece on the fold of the fabric.

3. Pin a sleeve piece to a shirt piece (for the front), right sides together, matching points T and S. Machine stitch between the points. Repeat for the other sleeve on the same shirt piece. (See Figure 16: Making the Shirt.)

4. Pin the other shirt piece (for the back) to the sleeve at points T and S and machine stitch between the points, keeping the front piece out of the way. Repeat for the other sleeve on the back. (See Figure 16: Making the Shirt.)

5. Pin the back shirt piece to the front shirt piece at the side seams, right sides together. Machine stitch from points S to points U. (See Figure 16: Making the Shirt.)

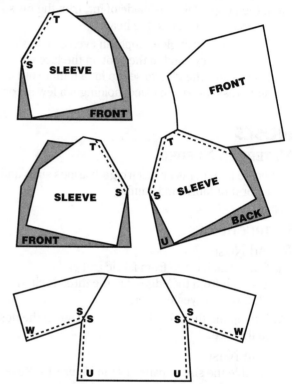

FIGURE 16: MAKING THE SHIRT

6. Pin sleeve edges together, and machine stitch from points S to points W. (See Figure 16: Making the Shirt.)

7. Narrow hem the sleeve, neck, and bottom openings.

8. Turn the shirt right side out.

9. Add any details to the shirt you want: collars, bows, ruffles.

10. Fit the shirt over the puppet's body. If the puppet has legs, the puppeteer's arm will go under the shirt and in the puppet's back opening.

Skirt

1. Gather a 30- by 7-inch piece of cloth on one of the 30-inch sides and pull threads to fit the waist of the puppet. Machine stitch when you have the desired size.

2. Right sides together, sew the 7-inch edges together, leaving 2 inches unsewn at the top for a back opening.

3. Narrow hem the back opening and the top, turning under a hem.

4. Determine the desired skirt length and cut off the excess. Narrow hem the bottom.

5. Place the skirt on the puppet and slip stitch the top edge of the skirt either to the waist of the puppet body or to the bottom edge of the shirt. Or you may use suspenders.

Dress

1. Follow the instructions for making the shirt, but cut off the front and back pieces about 1 inch below the underarm.

2. Follow the instructions for making the skirt and machine stitch the shirt bottom and skirt top.

Small Person Puppet

Finished length: about 13 inches

The instructions for the small person puppet are the same as those for the medium person puppet except for the hands. Instructions for them follow.

MATERIALS NEEDED

Small person pattern pieces 2A, 2B, 2D, 2E from chapter 13

20- by 26-inch piece of fabric for puppet body

One 5- by 6-inch piece of cotton or other thin fabric for mouth lining

For the mouth itself, one 5- by 6-inch piece of medium-weight, durable fabric (e.g., double-knit, velour) in a color contrasting with the puppet body fabric

One 4- by 5-inch piece of sturdy, medium-weight card-board, such as the back of a writing tablet

Thread that matches the puppet body fabric

Two 10-inch lengths of stiff but bendable galvanized steel wire (16 or 18 guage)

INSTRUCTIONS
Hands

1. Pin together the arm pieces, right sides together.

2. Machine stitch around hand and arm, leaving an opening from points J to K and between the squares.

3. Stuff the hands lightly and topstitch lines on pattern piece for fingers.

Large Person Puppet

Finished Length: 40 inches with legs;
25 inches without legs

The instructions for the large person puppet are the same as those for the medium person puppet, except that you will add shoulder pads to give more width at the shoulders. Because of the puppet's size, a back opening is needed for inserting the puppeteer's hand, whether or not legs are used.

MATERIALS NEEDED

Pattern pieces 3A, 3B, 3C, 1D, 1E from chapter 13

1 1/2 yards of 44-inch wide or 1 yard of 60-inch wide fabric for puppet body

Two 12- by 26-inch pieces of polyurethane foam for the body and four 2 1/2- by 4-inch pieces for shoulder pads

One 7- by 6-inch piece of cotton or other thin fabric for mouth lining

For the mouth itself, one 7- by 6-inch piece of medium-weight, durable fabric (e.g., double-knit, velour) in a color contrasting with the puppet body fabric

One 5- by 7-inch piece of sturdy, medium-weight card-board, such as the back of a writing tablet

Four 18-inch (for fingers and arms) and two 21-inch (for legs) lengths of stiff but bendable galvanized steel wire (16 or 18 guage) (If your wire comes in a roll, cut one 21-inch length for each leg. If it is in cut lengths—usually 18 inches—you will need to twist the ends of two wires together to equal 21 inches.)

Thread that matches the puppet body fabric

INSTRUCTIONS
Shoulder Pads

1. Cut two shoulder pads for one shoulder from polyurethane foam, leaving the 4-inch sides straight and rounding the 2 1/2-inch sides as in a shoulder pad for a dress. Tack the two pads together. Hand sew the pads to the finished puppet on one side of the puppet's neck, just above the top of the arm.

2. Repeat the preceding step for the other shoulder pad.

Enlarging Patterns

All patterns are as simple as possible, having very few pieces. They are drawn on graphs for enlarging. Each square on the graphs represents one inch.

MATERIALS NEEDED

See-through paper or cloth. You may use tissue paper, newsprint, tracing fabric.

Dressmaker's cutting board or paper marked off in 1-inch squares (at least 20- by 25-inch size)

Puppet patterns (from chapter 13)

Pins or tape

Pencil

Fine felt-tip pen

INSTRUCTIONS

1. Pin or tape see-through paper or cloth on the cutting board or marked paper.
2. Transfer the puppet pattern to the see-through fabric by first marking dots where the pattern lines touch the lines of the graph and then connecting the dots following the curves or lines of the pattern.
3. Transfer all pattern markings.
4. Trace over the pencil lines with a fine felt-tip pen.

Lining Puppets with Foam

To hold their shape, most puppet heads and bodies need foam lining.

MATERIALS NEEDED

Enlarged head and body pattern pieces

3/8- or 1/2-inch polyurethane foam for padding. If possible, get it with a thin plastic coating on one side, so the sewing machine needle will glide over it. Obtain this from department or craft stores. Carpet shops that use it for padding may sell or give you leftover pieces.

Pins

Felt-tip pen

Scissors

Contact cement (if you don't sew the foam pieces together)

Soft, thin fabric for foam lining, if desired

INSTRUCTIONS

1. Pin the enlarged body pattern pieces on the foam and trace around them with a felt-tip pen. Cut out 2. (If you are using the plastic-coated foam, reverse one of them before cutting.)
2. Trim the foam 1/2 inch around the mouth, squaring off the corners of the mouth. Cut a small *v* in the foam at the back of the head, opposite the mouth, for better mobility.
3. Machine stitch the darts and stitch the two head and body pieces together, following the directions for the fabric head and body. Use 1/2-inch seams. If the foam has the plastic coating, it should be facing up, directly underneath the needle.
4. If your machine presser foot won't glide over the foam, cut out a lining by the pattern from soft, thin fabric. Pin it to the foam before sewing, and with the fabric under the presser foot, stitch as one piece.
5. Turn the foam head right side out. Pull the finished fabric puppet over the foam, matching seams and pressing out all wrinkles. Tack the foam to the puppet body in a few places to hold it in place.
6. Instead of sewing the foam head and body, you may glue the edges together. First trim all seam lines by 1/2 inch. Using a stick or a small brush, spread a layer of contact cement on the edges that join together. Let the glue set until it is tacky; then press the edges together. If some curved edges won't stay together, use metal clamps to hold them until bonded. When dry, place the foam body into the head without turning the head inside out.
7. If you wish, you may make a lining to cover the foam on the inside of the puppet. Cut 2 body pieces from thin lining fabric, match notches, and stitch the pieces together. Turn back the raw edges 1/2 inch at the mouth and narrow hem. Leaving the lining wrong side out, insert it into the body and tack it in place over the foam.

Stuffing Puppets

Some puppets, especially the large ones, will need both a foam lining and stuffing. Places where stuffing might be necessary are the legs, arms, top of the head, bottom of the body.

MATERIALS NEEDED

A foot from nylon hose or a length of leg with one end sewn closed

Polyester fiber, shredded foam, cut-up nylon hose, or soft rags for stuffing

INSTRUCTIONS

1. Stuff the nylon foot or sewn leg with the stuffing. Add as much stuffing as necessary to get the desired effect in the puppet. (In the top of the head, leave just enough room to easily insert your fingers over the puppet's mouth. The stuffing will help to hold your fingers in place.)
2. When the stuffing pad is as large as you want, sew the opening closed.
3. Place the stuffing pad in the area to be stuffed. Tack it in place.

Making the Mouth

Most mouths are made the same way but are different sizes. See the specific instructions under each puppet you are making for any differences. See the specific materials list for the puppet you are making, which will indicate the amount of fabric and the patterns needed.

MATERIALS NEEDED

Enlarged pattern pieces for cardboard mouth and the cloth mouth

Cotton or other thin fabric for the mouth lining

For the mouth itself, medium-weight, durable fabric (e.g., double-knit, velour) in a color contrasting with the puppet body mouth fabric

Small pieces of sturdy, medium-weight cardboard, such as the back of a writing tablet

Pieces of felt or marking pens: dark for the throat, any color for the tongue

Scissors

Glue

INSTRUCTIONS

1. Using the enlarged cloth mouth pattern piece, cut one mouth from lightweight fabric for the lining and one from medium-weight fabric for the mouth surface.

2. Using the enlarged cardboard mouth pattern piece, cut a cardboard mouth.

3. Score the cardboard across the middle with the point of a scissors to allow the mouth to open and close.

4. Spread glue evenly over the back of the cardboard; let it dry slightly and then center the mouth lining over the cardboard and press it in place. (The lining will overhang the cardboard.)

5. Spread glue evenly over the front of the cardboard; let it dry slightly and then center the mouth surface fabric over the cardboard and press it in place. (The fabric will overhang the cardboard.)

6. Cut and glue or draw a throat "hole" below the center fold on the mouth, and a tongue, its back near the throat "hole" and its tip near the front of the mouth.

7. When the mouth is dry, bend it backwards and place it inside the puppet head, right side of the mouth facing the back of the puppet head (the puppet body should be stitched together and be wrong side out).

8. Pin the mouth in the puppet head, lining up the lettered notches. Clip the mouth corners on the puppet head to fit. Pin the mouth in place. (When you have pinned the mouth properly in place, you should see the wrong side of the mouth.)

9. Machine stitch the mouth to the puppet body, staying close to the cardboard. Don't let the cloth bunch up at the corners. Reinforce the seam.

Putting Wires in Arms and Legs

Wires in arms, fingers, and legs give the puppet more versatility and a greater lifelike appearance.

MATERIALS NEEDED

Stiff but bendable galvanized steel wire (16 or 18 guage). You can get this from a hardware store, or use floral wire from a craft store. Length varies depending on the puppet size. See the instructions for each puppet for the wire length needed for that puppet.

Pliers

Masking, cellophane, or duct tape

Polyester fiber or other filling

INSTRUCTIONS (See Figure 17: Inserting Wire.)

1. Bend a small loop in each end of the wire and wrap a piece of tape two or three times around the point at which the end of the wire touches the body of the wire.

2. Insert the wire in the arm or leg and fasten it at the lower end by sewing through the loop and over the toe or finger a number of times and at the other end through the loop and 1/2 inch from the top of the leg or arm. For wire in the fingers, sew each loop to a finger.

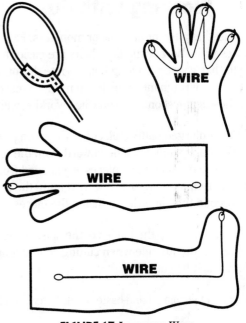

FIGURE 17: INSERTING WIRE

3. Lightly stuff polyester fiber or other filling on both sides of the wire to within one inch of the end of the wire.

4. Bend the wire at the ankle, knee, elbow, or finger as called for.

CHAPTER 9
Making Animal Mouth Puppets

One basic pattern will work for a variety of animals: cat, dog, mouse, rabbit, bear, lamb, lion. The kind of animal will be determined by the ears and other features you add.

Legs and feet are optional if you plan to use the animal in the stage only. If you use it for a ventriloquial routine you may want to add them.

Some basic instructions for making puppets have been detailed in the previous chapter. References are made to them when they are needed.

Working with Fur

Fur is used mostly for animals or monsters. Fake fur-like fabrics with short or medium hairs are easier to work with than those with long hairs. Some discount fabric shops sell remnants, which can reduce your cost.

Keep these suggestions in mind when working with fur:

Pin the enlarged pattern pieces to the wrong side of the fur. The hairs should run downward from the top of the pattern pieces. When two pieces are needed from the same pattern, cut one at a time, reversing the pattern the second time in order to match the pieces.

Take care to keep the blades of the scissors against the backing on the fur side when cutting so that long hair fibers won't be cut off.

To prevent slipping, hand-baste seams before stitching.

Shave or trim pile close to backing on seam allowance before or after stitching to reduce bulk.

Keep hairs pulled back away from the seam as much as possible when sewing fur. If short hairs get caught in the seams, run the tip of a large needle near the seam to loosen the hairs.

The Basic Animal Body

Finished length: 20 inches

MATERIALS NEEDED

Pattern pieces 4A, 4B, 1D, 1E for all animals

Additional pieces needed for
   rabbit: 4C, 4D, 4E, 4I
   dog: 4F, 4G, 4H
   cat: 4F, 4I, 4K
   bear: 4F, 4J, 4H, 4L
   mouse: 4J, 4F, 4H

See chapter 13 for pattern pieces.

A 24- by 44-inch piece of fur for the body, arms, legs (optional)

A 23- by 18-inch piece of fur for the chest, feet, and hands (contrasting with the color of the body fur)

A piece of felt (pink or other color) for the palms, inner ears, and bottoms of the feet

One 6- by 7-inch piece of cotton or other thin fabric for the mouth lining

For the mouth itself, one 6- by 7-inch piece of medium-weight, durable fabric (e.g., double-knit, velour) in a color contrasting with the puppet body (use white fabric glued on cardboard for the rabbit's teeth)

1 piece of 5- by 7-inch sturdy, medium-weight cardboard, such as the back of a writing tablet

Thread that matches the puppet body material

Two 12 1/2-inch lengths and two 15-inch lengths of stiff but bendable galvanized steel wire (16 or 18 gauge) from a hardware store, or use floral wire from a craft store

Polyester fiber filling for stuffing

Commercial wiggle eyes or small pieces of felt

A small pom-pom for the nose

64

INSTRUCTIONS

1. Enlarge all the pattern pieces needed for the animal you are making. (See "Enlarging Patterns," p. 61.)

2. Lay out all the pattern pieces needed for the puppet on your material.

   a. Cut 1 of piece 4A (head-back) from fur. Reverse the pattern and cut another one.

   b. Cut 4 pieces of fur 9 by 3 1/2 inches for arms.

   c. Cut 4 pieces of fur 11 by 3 1/2 inches for legs (optional).

   d. Cut 1 of piece 4B (face and chest) from contrasting fur. Reverse the pattern and cut another one.

   e. Cut 4 of other parts needed (ears, hands, feet), 2 of felt, 2 of contrasting fur.

   f. Cut 1 cardboard and 2 cloth mouth pieces using pattern pieces 1D and 1E from the medium person patterns.

Hands and Arms
(See Figure 18: Hand and Arm.)

1. Their right sides together, pin one felt hand to one arm. Stitch them together. Do the same with a fur hand and arm.

FIGURE 18: HAND AND ARM

2. Their right sides together, pin the arm-hands together and machine stitch, leaving the shoulder ends and 2 inches on one side of the arm open for inserting and wire and for stuffing.

3. Repeat the preceding steps for the other arm.

4. For hands with fingers, clip at the inner points. Turn the hand right side out.

5. Insert one 12 1/2-inch wire in each arm. (See "Putting Wires in Arms and Legs," p. 63.) Stuff the arms according to the directions on p. 62.

6. Slip stitch the opening.

7. On each of the 4A (head-back) pieces, cut the arm slit between points I and J. With the palms toward the body, insert the arms into the slits and pin them in place. Machine stitch.

Ears

1. For upright ears, bring the dotted lines together in the felt ear and sew a dart. (See Figure 19: Dart in Felt Ear.) Repeat this step for the other felt ear.

2. Their right sides together, sew around a fur and a felt ear, leaving the bottom open. Repeat this step for the other fur and felt ear. Turn the ears right side out.

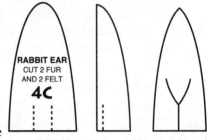

FIGURE 19: DART IN FELT EAR

3. Stuff the ears lightly if you wish. Sew across the bottom 1/4 inch from the edges.

4. Decide where the ears will go, depending on the kind of animal, and sew them into the head. (See Figure 20: Ear Placement.) For example:

For an animal with upright ears near the outside edge of the head (such as a cat, dog, bear), make the dart in the head 1 inch longer. With the inner ear facing the right side of the 4A (head-back) piece, pin the ear in the dart. Stitch it in when you sew the dart.

For an animal with upright ears close together (such as a rabbit), cut a slit in the end of the dart 1/2 inch. Sew in as for the above ear.

For an animal with floppy ears (such as a dog or lamb), sew in the dart according to the pattern. Hand sew the ears crosswise at the end of the dart when the puppet is finished.

FIGURE 20: EAR PLACEMENT

Head and Body

1. On the animal head-back, bring the dots of the dart together. Pin upright ears in place if you are using them. Machine stitch along the stitch lines in each head piece.

2. With right sides together, sew the two head-back pieces together from point A to point B. Sew the back from point C to notch D and from notch E to point F, leaving a space open between points D and E to insert your hand.

Face and Chest

1. Their right sides together, pin together the 4B (face-chest) pieces. Machine stitch from notch H to notch C and from point G to point A.

2. Prepare and sew in the mouth. (See "Making the Mouth," p. 63.) Be sure to stitch in the rabbit's teeth (4E) when you sew the mouth to the body.

3. Cut to the seam line of the face at notch C. Their right sides together, pin the face to the body, matching notches and seam lines. Machine stitch.

Foam Body (Optional)

1. Pin the 4A face pattern over the 4B head-back pattern at the seam lines. Using this pattern, cut and sew the foam stuffing, leaving the back open between notches D and E. (See "Lining Puppets with Foam," p. 62.)

2. Trim 1 inch off the bottom of the foam. Insert the foam body into the fur body.

Feet and Legs (Optional)
(See Figure 21: Foot and Leg.)

1. Their right sides together, pin one fur foot to one leg. Stitch together. Repeat with the other fur foot and leg.

2. Their right sides together, stitch one felt foot to one leg. Repeat with the other felt foot and leg.

3. Pin one fur foot and leg to one felt foot and leg, right sides together, and stitch around the edge, leaving the top of the leg and 2 inches on one side open for adding wire and stuffing. Repeat with the other foot and leg.

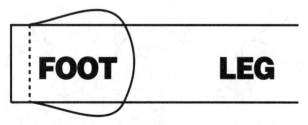

FIGURE 21: FOOT AND LEG

4. Insert a 15-inch wire in each leg. (See "Putting Wires in Arms and Legs," p. 63.) Stuff the legs following the directions on p. 62.

5. Insert the legs about 1/2 inch into the bottom of the puppet body, feet facing forward, and pin them in place, turning under the raw edges at the bottom of the body.

6. Topstitch the legs to the body, stitching through all pieces of material. Reinforce the seam.

7. To give the top of the head and the bottom of the body more shape and stability, add stuffing. (See "Stuffing Puppets," p. 62.)

Finishing Touches

Finishing touches will depend on the kind of animal you are making. Using real and cartoon animal pictures as guides, add pom-pom noses, eyes, chenille-wire whiskers, tufts of extra fur at the top of the head or the cheeks, etc. For an elephant, add a trunk over the nose area and floppy ears. For a lion, add a mane.

You may add clothing to your puppet by using the medium person pattern (p. 91) and instructions (p. 60).

Making Bird Mouth Puppets

With minor changes the bird mouth puppet pattern can be used for most birds. Beaks may be altered a little, such as adding a hook for a parrot, rounding the end of the beak for a duck, etc. The color of the fabric or fur can help indicate the bird species. Comb and wattle patterns are given for a rooster.

BASIC BIRD BODY

Finished length: 21 inches with legs;
13 inches without legs

MATERIALS NEEDED

Pattern pieces 5A, 5B, 5C, 5D, 5E, 5F, and 5G for all birds
  For rooster: Add 5H, 5I

See chapter 13 for pattern pieces.

One 15- by 18-inch piece of fabric or fur for body and wing

One 10- by 8-inch piece of fabric or fur for the beak

One 5- by 6-inch piece of cotton or other thin fabric for the mouth lining

For the mouth itself, one 5- by 6-inch piece of medium-weight, durable fabric (e.g., double-knit, velour) in a color contrasting with the puppet body material

One piece of 4- by 4-inch sturdy, medium-weight cardboard, such as the back of a writing tablet

One 12- by 10-inch piece of felt for the foot and leg

One 6- by 7 1/2-inch piece of red (or other color) felt for the wattle and comb (rooster only)

Two 10-inch lengths of bendable galvanized steel wire (16 or 18 guage)

Commercial wiggle eyes or small pieces of felt

INSTRUCTIONS

1. Enlarge all pattern pieces needed for the bird you are making. (See "Enlarging Patterns," p. 61.)

2. Lay out all pattern pieces needed for the puppet on your fabric.

a. Cut 1 of piece 5A head-body from cloth or fur. Reverse the pattern and cut another one.

b. Cut 4 of 5B (wing).

c. Cut 2 of 5C (mouth) of a color contrasting with the body.

d. Cut 2 of 5C (mouth), any color, for lining.

e. Cut 2 of 5D (upper beak) of yellow or other color.

f. Cut 2 of 5E (lower beak) of same color as upper beak.

g. Cut 4 of 5G (foot-leg) of felt.

Wings

1. Pin two 5B (wing) pieces together, their right sides facing, and stitch all around from point I to point J, leaving the end open. Turn the wing right side out. Repeat this step with the other wing.

2. Cut 2 wings from foam, trimming all edges by 1/2 inch. Insert them into the wing and tack them in place. Or stuff the wings lightly with polyester fiber.

3. On each 5A (head-body) piece, cut between the two squares, from point I to point J.

4. Insert the top of the wing into the slit of the body pieces, matching the wings with the body at the squares. Pin the wing in place. Machine stitch the wing in place on the inside. Repeat this step with the other wing.

Body

1. Their right sides facing, pin together the 5A head-body pieces, lining up notches and points. (If you are making a rooster, see "Rooster Wattle and Comb" section at this point.)

2. Stitch together from point B to point E and from point F to point G. Stitch the front from point C to point H. Leave the bottom open and the body wrong side out.

Mouth and Beak

1. Glue one 5F cardboard mouth between one 5C mouth and its cloth lining. Repeat with the other mouth and lining.

2. Stitch the two 5D upper beaks together from point K to point M, matching notches. (See Figure 22: Upper Beak.)

3. Right sides facing and matching out-

FIGURE 22: UPPER BEAK

side edges, stitch the sides of the upper beak and one 5C mouth piece together from point L to point K and on to the other point L. This will form a place to insert your hand. Trim seams. (See Figure 23: Upper and Lower Beaks.)

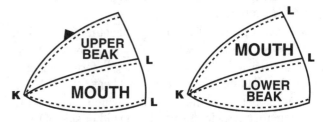

FIGURE 23: UPPER AND LOWER BEAKS

4. Right sides together, stitch the sides of the 5E lower beak and the other mouth piece together from point L to point K and on to the other point L. Trim the seams.

5. Stitch the mouth sections together at the back from point L to the other point L. Turn the entire beak right side out.

6. Pin the beak in the head, right sides together, being sure the upper beak seam matches the head seam and the lower beak notch N matches the chest seam. Stitch. Turn bird right side out.

Rooster Wattle and Comb
(See Figure 24: Wattle and Comb.)

1. Pin 5I (comb) pieces together. Topstitch from point A around comb top to point B, leaving the bottom open. Don't turn.

2. Lightly stuff the comb with polyester fiber. With the body right side out, pin the comb between the body pieces between notches A and B. Machine baste.

FIGURE 24: WATTLE AND COMB

3. Pin 5H (wattle) pieces together. Topstitch from point C to point D around the curve of the wattle. Pin the bottom of the wattle, between notches C and D. Machine baste.

4. As you pin the body pieces together, be sure to pin the wattle and the comb in between, matching letters.

Feet and Legs (Optional)

1. Topstitch two 5G (foot-leg) pieces together, leaving the top and 1 inch on one side open to add wire and stuffing.
2. Stuff a little fiber into the feet. Topstitch over the side opening.
3. Repeat the preceding steps for the other foot and leg.
4. Insert a 10-inch wire in each leg-foot. Bend the wire forward at the bottom of each leg to form the feet. (See "Putting Wires in Arms and Legs," p. 63.)
5. At the bottom of the bird, bring point G and point H together and pin. Insert a leg on either side of the pin, feet facing forward, and pin them in place, turning under the raw edges at the bottom of the body.
6. Topstitch the legs to the body, about 1/2 inch from the bottom of the body, stitching through all pieces of the material. Reinforce the seam.

Eyes

Glue or sew eyes to the head just above the beak. (See "Eyes," p. 58.)

BIRD CLOTHING

A bird puppet is easier to handle with no tail end. The lack of a tail will be less noticeable if the bird wears clothes. A simple vest and pants pattern are given on page 94. The color and design of the fabric used should be appropriate for the kind of bird (for instance, the rooster could wear cowboy clothes).

MATERIALS NEEDED

Pattern pieces 5J, 5K, 5L (from chapter 13)
An 18- by 18-inch piece of fabric for a vest
A 15- by 24-inch piece of fabric for pants
A 10- by 25-inch piece of fabric for a skirt

INSTRUCTIONS
Pants

1. Enlarge pattern piece 5J. (See "Enlarging Patterns," p. 61.)
2. Cut out 4 of piece 5J (pants), reversing 2.
3. Sew like the pants of the medium person puppet. (See p. 60.)
4. Put the pants on the bird and hand stitch them to the puppet.

Vest

1. With their right sides together, pin one front vest to the back vest, matching the points. Machine stitch between points A and B and then between points C and D.

2. Repeat the preceding step with the second front vest on the other side of the back vest.

Skirt

1. A pattern is not given for making a skirt. Sew the skirt fabric like the skirt of the medium person puppet. (See p. 60.)
2. Put the skirt on the bird and hand stitch it to the waist of the puppet.

Making Fish Mouth Puppets

Finished length: 15 inches

MATERIALS NEEDED

Pattern pieces 6A, 6B, 6C, 2D, and 2E from chapter 13
A 16- by 18-inch piece of fabric or fur for the fish
One 5- by 6-inch piece of cotton or other thin fabric for the mouth lining
For the mouth itself, one 5- by 6-inch piece of medium-weight, durable fabric (e.g., double-knit, velour) in a color contrasting with the puppet body
Small pieces of felt for tail and optional dorsal fin
One 4- by 5-inch piece of sturdy, medium-weight cardboard, such as the back of a writing tablet
One 16- by 18-inch piece of polyurethane foam (essential)
Thread that matches the puppet's body
Commercial fish or wiggle eyes or small pieces of felt

INSTRUCTIONS

1. Enlarge the fish pattern pieces. (See "Enlarging Patterns," p. 61.) This pattern is simple and can easily be made larger than the pattern given.
2. Lay out all pattern pieces needed for the puppet on your material.
   a. Cut 1 of piece 6A (body). Reverse the pattern and cut another.
   b. Cut 2 of piece 6B (tail) and 2 of 6C (dorsal fin) from felt.
   c. Cut mouth pieces, using pattern pieces 2D and 2E from the small person patterns.
   d. Cut 2 of piece 6A (body) from foam.

Body

1. With the right sides together, pin the two 6A body pieces together. Stitch from point A to point B, from point C to notch D, and from notch E to point F. Clip curves. (Leave a place open between points D and E to insert your hand.)

2. Using the mouth pattern for the small person puppet (p. 91) put in the mouth. (See "Making the Mouth," p. 63.)

3. Turn the fish right side out.

4. Sew the 6B (tail) pieces together. Do not turn. Insert the tail into the tail end of the fish, matching points B and C and turning in the raw edges of the fish. Topstitch.

Foam Body

1. Trim the mouth edges of the foam 1/2 inch on each side, squaring the corners of the mouth. Trim 1/2 inch between notches D and F.

2. Sew as for the fish. Turn right side out. Insert the foam into the fish, matching seams.

3. Slip stitch the opening from point D to point E, turning under a hem.

4. Glue or sew on eyes. (See "Eyes," p. 58.)

Dorsal Fin (Optional)

1. Pin the 6C dorsal fin pieces together. Topstitch.

2. Before sewing the 6A body pieces together, pin the fin to the fish on one outside piece, matching point G to notch G and point H to notch H. Machine baste. Proceed with sewing the fish.

CHAPTER 10
Making Special Mouth Puppets

The special mouth puppets described in this chapter are given names, and each has one or more dialogues in Part 3. Some of these puppets are made with the basic instructions given in chapter 8 but have special clothing or added features. References to instructions in chapters 8 and 9 are made where needed. Patterns for the rest of the puppets in this chapter are in chapter 13.

I have developed characters and have special uses for most of these puppets. (See chapter 4 on developing characters.) While you are not limited to the same use of them, these suggestions might give you more ideas for your puppets.

Croaker Frog can be used to tell Bible stories, such as in the dialogue in Part 3 where he tells the story of the plague of frogs in Egypt. He can also be used in contemporary stories or dialogues to teach lessons, such as in Dialogue 18.

S-s-sissel S-s-serpent is used in a dialogue in Part 3 to explain the salvation message by telling the story of the fall of man and the sacrifice of Jesus. Suggestions for developing other dialogues for the serpent puppet are given at the beginning of Dialogue 10.

Wiggly Worm is used to help children understand that God has a plan for each of them in "A Poor, Lowly Worm," Dialogue 11.

Betchacan Bee helps teach many scriptural admonitions, using the word "be." For example, he says, "Betchacan be kind, with God's help," "Betchacan be doers of the Word." See Dialogue 12 for other suggestions of Bible "be's."

Wilbur Whale and Jonah make a unique two puppets in one combination. Wilbur Whale tells the story of Jonah, with Jonah inside the stomach at the beginning of the dialogue and then making a surprise appearance. Wilbur can also be used for any other fish story or dialogue.

'Lijah Light Bulb is an unusual puppet that can be used when referring to Scripture verses about lights, shining, witnessing, etc. He can also be used as the "bright idea" puppet—making special announcements

or thinking up unusual things for children to do. He can help lead songs about shining and lights.

Hooray! Football could be your team mascot. The name of the football puppet can be anything you would like it to be to boost or advertise your school or other favorite team. In church services, he can be used to promote good sportsmanship in games and contests or to show that Christians should be much more fervent for Christ than sports fans are for their teams. (The football pattern may also be used to make a Humpty Dumpty puppet.)

Forgetful Fojo is a clown puppet. He writes notes to himself to remember the things he must do. But he even forgets to read his notes, which gets him into trouble. He can be used in the dialogues to help make announcements and to remind the children to memorize Bible verses.

Honey Dew is an extra large puppet. You place your right hand in Honey Dew's right glove to make her gesture, lead singing, pick up a phone or other objects, and do many things that other puppets can't. It will take some practice to learn to operate this puppet's mouth and hand at the same time. You must always remember that whatever actions are done with your right hand are not your own, but the puppet's. This puppet can sit on your lap or stand on a chair alongside and slightly in front of you. For the dialogues in Part 3, Honey Dew should be a teenager. But a puppet of any age or either sex could be made with the Honey Dew pattern.

Sock puppets are used in Dialogue 27 to encourage children to study hard now in order to give God their best. Dialogue 28 teaches the message of serving God joyfully in whatever place He puts you.

Sack puppets are very easy to make and can be used for either stage shows or ventriloquism. Their disadvantages: They don't really look much like people or animals and they are very fragile. There is a dialogue in Part 3 for Offering Envelopes. The instructions in this chapter are for making them, but other puppets can be made with minor adjustments.

Earlene Early Bird is a bird puppet that can be used

to greet the children as they arrive. Suggestions for the use of this puppet are found in chapter 6. (See "Ways to Use Puppets in the Classroom," pages 41-42.)

Booster Rooster is a loudmouth rooster who makes announcements and promotes special events. He frequently gets mixed up and must be corrected by the children. He can carry posters on sticks, which are taped under his wings.

Buffy Bunny is cheerful and charming, but she disobeys sometimes and gets into trouble for this, just as children do. If you prefer a boy rabbit, call him Tuffy Bunny and dress him as a boy.

Catastrophe Cat can be either a boy or a girl. As this cat's name implies, he is always getting into trouble.

Sugar Bear is a selfish bear who loves sweets and will do almost anything to get them.

Chucky Church Mouse is a mouse puppet with big ears who can help with discipline. (See how puppets can help with discipline, page 42, chapter 6.)

Cornpone D. Nutt is a farm boy who is sometimes dull-witted and other times very bright. He loves to act goofy and tell corny jokes. He can be made from a medium or large person puppet pattern. Given him a cowboy hat and Western clothes.

Croaker Frog

Finished length: 28 inches.

MATERIALS NEEDED

Pattern pieces 7A, 7B, 7C, 1A, 1D from chapter 13

1/2 yard of 60-inch wide or 7/8 yard of 45-inch wide green fabric or fur for the frog body

One 6- by 7-inch piece of cotton or other thin fabric for mouth lining

For the mouth itself, one 6- by 7-inch piece of medium-weight, durable fabric (e.g., double-knit, velour) in a color contrasting with the puppet body

One piece of 5- by 7-inch sturdy, medium-weight cardboard, such as the back of a writing tablet

Two 12-inch lengths of stiff but bendable galvanized steel wire (16 or 18 gauge)

Polyester fiber filling for stuffing

Commercial frog or wiggle eyes or small pieces of felt

Thread that matches the puppet body

INSTRUCTIONS

Follow the instructions for making the medium person puppet in chapter 8, with these exceptions:

Mouth

Use pattern piece 1D for the cloth mouth and pattern piece 7A for the cardboard mouth.

Upper Legs

1. With the right sides together, pin two 7B (upper leg) pieces together. Machine stitch them together from point H around the foot to point I, leaving the top open for stuffing.

2. Clip the curves and turn the leg right side out, pushing the points of the feet through.

3. Repeat the preceding steps with the other upper leg.

4. Put 12-inch wires in each upper leg. No extra wires are needed in the points of the feet. (See "Putting Wires in Arms and Legs," p. 63.)

5. Insert stuffing around the wires in the upper legs. Slip stitch the opening, turning under a hem.

6. Insert the upper legs into the slits of the body, matching points H and I.

Lower Legs

1. To make the lower legs, follow steps 1 through 5 of the upper legs, using pieces 7B.

2. Insert the legs into the body at the bottom, following the instructions for the medium person puppet legs.

Special Features

Use commercial frog eyes or make felt eyes. (See "Eyes," p. 58.) Place the eyes farther apart than the eyes of the person puppets.

Make tiny circles of felt for nostrils and glue them above the mouth.

Clothing

Use 1G (shirt) and 1H (shirt sleeve) from chapter 13. Follow the instructions for making the medium puppet shirt in chapter 8, but shorten the sleeve by 2 inches.

Use 5J (pants) from chapter 13. Follow the instructions for making the bird puppet pants in chapter 9.

S-s-s-sissel S-s-s-serpent

Finished length: about 58 inches

MATERIALS NEEDED

Pattern pieces 8A, 8B, 8C, 8D, 8E from chapter 13

One 14- by 60-inch piece of fabric or short-haired fur (If the cloth is wider than 60 inches, make the snake as long as possible.)

One 6- by 7-inch piece of cotton or other thin fabric for the mouth lining

For the mouth itself, one 6- by 7-inch piece of medium-weight, durable fabric (e.g., double-knit, velour) in a color contrasting with the puppet body

One piece of 5- by 7-inch sturdy, medium-weight cardboard, such as the back of a writing tablet

Small felt remnants for fangs and nostrils

Commercial snake, alligator, or other eyes

One 18-inch length of stiff but bendable galvanized steel wire (16 or 18 gauge)

Polyester fiber for stuffing

INSTRUCTIONS

1. Enlarge the pattern pieces. (See "Enlarging Patterns," p. 61.)

2. Lay out and cut pieces for the snake following these instructions:

   a. The 8A and 8B pattern pieces in chapter 13 are for the two ends of the snake (head and tail). A middle piece about 26 inches long is to be added. For the topside of the snake's body, lay pattern piece 8A (head) at one end of the 60-inch fabric (single layer of fabric) and piece 8B (tail) at the other end. Using a ruler, draw chalk lines between the pieces for a cutting line, indicated by the dotted lines on the pattern pieces. (See Figure 25: Layout of Snake Pattern Pieces.) Cut the snake's body as one piece.

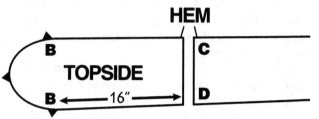

FIGURE 25: LAYOUT OF SNAKE PATTERN PIECES

   b. For the underside of the snake's body, repeat the above step, except move the two pattern pieces 1 inch closer together.

   c. Cut out the mouth pieces, using pattern pieces 8C and 8D.

   d. Cut 8E (fangs) and two small circles for nostrils from felt.

3. Cut apart the topside piece only of 8A, from point C to point D. This will make an opening for you to insert your arm up to your elbow to manipulate the puppet's mouth. If your arm is long or short, you may want to cut the slit at a different place. (Do not cut apart the underside piece.) Sew a 1/2-inch hem in both raw edges of the cut. (See Figure 26: Cutting the Topside of the Snake.)

4. With the right sides together, pin the topside to the underside, matching notches and bringing the two hems of the cut on the topside close together. Machine stitch the entire body from point B to point B on the other side, going around the tail. Come to a point at the tail, and leave a 6-inch opening on one side for adding stuffing near the tail. Trim the point of the tail.

FIGURE 26: CUTTING THE TOPSIDE OF THE SNAKE

5. Put in the mouth. (See "Making the Mouth," p. 63.)

6. Turn the snake right side out.

7. Loop each end of an 18-inch wire. Insert the wire in the snake body. Tack one loop to the tail and the other loop where it ends (about 16 inches into the body). (See "Putting Wires in Arms and Legs," p. 63.)

8. Stuff the tail and middle section of the serpent with polyester fiber (firmly at the end and lightly up to points C and D). Slip stitch the side opening, turning under a hem.

FIGURE 27: CLOSING THE BACK END OF THE SNAKE BODY

9. Slip stitch the edge of the topside from point C to point D to the underside on the back section to keep the stuffing in place. (Do not sew front section, since this is where you will insert your arm. See Figure 27: Closing the Back End of the Snake Body.)

10. Add snake, frog, or wiggle eyes.(See "Eyes," p. 58.)

11. Glue nostrils in the center of the face, above the mouth. Glue fangs inside the lower mouth, with the points hanging out.

12. To use the puppet, place your hand inside the puppet's body between points C and D. Curl the snake around your arm. Rest your elbow on your hand, a table top, or the ledge of the puppet stage.

Wiggly Worm

Finished length: 28 inches

MATERIALS NEEDED

Pattern pieces 8A, 8B, 8C, 8D from chapter 13

One 14- by 36-inch piece of fabric or light-weight fur for the body

One 6- by 7-inch piece of cotton or other thin fabric for mouth lining

For the mouth itself, one 6- by 7-inch piece of medium-weight, durable fabric (e.g., double-knit, velour) in a color contrasting with the puppet body

One piece of 5- by 7-inch sturdy, medium-weight cardboard, such as the back of a writing tablet

Commercial wiggle eyes or small pieces of felt

One 8-inch length of bendable galvanized steel wire (16 or 18 gauge)

Polyester fiber filling for stuffing

Thread that matches the puppet body

INSTRUCTIONS

1. Enlarge the pattern pieces. (See "Enlarging Patterns," p. 61.)

2. Lay out and cut pieces for the snake following these instructions:

   a. For the underside of the body, lay pattern pieces 8A (head) and 8B (tail) on a single layer of fabric as in the instructions for the snake, but only 4 inches apart. Draw chalk lines between the two pieces.

   b. For the topside of the body, lay pattern pieces 8A (head) and 8B (tail) as for the underside, but only 3 inches apart. (The underside of the worm body is to be 1 inch longer than the topside, reversing the snake layout.)

3. Complete by the instructions for the snake, cutting apart the underside from points C to D to make the opening for your hand on the bottom. Use an 8-inch wire in the tail.

4. To use the puppet, insert your hand in the opening on the underside of the worm. The worm rests on the top of your arm. (See Figure 28: Worm on Arm.)

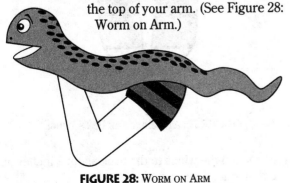

FIGURE 28: WORM ON ARM

Betchacan Bee

Finished length: 18 inches

MATERIALS NEEDED

Pattern pieces 2A, 2D, 2E, 9A, 9B, 9C, 9D from chapter 13

One 15- by 20-inch piece of black short-haired fur for head and neck, body stripe, and tail

One 14- by 15-inch piece of yellow or gold short-haired fur for 2 body stripes

One 10- by 18-inch piece of shiny gold or white fabric for wings

One 7- by 16-inch piece of black felt for legs and feet

One 5- by 6-inch piece of cotton or other thin fabric for mouth lining

For the mouth itself, one 5- by 6-inch piece of medium-weight, durable fabric (e.g., double-knit, velour) in a color contrasting with the puppet body

One 4- by 5-inch piece of sturdy, medium-weight cardboard, such as the back of a writing tablet

One 6- by 17-inch piece of polyurethane foam for wings

Commercial wiggle eyes or small pieces of felt

One 7-inch piece of black chenille wire for feelers

A small gold or yellow pom-pom for the nose

Polyester fiber filling for stuffing

Two 8-inch and two 9-inch lengths of stiff but bendable galvanized steel wire (16 or 18 gauge)

Black thread

INSTRUCTIONS

1. Enlarge the pattern pieces. (See "Enlarging Patterns," p. 61.)

2. Lay out all pattern pieces needed for the puppet on your material.

   a. Cut 1 of piece 2A (small person body) from black fur, using the dotted line on the pattern for the bee. Reverse the pattern and cut another one. These will make the bee's head.

   b. The body is made of black and gold stripes. For measurements, see Figure 29: Bee Stripes. Cut 2 each of the 3 stripes (9E, 9F, 9G on page 74).

   c. Cut 2 of 9A (tail) from black fur.

   d. Cut two 9B (wing) pieces on the fold from shiny gold or white fabric.

   e. Cut one 9B (wing) from polyurethane foam, cutting one half to the fold, reversing the pattern, and cutting the other half.

   f. Cut four 9D (leg) pieces from black felt.

   g. Cut four 9C (arm) pieces from black felt.

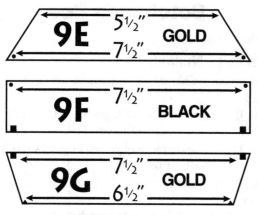

FIGURE 29: BEE STRIPES

Head and Body

For the following instructions on the body, see Figure 30: Assembling the Bee Body.

1. With right sides together, pin and then machine stitch the 5 1/2-inch edge of one of the 9E stripes to the neck edge of one of the 2A (head) pieces.

2. With right sides together, pin and then machine stitch the 7 1/2-inch edge of one of the 9F stripes to the raw edge of the 9E stripe (now attached to the head piece), matching the small circles.

3. With right sides together, pin and then machine stitch one edge of one 9G stripe to the raw edge of the 9F stripe (as in the previous step), matching squares.

4. With right sides together, pin and then machine stitch one 9A (tail) piece to the 9G raw edge, matching triangles.

5. Repeat steps 3 through 6 with the remaining head, stripe, and tail pieces to form the other half of the body.

6. On each headpiece (2A), bring the circles of the dart together and machine stitch along the stitch lines. Press the darts open.

7. Right sides together, pin together the two head and body pieces, carefully lining up points and seams of the stripes.

FIGURE 30: ASSEMBLING THE BEE BODY

8. Machine stitch completely around the body from point A to point E, leaving the back open from the top edge of the top gold piece to the bottom edge of the black stripe for your hand to be inserted. (See Figure 31: Stitching the Bee Body.)

9. Put in the mouth. (See "Making the Mouth," p. 63.)

10. Turn the bee right side out. Slip stitch the back opening, turning under a hem.

11. Stuff the tail and head. (See "Stuffing Puppets," p. 62.)

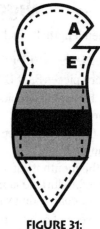

FIGURE 31: STITCHING THE BEE BODY

Wings

1. Right sides together, pin the two 9B (wing) pieces together, matching notches. Machine stitch, leaving an opening at the bottom between the notches. Trim the seams. Turn right side out.

2. Insert the foam wings into the fabric wings. Topstitch 1/4 inch from the edge around the wings, folding the raw edges to the inside between the notches.

3. Center the wings on the back seam line just above the back opening. Pin the wings in place. (See Figure 32: Attaching the Bee's Wings.)

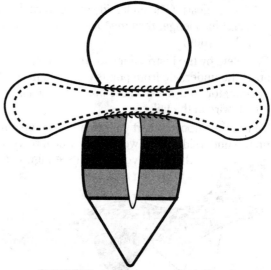

FIGURE 32: ATTACHING THE BEE'S WINGS

4. Slip stitch the wings to the back about 2 inches on either side of the seam line.

Legs and Feet

1. Pin two 9C (arm) pieces together. Topstitch, leaving the top edge open. Repeat with the other 9C pieces.
2. Repeat step 1 with the 9D (leg) pieces.
3. Put 8-inch wires in the arms and 9-inch wires in the legs. (See "Putting Wires in Arms and Legs," p. 63.)
4. Hand stitch the arms to the side of the body just above the top gold stripe. Bend each arm forward at the middle.
5. Hand stitch the legs to the side of the body just above the lower gold stripe. Bend the feet forward at the ankles.

Special Features

For a nose, sew on a small gold or yellow pom-pom.

For eyes, cut 2 circles, 2 inches in diameter, of gold fur. Glue them to the face on either side of the nose. Glue small wiggle or black felt eyes to the middle of the gold circles. (See "Instructions for Felt Eyes" on p. 58.)

For feelers, loop each end of a 7-inch piece of chenille wire to make a small ball. Measure 1/2 inch on either side of the middle of the wire and bend those places, making 2 right angles. Sew the middle inch to the center head above the gold circles. (See Figure 33: Adding Features.)

FIGURE 33:
ADDING FEATURES

Wilbur Whale

Finished Length: 25 inches

MATERIALS NEEDED

Pattern pieces 10A, 10B, 10C from chapter 13

One 16- by 25-inch piece of gray or black fabric or short-haired fur

One 8- by 12-inch piece of white fabric or short-haired fur

One 6- by 9-inch piece of white felt

One 12- by 18-inch piece of red fabric

One 12- by 33-inch piece of blue velour or felt

One 25- by 32-inch piece of polyurethane foam

Commercial fish, frog, or wiggle eyes or small pieces of felt

Polyester fiber filling for stuffing

1 metal ring about 1 inch in diameter

Thread that matches puppet body

INSTRUCTIONS

1. Enlarge all pattern pieces. (See "Enlarging Pattern Pieces," p. 61.)
2. Lay out all the pattern pieces needed for the puppet on your material.
   a. Cut 2 of piece 10A (body) from gray or black fabric or short-haired fur and 2 from polyurethane foam.
   b. Cut 1 of 10B (mouth) from white fabric or short-haired fur, 2 from red fabric, 2 from foam, trimming 1/2 inch around on the foam.
   c. Cut 2 pieces of 10C (tail fin) from white felt.
3. In each body piece, bring the circles of the dart together and machine stitch along the dotted lines. Press the darts flat.
4. Right sides together, pin the 10A (body) pieces together, lining up notches and points. Machine stitch from point A to point B around the head, and then from point C to notch D near the back of the body. (This will leave openings between points B and C on the tail, and between point A and notch D for the mouth.) Clip curves.
5. Wrong sides out, pin one red fabric piece 10B (mouth) to the body, matching notch A to point A. This will form the roof of the mouth. (See Figure 34: Attaching the Mouth Roof.) Machine stitch together from point E to point F, going through notch A. Stop about 1/2 inch from points E and F. Turn the mouth and body right side out.
6. On the foam body pieces, trim 1/2 inch from the tail ends and from notch D to point A. Stitch together the foam body pieces as in step 4. Clip the curves. Insert the foam body into the fabric body, matching

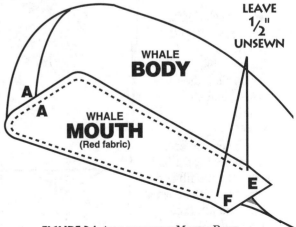

FIGURE 34: ATTACHING THE MOUTH ROOF

seams. Insert one foam mouth on top of the fabric mouth on the inside.

7. Stuff the tail and the upper body. (See "Stuffing Puppets," p. 62.)

8. Stitch the roof of the mouth to the body from points E to F, turning under a hem.

9. Pin the two pieces of 10C (tail fin) together. Topstitch.

10. Bring together points B and C of the whale body and insert the tail fin into the opening, matching points B and C with point B-C. Topstitch. (See Figure 35: Attaching the Tail Fin.)

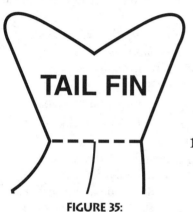

FIGURE 35:
ATTACHING THE TAIL FIN

11. Right sides together, pin the red fabric piece 10B (mouth) to the gray or black fabric piece 10B matching points and notches. Stitch together, leaving open between point E and point F. Turn right side out. Insert the foam mouth piece in the opening. Topstitch between point E and point F. This is the bottom of the mouth.

12. Pin the bottom of the mouth to the roof of the mouth, lining it up exactly. On either side of the mouth, measure 5 inches back from the front of the mouth. Beginning there, join the two mouths by hand stitching toward the back 3 inches. Then remove all pins. (See Figure 36: Attaching the Mouth.)

13. Sew a small ring on the underside of the mouth, 4 inches from the front. Slip your finger through the ring to open and shut the mouth.

14. Glue an eye on each side of the head 1 inch above the mouth and 2 inches from the corner of the mouth. (See "Eyes," p. 58)

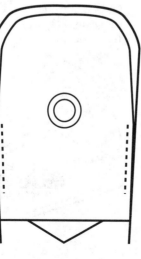

FIGURE 36:
ATTACHING THE MOUTH

FIGURE 37: ATTACHING THE WATER

Water

The water hides the puppeteer's arm. With it, the whale will appear to be swimming in water, with his head and tail held above it.

1. Cut scallops along one 33-inch side of the blue velour or felt to represent waves.

2. Find the middle of the scalloped edge and pin it about 1 1/2 inches closer to the front of the mouth than the ring that is sewn under the mouth. Continue to pin the waves on each side of the whale. (See Figure 37: Attaching the Water.)

3. Slip stitch the water to the whale body.

Jonah

Finished length: 12 inches

MATERIALS NEEDED

Pattern pieces 2A, 2D, 2E from chapter 13

One 16- by 20-inch piece of flesh or tan fabric for head and body

One 19- by 30-inch piece of red fabric (the same color as the whale's mouth)

One 5- by 6-inch piece of cotton or other thin fabric for mouth lining

For the mouth itself, one 5- by 6-inch piece of medium-weight, durable fabric (e.g., double-knit, velour) in a color contrasting with the puppet body

One 4- by 5-inch piece of sturdy, medium-weight cardboard, such as the back of a writing tablet

Small pieces of felt for eyes

Polyester fiber filling for stuffing

Thread that matches puppet body

INSTRUCTIONS

Body

1. Make a small person puppet following the instructions in chapter 8. In order to move Jonah easily through the whale's mouth, the puppet has no arms or nose.

2. Glue on felt eyes. (See "Instructions for Felt Eyes," p. 58.)

3. Lightly stuff the head. (See "Stuffing Puppets," p. 62.)

Clothing

Jonah's clothing must be of the same material and color as the whale's mouth to keep him from being seen when the whale opens his mouth.

1. Cut 2 rectangles, 9- by 13-inches for the headpiece and 9- by 15-inches for the robe. Cut one band, 2- by 12-inches.

2. Fold the band in the middle, lengthwise, with right sides together. Stitch near all edges except one end. Turn right side out.

3. Narrow hem all raw edges on both rectangles.

4. Gather the top of the robe to fit the neck. Hand stitch the robe to the neck, with one side lapping over the other.

FIGURE 38: JONAH

5. Pin the middle of one long side of the headpiece to the forehead. Wrap the band around the headpiece, gathering the headpiece where needed, and sew the band to the head. (See Figure 38: Jonah.)

How to Position and Operate Wilbur Whale and Jonah

1. Place Jonah on your hand and put him inside the whale's mouth with his head at the back of the tongue and bent down so that his face is covered. Put your other hand, which will be hidden by the water, under the whale's body to control the whale's mouth with the ring.

2. To make Jonah come out, let go of the ring and grab the back end of the whale's lower body with your free hand. Pull the whale's body toward you and, at the same time, push Jonah out of the mouth as far as his waist. (See Figure 39: Jonah Comes Out of the Whale.)

FIGURE 39: JONAH COMES OUT OF THE WHALE

'Lijah Light Bulb

Finished length: 15 inches

MATERIALS NEEDED

Pattern pieces 11A, 11D, 11E from chapter 13

One 17- by 30-inch piece of white fabric or fur for the head

One 3- by 13-inch piece of yellow or orange felt for the bottom screw ring

One 6- by 7-inch piece of cotton or other thin fabric for mouth lining

For the mouth itself, one 6- by 7-inch piece of medium-weight, durable fabric (e.g., double-knit, velour) in a color contrasting with the puppet body

One 4- by 5-inch piece of sturdy, medium-weight cardboard, such as the back of a writing tablet

Commercial wiggle eyes or small pieces of felt

One large pom-pom for the nose

One 5- by 30-inch piece of fabric (any color) for a beanie (optional)

One 2- by 4-inch piece of black felt for bow tie (optional)

One 17- by 30-inch piece of polyurethane foam for body lining

Polyester fiber filling for stuffing

Thread that matches puppet body

INSTRUCTIONS

1. Enlarge pattern pieces. (See "Enlarging Patterns," p. 61.)

2. Lay out all pattern pieces on the material.

   a. Cut 5 pieces of 11A (head) from white fabric or fur, and 5 from polyurethane foam, trimming 1/2 inch off the bottom of the foam.

b. Cut 2 pieces of 11D (cloth mouth) from fabric—one for the lining and one for the mouth itself.

c. Cut a cardboard mouth using pattern 11E.

3. Glue the cloth mouth (11D) pieces to the cardboard mouth piece (11E) following the instructions in chapter 8, page 63, steps 3 through 6..

4. To make an opening for the mouth, cut the line marked on the pattern piece 11A (head) from point B to point B through A-C on one of the fabric pieces and one of the foam pieces. Then cut the foam slit 1/2 inch bigger all around the mouth, coming to a point 1/2 inch from each point B.

5. Right sides together, pin the top half of the mouth to the head, matching points A. Machine stitch the top of the mouth to the head.

6. Push the mouth through the mouth slit and pin the bottom half of the mouth to the head, matching points C, right sides together. Machine stitch the bottom of the mouth to the head.

7. Right sides together, pin one side of an 11A (head) fabric section to one side of another section. Machine stitch the sides but leave the bottom open. Repeat with the other 4 sections. Turn the body right side out.

8. Repeat step 7 with the foam sections.

9. Insert the foam head into the fabric head, matching seams and mouth opening. Tack the foam to the fabric at the seams.

10. Slip stitch the fabric to the foam along the bottom, turning under a hem.

11. Pin a yellow or orange felt strip to the bottom of the head for a screw ring, and slip stitch it in place.

12. Stuff the top of the head, leaving just enough room for your hand to be placed in the mouth. (See "Stuffing Puppets," p. 62.)

Special Features

Glue eyes in place. (See "Eyes," p. 58.)

Glue or sew on a large pom-pom for a nose.

Pin and stitch together the sections you cut for a beanie, following the instructions for making the head. Narrow hem the bottom of the beanie. Place a pom-pom at the center top. Tack the beanie to the head.

For the bow tie, wrap the 1- by 2-inch piece of black felt around the center of the 2- by 4-inch piece, pulling tightly, to simulate a knot. Slip stitch the tie at the knot to the head 2 inches below the mouth.

Hooray! Football

Finished length: 18 inches, including legs

MATERIALS NEEDED

Pattern pieces 11A, 11B, 11C, 11D, 11E from chapter 13

One 14- by 24-inch piece of brown fabric or short-haired fur for football

One 8- by 12-inch piece of felt (any color) for arms and legs

One 6- by 7-inch piece of cotton or other thin fabric for mouth lining

For the mouth itself, one 6- by 7-inch piece of medium-weight, durable fabric (e.g., double-knit, velour) in a color contrasting with the puppet body

One 4- by 5-inch piece of sturdy, medium-weight cardboard, such as the back of a writing tablet

Commercial wiggle eyes or small pieces of felt

Two 9- by 12-inch pieces of felt in your team's colors for beanie, bow tie, and pennant

Two small pom-poms, for the nose and for the top of the beanie

One 14- by 24-inch piece of polyurethane foam for lining

Polyester fiber filling for stuffing

Four 7-inch lengths of stiff but bendable galvanized steel wire (16 or 18 gauge)

Thread that matches puppet body

INSTRUCTIONS

1. Enlarge pattern pieces. (See "Enlarging Patterns," p. 61.)

2. Lay out all pattern pieces on the material.

a. Cut 4 pieces of 11A (body) from brown fabric or fur, and 4 from polyurethane foam, trimming 1/2 inch off the bottom.

b. Cut 2 pieces of 11D (cloth mouth) from fabric—one for the lining and one for the mouth itself.

c. Cut a cardboard mouth using pattern 11E.

d. Cut 5 pieces of fabric using the top 5 inches of 11A (body) for the beanie.

e. Cut one 2- by 4-inch piece and one 2- by 2-inch piece of black felt for the bow tie.

3. Cut a slit between dot D and dot E in one section of 11A (body) in one fabric and one foam piece (where you will insert your hand at the back to work the puppet's mouth). Trim the foam piece an extra 1/2 inch on either side of the slit.

4. Follow steps 4 through 10 for making 'Lijah Light Bulb, with these exceptions: In steps 7 and 8, stitch the football body at both ends (don't leave the bottom open).

Make sure the opening for your hand is in the back and the mouth is in the front.

5. Slip stitch the fabric over the foam in the opening in the back, turning under a hem.

6. Stuff firmly both the top and the bottom of the body, leaving only enough room to place your hand in the mouth.

7. Pin 2 of the 11B (leg) pieces together. Topstitch near the edges, leaving the top edge open.

8. Loop the ends of one 7-inch wire and insert the wire into the leg. (See "Putting Wires in Arms and Legs," p. 63.)

9. Repeat steps 7 and 8 with the other leg.

10. Hand sew the tops of the legs on either side of the center bottom of the football body. Bend the feet forward at the ankles.

11. Follow steps 7 and 8 for the arms.

12. Hand sew each arm to the center of a side section, 1 inch below the lower point of the mouth. Bend the arms at the elbows.

13. Make the beanie, following the instructions under "Special Features" for 'Lijah Light Bulb, alternating the contrasting colors.

14. Make the bow tie, following the instructions for 'Lijah Light Bulb, using one color for the tie and one for the bow.

15. Cut a small pennant from felt and glue it to the end of a small stick. Glue the stick to the inside of one hand.

16. Cut a pom-pom from crepe paper and glue it to the end of a small stick. Glue the stick to the inside of the other hand.

Forgetful Fojo

Make a medium or large person puppet, following the instructions in chapter 8. Use white fabric for the face. Add the following clown features.

For oversized lips, trace around the cardboard mouth pattern on red felt. Measure 1 inch beyond that line for the lips. Cut out the lips (it will form a ring). Pin the felt lips around the mouth of the finished puppet and slip stitch it to the face.

For hair, follow the instructions for the girl's short yarn hair in chapter 8, using red yarn.

If desired, add streaks or circles of color to the face with a felt pen or by cutting out felt pieces and gluing or sewing them onto the face.

Use bright colors for clothing and add a big ruffle at the neck. You could cut the shirt pattern (chapter 8) in

half at the fold and make each side a different color.

For the eyeglasses, which are called for in the dialogues for Forgetful Fojo, make oversized ones by twisting two wires together or use the frames from sunglasses.

Honey Dew

Finished length: about 46 inches

MATERIALS NEEDED

Pattern pieces 3A, 3B, 3C, 1D, 1E from chapter 13

Two yards of 44-inch wide or 1 1/2 yards of 60-inch wide fabric for the puppet body

One 24- by 29-inch piece of polyurethane foam for body lining and four 4- by 3-inch pieces for shoulder pads

One 6- by 7-inch piece of cotton or other thin fabric for mouth lining

For the mouth itself, one 6- by 7-inch piece of medium-weight, durable fabric (e.g., double-knit, velour) in a color contrasting with the puppet body

One 5- by 7-inch piece of sturdy, medium-weight cardboard, such as the back of a writing tablet

Commercial wiggle eyes or small pieces of felt

Pom-pom or small piece of puppet body fabric for nose

Yarn, fur, or a wig for hair

Polyester fiber filling for stuffing

Two 18-inch and four 24-inch lengths of stiff but bendable galvanized steel wire (16 or 18 gauge). Twist two wires together, if necessary, to get the proper length.

A pair of dress gloves that fit the puppeteer

Thread that matches the puppet body

INSTRUCTIONS

1. Enlarge pattern pieces, making the following adjustments. (See "Enlarging Patterns," p. 61.)

    a. Add 3 inches to the length of piece 3A (body) at the bottom, and 1 1/2 inches to the width. Then using a ruler, taper the sides from the wider bottom to the original lines at the neck.

    b. Lengthen the legs to 21 inches and add 1 1/2 inches to the width. Make the feet 2 inches longer.

    c. When cutting the arms (3B) do not cut hands. Cut off the left arm at the wrist and the right arm at the elbow. Add 1 1/2 inches to the width of each arm. Add 4 inches to the length of the left arm and 2 inches to the length of the right arm.

2. Make the puppet following the instructions for the medium person puppet in chapter 8, with these differences:

3. Round off the 3-inch sides of the foam shoulder pads and attach them to the puppet as in the instructions for the large puppet in chapter 8.

4. For the left arm and hand, leave the wrist end open. Lightly stuff the left glove to look as much like the puppeteer's hand as possible. Slip stitch the glove to the wrist. Insert an 18-inch wire in the arm and glove. (See "Putting Wires in Arms and Legs," p. 63.) Stuff the arm, slip stitch the opening between points J and K, and sew the arm into the puppet body as in the medium person puppet instructions for arms in chapter 8.

5. For the right arm and hand, stitch the sides and bottom of the right arm stub, leaving the top between point H and point I open. Stuff the arm with filling and sew the arm stub to the body. To complete the rest of the right arm and hand, obtain a shirt, blouse, or dress with long, full sleeves with cuffs at the wrist. The cuff must be loose enough for you to put your hand through it easily. Hand sew the right cuff very securely over the right glove at the wrist. Cut a slit in the right sleeve at the back of the elbow large enough for your hand and arm to be inserted there. Slip stitch the raw edges of the opening, turning under a hem.

Sockem and Sockette

These instructions are for person sock puppets. To make animal sock puppets, use larger-sized socks, increase the length of the mouth, and put more stuffing at the heel. Add ears and other details. Materials are given for one sock puppet.

MATERIALS NEEDED

Pattern pieces 2D, 2E from chapter 13

One men's heavy sock, medium size

One 5- by 6-inch piece cotton or other thin fabric for mouth lining

One 5- by 6-inch piece of medium-weight, durable fabric (e.g., double-knit, velour) in a color contrasting with the sock

One 4- by 5-inch piece of sturdy, medium-weight cardboard, such as the back of a writing tablet

Commercial wiggle eyes or small pieces of felt

A small pom-pom for a nose

Yarn or fur for hair

Small pieces of felt, lace, ribbon, etc., as needed for clothing

Polyester fiber filling for stuffing

Thread to match the sock

INSTRUCTIONS

1. Enlarge the pattern pieces. (See "Enlarging Patterns," on p. 61.)

2. Attach the cloth mouth pieces to the cardboard piece following the instructions in chapter 8.

3. Place the sock on your hand with the heel on top of your wrist. If the toe of the sock is longer than the tip of your fingers, cut it off to fit. If the sock is the right length, cut a slit in the toe from one side to the other.

4. Lay the sock flat and place the mouth in the toe, aligning notch A with the exact middle of the slit. Place a pin on either side of the sock at notches G of the mouth. Cut a slit in the toe of the sock down to the pins. (See Figure 40: Sock Mouth and Head.)

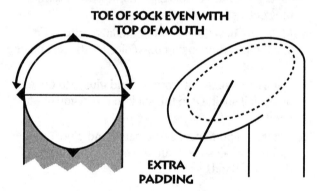

TOE OF SOCK EVEN WITH TOP OF MOUTH

EXTRA PADDING

FIGURE 40: SOCK MOUTH AND HEAD

5. Put in the mouth. (See "Making the Mouth," p. 63.)

6. Make a pad of stuffing for the top of the sock from the back of the heel to 1 inch from the mouth. Insert the pad into the sock and add extra stuffing above the pad in the heel area. Slip stitch the pad to the sock. (See Figure 40: Sock Mouth and Head.)

Special Features

Add eyes, eyebrows, and a pom-pom nose. (See "Eyes," p. 58.)

Put boy's hair on Sockem and girl's hair on Sockette. (See "Hair," p. 56.)

Add a collar and bow tie for Sockem and a lace ruffle and ribbon bow for Sockette.

Offering Envelopes

MATERIALS NEEDED

Two number 6 grocery sacks

Two 2- by 6-inch pieces of cardboard

Acrylic paints, colored felt pens, or crayons

Yarn for hair and mustache (optional)

Staples

INSTRUCTIONS

(See Figure 41: Sack Puppets.)

1. With the flat bottom of each bag facing up, print "No. 26" near the top of one and "No. 3" near the top of the other. (These are the names of the envelopes.)

2. Underneath the number, draw eyes, a nose, and the top part of a mouth.

3. Lift up the bottom flap and continue drawing a long, open mouth on the portion under the flap. Put the flap down and draw the remainder of the mouth.

FIGURE 41: SACK PUPPETS

4. Underneath the mouth print in large letters, "TITHES AND OFFERINGS."

5. Color in some hair or glue on strands of yarn for hair. Add ears and a mustache, if desired.

6. Glue a piece of cardboard across the flap at the bottom on the inside. Staple together the sides opposite the lower mouth, leaving just enough room for your hand to be inserted.

7. Operate the puppet by placing your hand in the sack with your fingers inside the flap. Open and close your hand to make the puppet talk.

CHAPTER 11
Making Hardhead Puppets

Hardhead puppets, particularly furry animals, can sometimes be bought in toy stores or department stores.

Some ready-made dolls and stuffed animals can be converted into puppets.

While there are several ways you can make hardhead puppets from raw materials, the suggestions in this chapter will be for making them by using a Styrofoam ball as a base and covering it with your choice of materials.

Converting Dolls to Puppets

MATERIALS NEEDED

Patterns 12A and 12B from chapter 13

A doll head about 3 to 4 inches in diamater—large enough to be seen easily by the audience but not so large that it is out of proportion to the puppeteer's hand, since the puppet's body gets its shape from the puppeteer's hand

One 15- by 20-inch piece of durable, flexible fabric for costume (e.g., knit, velour)

One 8- by 10-inch piece of fabric the color of the puppet's face for hands

One 5- or 6-inch length of narrow elastic

A small amount of polyester fiber filling for the hands

Thread to match the puppet's costume

INSTRUCTIONS

1. If the doll's head is still attached to a body, cut it from the body at the base of the neck, leaving a little of the shoulder area to make a projecting edge, or flange, on which to fasten clothing.

2. Follow the instructions for making the basic costume for hardhead puppets on p. 85. Enlarge the neck area when cutting the pattern if the neck of the doll is too big for the pattern.

Converting Stuffed Animals to Puppets

MATERIALS NEEDED

A small stuffed animal

A piece of fabric for lining

Polyurethane foam, if needed, for shaping the legs, neck, and front of the face

Thread to match the animal's color

INSTRUCTIONS

1. If the animal is one that sits upright, cut a 6-inch slit in the middle of the back. If it lies down or stands on its legs, make a 6-inch slit on the underside.

2. Remove the stuffing from the front legs, the upper chest area, the neck, and the front of the face to just above the nose, making room for your index and middle fingers to go in the mouth area, your other two fingers in one leg, and your thumb in the other leg.

3. Enclose the exposed stuffing in the head and chest by hand sewing pieces of fabric to the inside.

4. For shaping, if necessary, line the legs, neck, and front of the face with polyurethane foam and tack it into place.

5. Narrow hem the back opening, turning under a hem.

A Puppet from Scratch
HEAD
MATERIALS NEEDED

One 4-inch Styrofoam ball

A cardboard tube (like that in a paper towel roll), about 1 1/2 inches in diameter and 2 1/2 inches in length for the neck

A small piece of cardboard or a 6-inch length of
1/4-inch rope for a bottom flange on the neck

Strapping tape

A ball-point pen

A pea-sized ball of Styrofoam

A sharp knife

Straight pins

A nickel

INSTRUCTIONS

1. Find the exact center of the Styrofoam ball by measuring from the top to the bottom of the ball. Mark
this point with a pen. At this point, draw a horizontal
line a little less than halfway around the ball. (See A
of Figure 42: Shaping the Styrofoam Ball.)

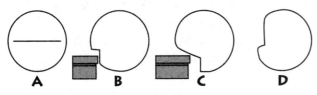

FIGURE 42: SHAPING THE STYROFOAM BALL

2. Roll the ball on a sharp table edge along the line.
Press hard. (See B of Figure 42.) Above this line is
the forehead, which should be flattened by pressing
it on the table edge. (See C and D of Figure 42.)

3. Smooth out the cheeks by pressing the Styrofoam
with your thumbs. For an adult puppet, flatten the
cheeks and the sides of the head. For a child, leave
the face rounder.

4. Find the exact center at the bottom of the ball and
mark it with a pen. Measure 1/2 inch in front of that
and mark that point. Press the tube into the foam
hard enough to make an indentation, putting the
second mark in the center of the tube. (This will put
a little more of the head in the back than in the
front.) With a sharp knife, make a hole in the ball
the diameter of the indentation and about 1 1/2
inches deep. Push the cardboard tube into the hole,
leaving about 1 inch protruding. Push your middle
and index fingers into the tube to see if the hole is
deep enough to control the head. If not, hollow it
out some more. (See E and F of Figure 43: Placing
the Neck in the Ball.)

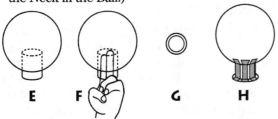

FIGURE 43: PLACING THE NECK IN THE BALL

5. On a piece of cardboard, draw around the outside of
the neck tube. Draw a second circle, 3/8 inch bigger than the first, making a ring. (See G of Figure
43.) Cut out the ring and slip it over the bottom of
the neck as a flange on which to attach clothing.
(Instead of the cardboard flange, you may glue a 6-
inch piece of 1/4-inch rope around the bottom of
the neck.) To reinforce the neck, attach strapping
tape strips all around, from the bottom of the head
on the outside, across the neck, over the ring or
rope, and into the neck on the inside. (See H of Figure 43.)

6. For a nose, take a small piece of Styrofoam and
squeeze it into a ball about the size of a pea. Place it
on the upper edge of the cheeks in the middle. Push
a straight pin down through it and into the ball. (See
I of Figure 44: Facial Features. If you are using papier-
mache for the
head covering,
see step 2 of
those instruc-
tions for adjust-
ing the size of
the nose.)

7. For eyes, make
deep indenta-
tions by press-
ing a nickel hard into the Styrofoam just above the
cheek lines on either side of the nose, a little more
than a nickel-width apart. (See J of Figure 44. If you
will be covering your puppet's head with papier-
mache and you want regular-shaped eyes, don't use
the nickel. See step 2 of the instructions for making
a papier-mache head covering.)

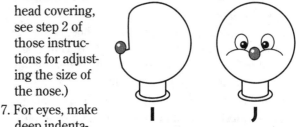

FIGURE 44: FACIAL FEATURES

8. For the mouth, mark with a pen the shape you wish
the mouth to be and then cut the shape into the
foam with a sharp knife. (The mouth should be
located in the middle of the space between the nose
and the bottom of the chin.)

COVERING THE HEAD

There are several ways to cover the Styrofoam head
now that you have shaped it into the desired form. The
following are three methods: fabric covering, sock covering, and papier-mache covering.

Fabric Head Covering

MATERIALS NEEDED

Craft foam, felt, or stretchable fabric in the skin color
of the puppet: one 6- by 6-inch piece for the face,
one 2- by 6-inch piece for the neck, and 2 circles (2
inches in diameter), for the ears, if needed

A small piece of red chenille wire or felt for the mouth

20mm commercial wiggle eyes or small pieces of black and white felt

Yarn or fake fur for hair

Straight pins

Tacky craft glue

INSTRUCTIONS

1. Pin the center of the face-covering material over the nose. Push small straight pins into the Styrofoam around the upper part of the nose and all around the edges of the eye and mouth indentations.

2. Stretch the material to cover the face and head area smoothly, pinning behind the hair line and keeping all wrinkles at the edges. (It won't matter if there are wrinkles where the hair will cover the head.) If you are using felt, dampen it slightly so it will stretch better.

3. Insert pins under the chin and jaw line, being sure that the points do not protrude where your fingers will be in the neck. Proceed slowly in getting out the wrinkles and use many pins.

4. Fold the 2- by 6-inch strip of fabric in half, lengthwise. Stretch it around the neck and glue it to the cardboard tube.

5. Glue a red chenille wire or little piece of red felt to the mouth over the pin heads.

6. Make round eyes the size of a nickel from felt or use 20mm wiggle eyes. (See "Eyes," p. 58.) Glue the eyes over the pin heads.

7. For a male puppet, cut 2 circles, 2 inches in diameter, for the ears. (See "Ears," p. 59.) Sew the ears to the sides of the head.

8. Glue on hair. (See "Hair," p. 56. Adjust the measurements to fit the smaller head.)

Sock Head Covering

This is the simplest of all coverings. It is especially good because you can obtain a match for almost any skin color.

MATERIALS NEEDED

A man's large-size, stretchy dress sock in the color of the puppet's skin

A small piece of red chenille wire or felt for the mouth

20mm commercial wiggle eyes or small pieces of felt

Yarn or fake fur for hair

Small straight pins

Tacky craft glue

INSTRUCTIONS

1. Pull the sock over the Styrofoam head, with the toe at the top. If the sock is smooth on the underside, use this for the face.

2. Push small straight pins into the Styrofoam around the upper half of the nose and into the edges of the eye and mouth indentations. Push pins upward into the Styrofoam all around above the top of the neck, smoothing out the wrinkles in the sock as much as possible.

3. Cut off the sock at the bottom of the neck. Cut a 2- by 6-inch strip from the remaining sock material. Fold it in half lengthwise, stretch it tightly around the neck, and glue it in place.

4. For a male puppet, cut 2 circles, 2 inches in diameter, from the sock material, for the ears. (See "Ears," p. 59.)

5. Glue on hair. (See "Hair," p. 56. Adjust the measurements to fit the smaller head.)

Papier-Mache Head Covering

This is by far the most durable covering. Some of my papier-mache puppets have lasted for about 20 years and have seen a great deal of use, only needing occasional touch-ups of paint. Papier-mache is also more versatile, because you can make a greater variety of head shapes and facial expressions. A little more time and creativity is needed, but the results make the efforts worthwhile.

MATERIALS NEEDED

Instant papier-mache, found in craft and department stores (It is a dry mixture of finely cut-up paper and glue sold by the pound, each pound making about 6 puppets.)

Water

Sandpaper

Gesso, or modeling paste, found in craft stores

Acrylic paints

Clear acrylic finishing spray

Yarn or fake fur for hair

Thick craft glue

INSTRUCTIONS

1. Mix 8 cups of papier-mache with 2 cups of warm water in a large plastic bag. Close the bag, letting all the air out, and then squeeze and knead the mixture until it is like thick modeling clay. (A bowl may be used instead of a bag for mixing, but there will be a lot of dust.) If necessary, add more water; but be careful not to get too much, because water causes

the papier-mache to shrink. If the papier-mache does not have enough adhesive quality to hold together well as you use it, add some thick craft glue.

2. In preparing the Styrofoam ball, don't use a nickel for the eye indentations if you want regular-shaped eyes. Instead, carefully carve out with a sharp knife the size and shape of eye you want. If you want a large nose, shape a bigger ball or triangle from Styrofoam and pin it in place. (Remember that the papier-mache will add to the size.)

3. Starting at the top of the head, spread a layer of papier-mache evenly over the entire head and neck. Let this dry for several hours.

4. Add features by first marking their positions with a pen. To keep the features even, mark a vertical line down the middle of the face. You can vary the placement of the features since people differ somewhat and so can puppets. These are general rules for placing the nose and ears. A nose—other than a child's turned-up one—should have its tip halfway between the eye line and the bottom of the chin. Line up the ears by making the top of the ear even with the eyebrows. The bottom of the ears should be even with the tip of the nose. Using bits of papier-mache, mold the features and add them to the face. They can be exaggerated to be seen better or to give comic effect.

5. Place the puppet neck over a weighted pop bottle for drying. Brace the bottle so it can't be tipped over. Air dry the head, in the sun if possible. This will take two or three days. Don't put the puppet in an oven to dry or the Styrofoam will melt and produce a misshapen head.

6. When the head is dry, the papier-mache will have a pitted look and may have shrunk some. Sandpaper any large, rough spots and use small amounts of papier-mache to improve the features. Let the head completely dry again. Then brush on a coat of gesso, or modeling paste. (This smooths the surface and protects the papier-mache.) It will dry fast.

7. Paint the entire face, neck, and head (except where the hair will go) with acrylic paint, in any color you wish your puppet to be. Let it dry.

8. Paint the facial features: eyes, eyebrows, mouth, etc.

9. When everything is dry, spray the entire head with a protective coat of clear acrylic finisher. Let the head completely dry before adding the hair.

10. Glue on hair. (See "Hair," p. 56. Adjust the measurements to fit the smaller head.)

CLOTHING

Since hardhead puppets are seldom seen much below the waist, costume details are needed above the waist only. The bottom of the costume is open like a dress for inserting the puppeteer's hand. Add accessories to make the costume fit the puppet's age, sex, and character.

You may want to permanently attach a basic costume to the puppet and then add other pieces depending on the puppet's character in a play or dialogue, such as a coat, robe, gathered skirt. I prefer having an entire costume already put together so I can quickly dress my puppets. This is done by putting elastic in the necks of the costumes, which can then be changed in seconds.

You may want a few basic costumes on which you may pin additions or drape robes before a show. Other costumes may have permanently attached accessories.

MATERIALS NEEDED

Pattern pieces 12A and 12B from chapter 13

One 15- by 20-inch piece of durable, flexible fabric for the costume (e.g., double-knit, velour)

One 8- by 8-inch piece of fabric the color of the puppet's face for hands

One 5-inch length of narrow elastic

A small amount of polyester fiber filling for stuffing hands

Thread that matches clothing

Thread that matches the hands

INSTRUCTIONS

1. Enlarge the pattern pieces. (See "Enlarging Patterns," p. 61)

2. Lay out the pattern pieces needed on your fabric.
   a. Cut 2 pieces of 12A (basic costume) on the fold
   b. Cut 2 pieces of 12B (hand). Reverse the pattern and cut 2 more.

3. Right sides together, pin one hand piece to one sleeve, matching points A and B. Be sure the thumb is pointing up toward the neck. Machine stitch. (Use 1/2-inch seams throughout these instructions.)

4. Repeat step 3 with the other 3 hand pieces.

5. Right sides together, pin the 2 costume pieces together. Machine stitch around each side from point C to point D, including the outside edges of the hands. Be sure to leave the bottom open. Turn the costume right side out.

6. Lightly stuff the finger area of the hands. To indicate fingers, topstitch along the stitch lines on the pattern with thread the color of the hands.

7. On the inside, turn down the neck edge, making the fold big enough for the elastic to go in it. Machine stitch, turning under a hem and leaving an opening to insert the elastic. Attach a safety pin to one end of the elastic, insert it in the opening, and pull the elastic through the hem. Stitch the ends of the elastic together and then slip stitch the opening.

8. Narrow hem the bottom of the costume.

Making a Scarecrow

This puppet is needed for the play "Sir Stumpy" (Dialogue 39). It can be used for other dialogues or plays you create.

MATERIALS NEEDED

3- to 4-inch Styrofoam ball
6- by 6-inch piece of orange felt to cover Styrofoam ball
2 dowels
yellow yarn for hair
string or twine
wood-base glue

INSTRUCTIONS

1. Determine the length of the dowels you will need by measuring from where the scarecrow base will stand (for example on the ledge of your puppet stage) to the height you want the head of the puppet to be. Cut one dowel to that length. Cut the other dowel to half that length.

2. Push one end of the long dowel about 2 inches into the Styrofoam ball.

3. Determine the side of the Styrofoam ball you will use for the puppet's face. Pin the center of the orange felt to the center of that side. Stretch the material to cover the ball smoothly. (Dampen the felt slightly so it will stretch better.) Push straight pins through the felt into the ball to hold the felt in place.

4. Glue the other end of the dowel into a hole in the wooden base to allow the scarecrow to stand on its own.

5. Tie the short dowel horizontally onto the first dowel, leaving just enough room between the head and the dowel for a neck. This dowel will support the scarecrow's arms.

6. Put a shirt on the crosspiece. Hang the overalls from the crosspiece.

7. Glue yellow yarn on the head and at the sleeve ends to represent straw.

8. To make the scarecrow walk, hold the bottom of the vertical dowel and move it up and down. When he talks, move the dowel back and forth slightly in a swaying motion.

CHAPTER 12
Making the Talking Bible

The Talking Bible is a visual aid that can be used in a variety of ways to teach Bible truth and memory work to children. It is similar to a puppet in its mode of operation, but it should be handled with the seriousness and respect that is due the Word of God. It can be used equally well by a ventriloquist or by a puppeteer. Even the children can operate it sometimes when they repeat memory verses.

A dialogue with the Talking Bible would be handled like an interview, with questions and answers. Usually the answers by the Bible would either be exact scriptural quotations or facts about the Word. A ventriloquist would hold the Bible in his/her hand. A puppeteer would stand behind a stage or curtain to operate the Talking Bible, speaking for it while hidden from view.

The Talking Bible is simple and inexpensive to make, and any church worker who teaches children should find it well worth the small amount of time and money spent on its construction. Children are fascinated with it and listen much more attentively to the Scriptures when they are repeated by the Talking Bible.

Suggestions for Using the Talking Bible

Use the Talking Bible to teach Bible truths and to inspire children to love, read, and respect God's Word. Use it occasionally instead of your regular Bible for a short devotional reading. As a reward for excellent work in memorizing, let children hold and operate it while repeating their memory work.

Be careful about using the Talking Bible so much that it loses its appeal. Also, don't ever let children play with it. Avoid letting them overuse it. You don't want their familiarity with it to lessen their respect for the Word of God.

In some of the dialogues given in Part 3, the Talking Bible gives direct Bible quotations. Every time this is done, be exact and correct with each word, and give the reference. While you should be familiar with the verses, you wouldn't need to memorize them thoroughly, unless you wish to. Just place a copy of them where you can easily see the words and refer to them as necessary during your presentation. Know the verses well enough to put feeling and expression in the words.

Some of the dialogues are examples of ways to use the Talking Bible. Similarly, you can develop your own questions and scriptural answers on almost any subject in the Bible. Use a concordance, a chain-reference Bible, Sunday school quarterlies, etc., to help you find related verses. But keep such dialogues short and to the point.

Making the Puppet

MATERIALS NEEDED

A hardcover book that is about 2 inches thick (A thicker book will be heavy and harder to operate. The book doesn't have to be a Bible, because only the two middle pages are visible. Two pages from an old Bible could be glued in the middle.)

Sturdy corrugated cardboard, such as from a grocery box

A piece of fabric (velour or felt) of any color (black, blue, or red are most appropriate) that is 4 inches bigger all around than your open book

87

Small pieces of felt: red for the mouth, pink for the tongue, and black for the eyelids

A small pom-pom for the nose

Commercial wiggle eyes or small pieces of felt

A ribbon bookmark (optional)

Cellophane tape

Glue

INSTRUCTIONS

1. Make a false cover over the regular cover of the book by following the next several steps. The strips on the front cover will raise the false cover above the regular one high enough for you to put your fingers in between them and operate the book. If the cardboard that you use is not very thick, you may need more strips than called for. Measure with your fingers to make sure the height is adequate. The strips on the back cover will make the false cover uniform in appearance.

2. Lay the book down on the cardboard and trace around the front cover and cut out the piece. Do the same for the back cover. These pieces will be the false cover of the book.

3. Cut out 12 strips of the cardboard, 1 inch wide and as long as the width of the book cover. Glue 3 of the strips, one on top of the other, along the top edge of the front cover. Repeat for the bottom edge, using 3 more strips. Turn the book over and do the same on the back cover.

4. Cut out 6 strips, 1 inch wide and as long as the length of the cover, minus 2 inches. Glue 3 of these, one on top of the other, along the leading edge of the front cover between the other strips. (See Figure 45: Strips for the False Cover.) Turn the book over and do the same for the back cover.

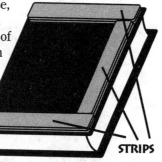

FIGURE 45:
STRIPS FOR THE FALSE COVER

5. Glue the false covers on top of the strips, one on the front and one on the back.

6. Center the open book on the wrong side of the fabric to be used for the cover. At both ends of the spine, cut the fabric the width of the spine, up to 1 inch from the book itself. (See Figure 46: Preparing the Fabric Cover.)

7. Fold the edges of the cloth over the inside of the real covers, front and back, pleating the corners to fit. Tape the cloth to the covers.

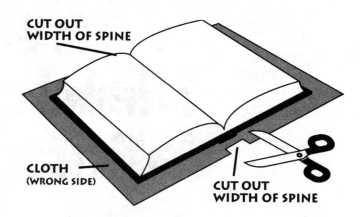

FIGURE 46: PREPARING THE FABRIC COVER

8. Glue the front and back pages of the book to the inside cover to conceal the tape and cloth edges.

9. In the center of the spine, cut an opening wide enough for you to insert all four fingers. (See Figure 47: Opening in the Spine.)

10. Open the book to the middle. If the book you're using is not a Bible, glue pages from an old Bible over the middle pages.

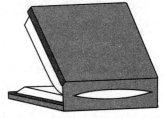

FIGURE 47:
OPENING IN THE SPINE

11. Enlarge the mouth and tongue patterns (Figure 48: Mouth and Tongue Patterns) to the size indicated on the patterns. Place the mouth pattern on a piece of red felt and the tongue pattern on pink felt and cut around the patterns. Glue the tongue to the mouth as shown in the illustration on page 87.

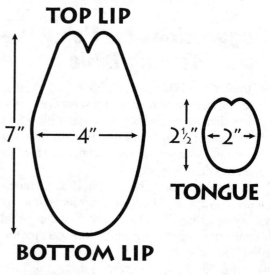

FIGURE 48: MOUTH AND TONGUE PATTERNS

12. With the book opened to the Bible pages in the middle, place the curved lips of the mouth near the center edge of one side of the book, extending slightly over the edge. Staple the mouth to a few of the middle pages. Do the same with the bottom of the mouth. (See Figure 49: Inserting the Mouth.)

13. Tape together with cellophane tape all the pages that are not stapled. Then glue the lips that extend over the edge to the pages.

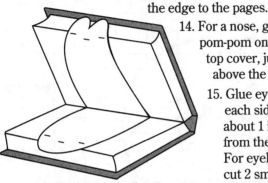

FIGURE 49: INSERTING THE MOUTH

14. For a nose, glue a pom-pom on the top cover, just above the lips.

15. Glue eyes on each side, about 1 inch from the nose. For eyelashes, cut 2 small pieces of black felt for eyelids, rounded on one edge and slashed in thin strips on the other. Glue these over the eyes.

16. Glue a ribbon bookmark in the center of the book (optional).

How to Operate the Talking Bible

1. Place all four fingers up to the second knuckles in the opening at the spine between the real and false covers. Rest your thumb on the outside of the back cover of the book.

2. Open and close your fingers with each word to make it appear that the book is talking. Open widely on heavily-accented syllables and only part-way on other syllables.

3. Hold the book toward the audience, slanted down slightly if their eye level is below you.

Making the Gospel Bookmarks

Some dialogues for the Talking Bible in Part 3 require bookmarks for visuals. Instructions for these bookmarks are given here. You can make other bookmarks to accompany other lessons from the Bible you teach with the Talking Bible.

MATERIALS NEEDED

Six pieces of lightweight cardboard or heavy construction paper, each approximately 5 inches square, in colors as indicated

Six 10-inch lengths of ribbon

Black and red felt pens

Gold glitter; sequins or stars

Glue

INSTRUCTIONS

Use the following illustrations as patterns for the bookmarks. Adjust the size to fit your Talking Bible. Also consider whether your audience will be able to see the bookmarks.

For the heaven bookmark, cut two pieces from yellow paper in the shape of a cloud. On one piece, draw the lines as indicated and run glue over each one. Sprinkle the lines with gold glitter. Glue the back of this piece to the plain piece with the ribbon between them.

HEAVEN BOOKMARK

HELL BOOKMARK

BELIEVER'S CLEAN HEART BOOKMARK

OUTSIDE

INSIDE

SINNER'S HEART BOOKMARK

CROSS BOOKMARK

For the hell bookmark, cut two flame shapes from yellow paper. On one piece, color the flames red. Glue the back of this piece to the plain piece with the ribbon between them.

For the believer's clean heart bookmark, cut two hearts from white paper and glue them together with a ribbon in between.

For the sinner's heart bookmark, cut one heart from colorful paper or use shiny paper on which you glue sequins or stars. This represents the sinner's outward appearance. Cut one heart from gray paper. Add spots with a black marker. This represents the inside of the sinner's heart—his true condition in God's sight. Glue the two hearts together, *back sides facing*, with a ribbon in between.

For the cross bookmark, cut two red crosses and glue them together with a ribbon in between.

CHAPTER 13
Puppet Patterns

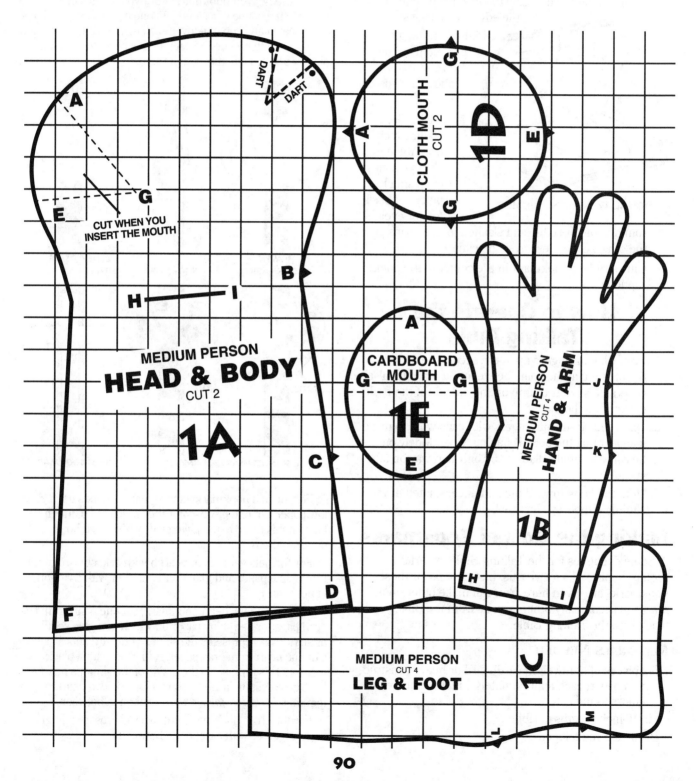

DART

DART

A

E G

CUT WHEN YOU
INSERT THE MOUTH

H I

B

MEDIUM PERSON
HEAD & BODY
CUT 2

1A

C

D

F

G
CLOTH MOUTH
CUT 2
A
1D
E
G

A
CARDBOARD
MOUTH
G G
1E
E

MEDIUM PERSON
CUT 4
HAND & ARM
J

K

H

I

1B

MEDIUM PERSON
CUT 4
LEG & FOOT

1C

L M

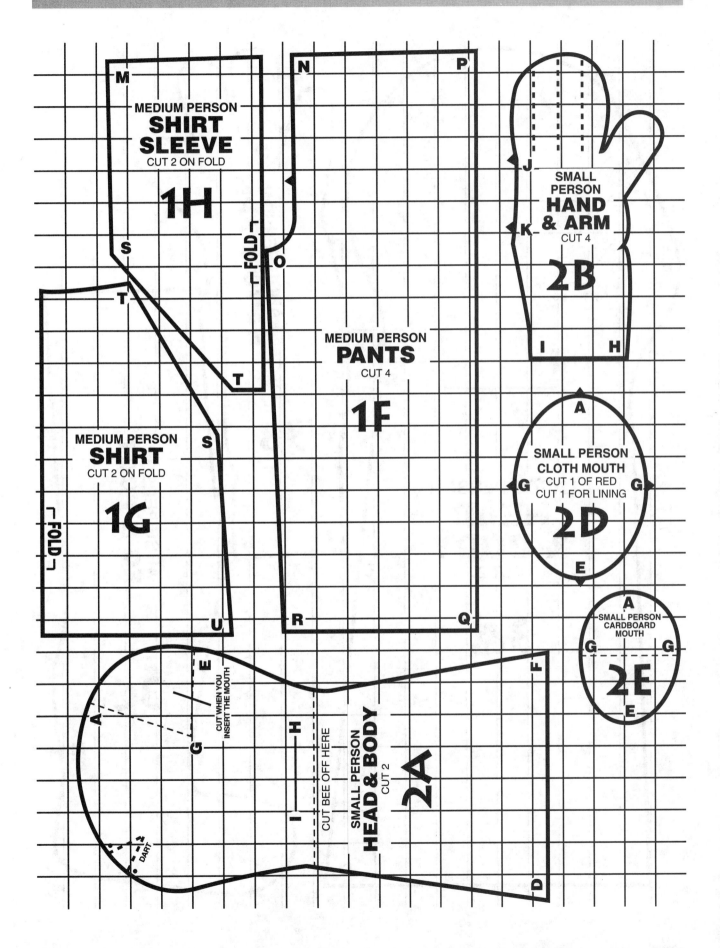

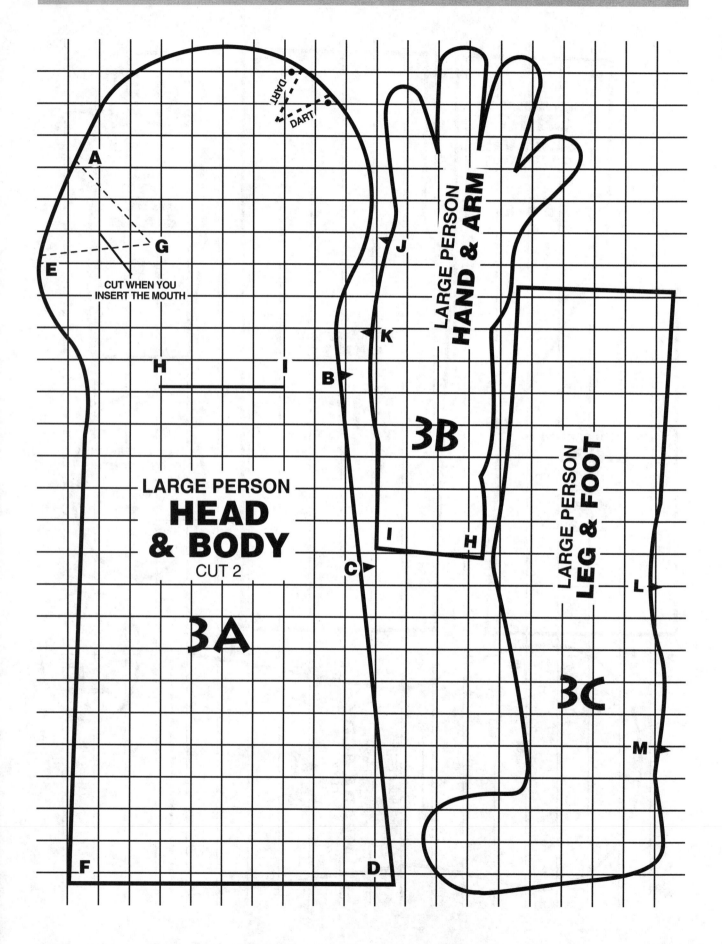

DART

DART

A

G

E

CUT WHEN YOU
INSERT THE MOUTH

H　　　　I

B

J

K

LARGE PERSON
HAND & ARM

3B

I　　　H

LARGE PERSON
**HEAD
& BODY**
CUT 2

3A

C

LARGE PERSON
LEG & FOOT

L

3C

M

F　　　　　　　　D

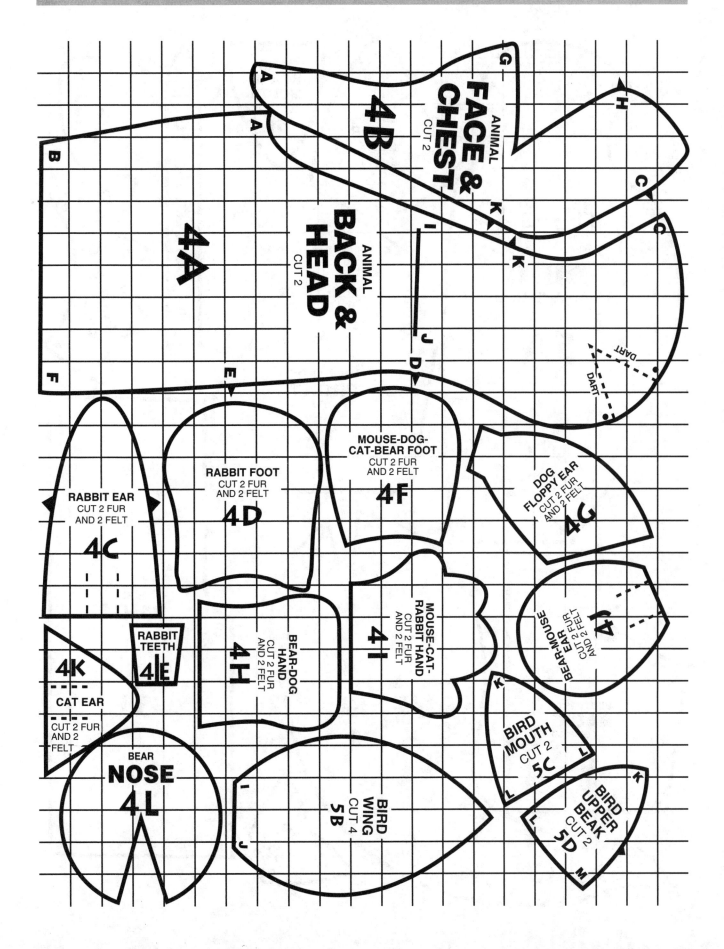

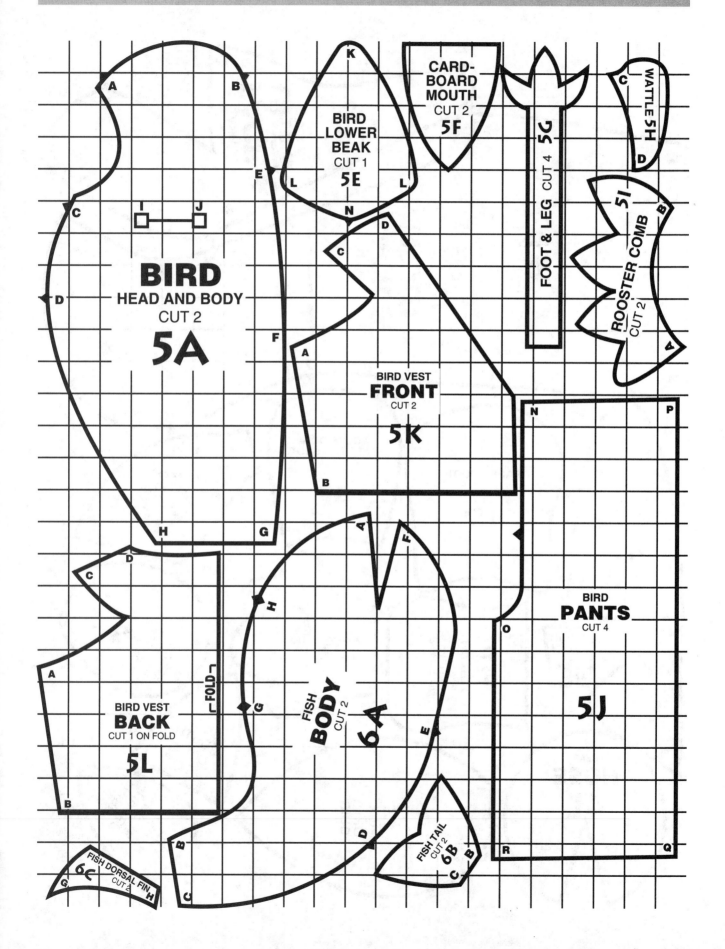

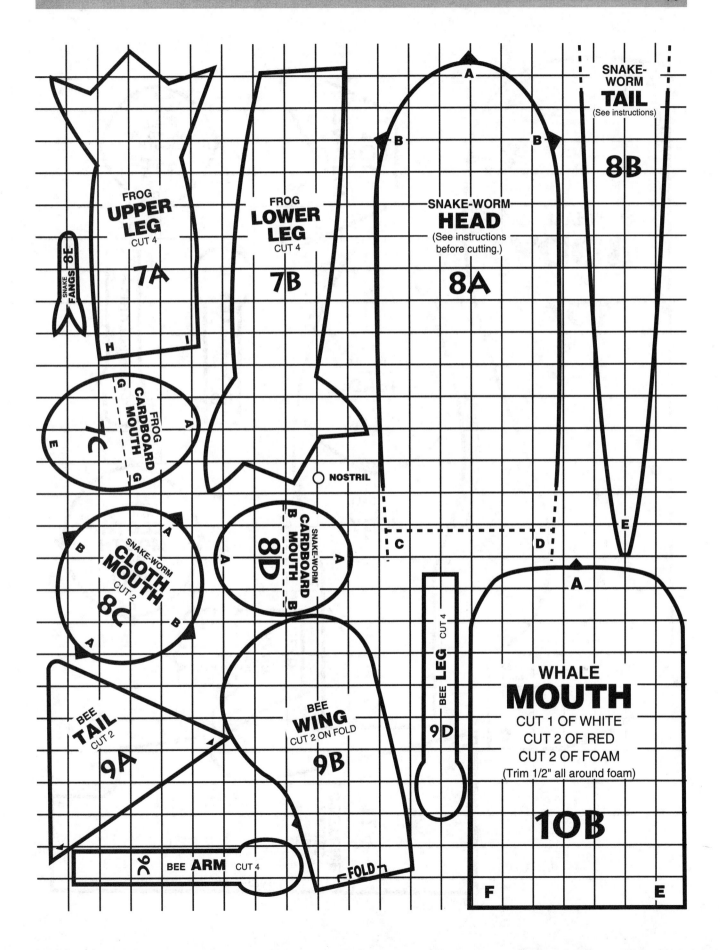

FROG **UPPER LEG** CUT 4   **7A**

SNAKE **FANGS** 8E

FROG **LOWER LEG** CUT 4   **7B**

SNAKE-WORM **HEAD** (See instructions before cutting.)   **8A**

A

B   B

SNAKE-WORM **TAIL** (See instructions)   **8B**

E

FROG **CARDBOARD MOUTH**   **7C**   G   A   E   G

NOSTRIL

C   D

SNAKE-WORM **CLOTH MOUTH** CUT 2   **8C**   A   B   B   A

SNAKE-WORM **CARDBOARD MOUTH**   **8D**   A   B   A   B

BEE **LEG** CUT 4   **9D**

WHALE **MOUTH** CUT 1 OF WHITE CUT 2 OF RED CUT 2 OF FOAM (Trim 1/2" all around foam)   **10B**   A

BEE **TAIL** CUT 2   **9A**

BEE **WING** CUT 2 ON FOLD   **9B**

BEE **ARM** CUT 4   **9C**

FOLD

F   E

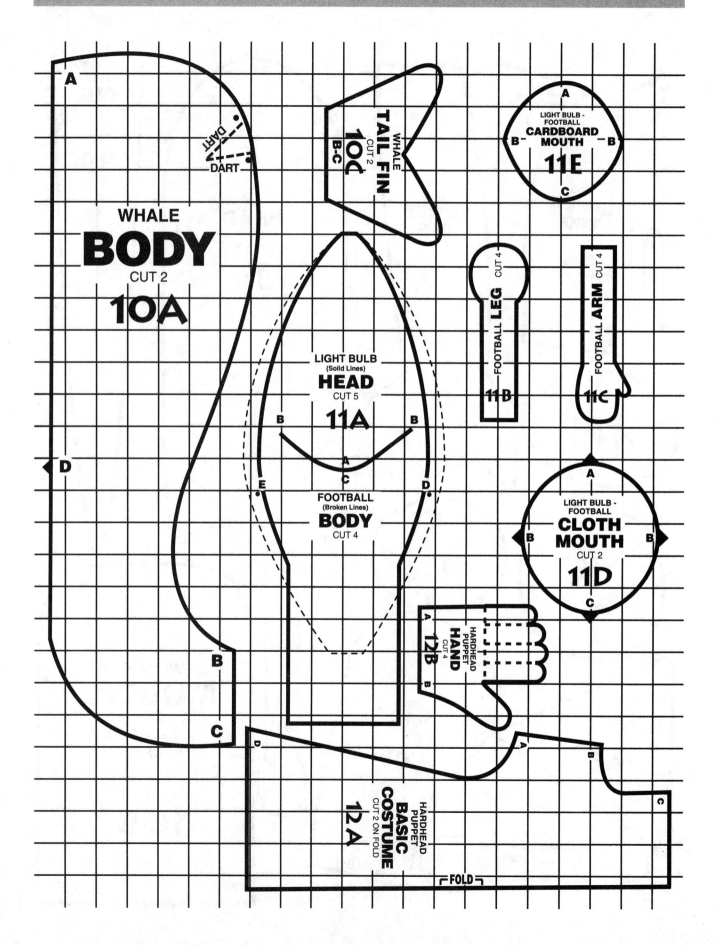

PART THREE

Dialogues and Plays

Introduction to Puppet Dialogues and Plays

The puppet dialogues in this book may be used in three ways:
1. They may be performed by a ventriloquist and one or two puppets, except for "You'll Get Hooked, Filbert," which needs a stage.

2. They may be performed by two people—an interviewer who stands outside the stage and a puppeteer who works one or two puppets behind the stage.

3. Some of them may be performed by two puppets behind the stage.

Puppets Needed

You can use almost any person puppet for the first nine dialogues. The remaining dialogues each mention a specific puppet to be used. Puppets different from the ones called for could be used with some alteration to the script. Patterns and instructions for making all of these mouth puppets are found in Part 2.

Preparing for the Performance

If you are looking for a puppet dialogue that will fit the particular Bible verse or lesson you are teaching, see the indexes for Part 3: Scripture References and Lesson Themes. You can also alter a dialogue to teach a different lesson than is represented in the dialogue.

Once you have selected a puppet dialogue or play, read it to get a feel for the puppets' attitudes and characteristics as portrayed by the words. You may need to change some of the wording to suit your own personality and that of your particular puppet. Words in the dialogues that are italicized are instructional, for example, giving direction for how something should be said or what the puppets should be doing. Words that are capitalized should be said with emphasis.

Memorize the script and practice the words and actions. (See Part 1 for tips on doing this.)

DAVID, THE GIANT-KILLER

Scripture References: 1 Samuel 17:15-50; Psalms 3:6; 118:6-8

Lesson Theme: Be counted as God's soldier. Fight the devil. God will deliver.

Puppet Used: Any puppet will do, but a boy is best.

INTERVIEWER: Andy, would you like to hear a Bible story?

ANDY: Sure.

INTERVIEWER: This one is about David, the shepherd boy.

ANDY: What kinda boy is that?

INTERVIEWER: A shepherd looks after the sheep.

ANDY: Oh, I know where HE is.

INTERVIEWER: You know where WHO is?

ANDY: David—the little boy who looks after the sheep. He's under the haystack, fast asleep.

INTERVIEWER: That's Little Boy Blue, not David.

ANDY: Well, what color was David? Was he Little Boy Red?

INTERVIEWER: This isn't a nursery rhyme. It's a true Bible story. David was a shepherd boy who lived in the hills of Judea long ago. David's older brothers had gone off to try to defeat the Philistines. Do you know about the Philistines?

ANDY: If they didn't play against the Dallas Cowboys, I didn't watch the game.

INTERVIEWER: This was a war. The Philistines were fighting against God's people. And there was a giant who came out from the Philistine camp each day and challenged any Israelite to fight him. Do you remember the giant's name?

ANDY: Uh . . . galoshes?

INTERVIEWER: Almost right. His name was Goliath.

ANDY: Knock! Knock!

INTERVIEWER: Now, Andy, we're not playing any knock-knock games.

ANDY (louder): KNOCK! KNOCK!

INTERVIEWER: Not now.

ANDY (very loudly): KNOCK! KNOCK!

INTERVIEWER (gives a big sigh): Who's there?

ANDY: Goliath.

INTERVIEWER: Goliath who?

ANDY: Go lieth down. You looketh tired.

INTERVIEWER: Let's get back to the story. David's father sent him down to the battlefront to bring his brothers some food and to see how they were doing.

ANDY: Was one of them fighting Goliath?

INTERVIEWER: No. But when David got there, he saw the giant.

ANDY: And he got scared and ran away.

INTERVIEWER: David didn't get scared. It was the Israelite soldiers who were afraid to fight the giant.

ANDY: What did David do?

INTERVIEWER: He offered to fight the giant.

ANDY: Get outta here! He DIDN'T. He was too little to fight.

INTERVIEWER: Even though he was too young to be a soldier, David said, "I will go. God will help me." So he went to a brook and got five smooth stones for his sling.

ANDY: I know why he got SMOOTH stones.

INTERVIEWER: Why?

ANDY: 'Cause he didn't want to HURT the giant. He just wanted to kill him.

INTERVIEWER: Well, David walked up to Goliath. And that giant was ANGRY when he saw it was just a young boy who'd come to fight him. He roared, "Do you think I am a dog, that YOU come at me with a stick! Come here and I'll give your body to the birds and the animals to eat."

ANDY: And David ran away fast.

INTERVIEWER: No, he didn't.

ANDY: I would have.

INTERVIEWER: David said, "I come to you in the name of the Lord. He will deliver me. And I'LL give YOUR flesh to the birds and dogs."

ANDY: Wow! He sure was brave!

INTERVIEWER: He was trusting God to help him. He put a stone in his sling and—

ANDY: And he turned the sling round and round and round (rotates his head or arm) and round—

INTERVIEWER: That's enough.

ANDY: And round and round and round—

INTERVIEWER: Are you through?

ANDY: Not yet—And round and round and round. And that stone went WHOOOOSH through the air and hit the giant in the teeth.

INTERVIEWER: No. It hit him in the forehead, right between the eyes; and the giant fell to the ground. David got the giant's sword and—

ANDY: He cut out his gizzard.

INTERVIEWER: No. He did something with his head.

ANDY: He whacked off his head!

INTERVIEWER: That's right. And the Israelites won a great victory over the Philistines that day. You see, GOD gave the victory, but He had to have someone who was willing to step out and fight.

ANDY: And only David would do that. And all he had was just a little sling to fight with.

INTERVIEWER: Yes. Our mighty, powerful God can do great things through believers who will let Him take charge.

ANDY: Even if they're only boys and girls?

INTERVIEWER: Yes. God wants boys and girls to fight the devil and let everyone know they're on God's side.

ANDY: And God will help them.

INTERVIEWER: Yes, He will. Now it's time for you to help me say the poem we practiced. I'll do the part of the voice of God, and you do the part of David.

ANDY: Okay.

INTERVIEWER: Oh, what is that in thine hand, son? Please give it unto Me.

ANDY: It's only a little sling, Lord, but what is that to Thee? The giant's tall, and he is strong; I see all Israel flee.

INTERVIEWER: Just go and face the giant, son, the rest is up to Me.

ANDY: Oh, Lord, the giant's fallen, thy glory I do see! 'Twas only a little sling, Lord; but it was much with Thee.

WHAT'S THAT IN YOUR HAND?

Scripture References: Numbers 32:23; Proverbs 15:3; Hebrews 12:5-7; 1 John 1:5 to 2:2

Lesson Theme: God sees sin and will punish unconfessed sin.

Puppet Used: Any puppet can be used.

Preparation: The puppet's hand is closed over a dollar. Tape the fingers over the dollar if necessary.

ANDY: Hi, everyone! Remember me? I are Andy.

INTERVIEWER: No, I AM Andy.

ANDY: Why, you ain't neither. I are Andy.

INTERVIEWER: But you should say, "I AM Andy."

ANDY: I ain't gonna say that YOU am Andy.

INTERVIEWER: No. YOU are Andy.

ANDY: Well, now you got it right. Ain't that nice?

INTERVIEWER: Don't say "AIN'T." Where's your grammar?

ANDY: My "GRAMMER"? Oh, she's home with grandpa.

INTERVIEWER: Andy, I've been noticing that you have your hand closed up tight. Do you have something in your hand?

ANDY: Uh. . . no. I just feel like making a fist.

INTERVIEWER: Open up your hand.

ANDY: Oh, I don't feel like doing that.

INTERVIEWER: You're trying to hide something, aren't you?

ANDY: Me? Hide something? Why should I do that?

INTERVIEWER: That's what I want to know, and I'm going to open your hand. *(Does so and discovers a dollar.)* Why, you have a dollar in there!

ANDY: Why, imagine that! Thanks for finding me a dollar.

INTERVIEWER: How did it get in your hand?

ANDY: Uh . . . well, it was flying through the air, and I grabbed it; and I was holding it tight to keep it from flying away again.

INTERVIEWER: Now let's try for the truth. Where did you get the dollar?

ANDY: Um . . . I sort of borrowed it from your pocketbook.

INTERVIEWER: You mean you STOLE it. Did you think you could hide it from me?

ANDY: I almost did.

INTERVIEWER: But I found out, didn't I? Did you know that children try to hide things sometimes, too?

ANDY: You mean like when they play games?

INTERVIEWER: No. I mean when they try to hide their SINS.

ANDY: Give me a fer-instance.

INTERVIEWER: One time a boy took five dollars from his father's wallet. His father didn't notice the money was missing.

ANDY: So the boy got away with stealing?

INTERVIEWER: No. The teacher saw the boy spending a lot of money around school, and she told the father she thought something was wrong.

ANDY: Uh-oh! What did the father do?

INTERVIEWER: He questioned his boy until he got the truth out of him. The boy was punished, of course. But Someone else knew that the boy had stolen the money.

ANDY: Really? Who?

INTERVIEWER: God.

ANDY: Oh, yeah. He knew all along, didn't He?

INTERVIEWER: Yes. The Bible says "You . . . have sinned against the Lord, and you may be sure that your sin will catch up with you."* We can't hide from God.

ANDY: Like I couldn't hide that dollar from you.

INTERVIEWER: Exactly. And God punishes people who won't confess their sins to Him.

ANDY: Are going to punish me?

INTERVIEWER: I think I should take away your allowance this week.

ANDY: Please don't! I'm sorry I took the dollar. Please forgive me.

INTERVIEWER: Are you going to steal from me again?

ANDY: No—not ever.

INTERVIEWER: Then I forgive you, and you may have your allowance.

ANDY: Thank you! Thank you! I feel lots better inside now.

INTERVIEWER: Do you know what can keep you feeling that way?

ANDY: Yeah. Don't do wrong in the first place.

*Numbers 32:23, *The Living Bible*.

VOLUNTEERS FOR JESUS

Scripture References: Isaiah 6:8; Jonah 1:1-3; 2:17; 3:1-3; Mark 16:15,20

Lesson Theme: Volunteering to give and go in God's service

Puppet Used: Any person puppet.

Preparation: The puppet is to wear a disguise—a veil over the top of colored glasses, a bandanna over a mask, or something similar.

INTERVIEWER: Andy, why are you dressed like that?

ANDY *(using a disguised voice)*: **I'm not Andy.**

INTERVIEWER: Why, of course you're Andy.

ANDY *(disguised voice)*: **No, I'm not. Andy's gone away.**

INTERVIEWER: Andy is right here. YOU are Andy. Now I'll just take off that silly bandanna. *(Does so and is startled to see a mask underneath.)*

ANDY: **Please don't take off my mask, too!**

INTERVIEWER: What's the matter? Are you trying to hide from someone?

ANDY: **Yeah.**

INTERVIEWER: Who is it?

ANDY: **I'm hiding from** *(names a person in the audience)***.**

INTERVIEWER: Why are you hiding from him/her?

ANDY: **He's trying to get some kids to help him sing at the nursing home. I know he'll call on me, and I don't want to go.**

INTERVIEWER: So you are hiding.

ANDY: **Yeah. I'd rather play ball. Yikes! He's looking right at me.** *(Tries to hide his face.)*

INTERVIEWER: You can't hide, Andy. You're just like a man who didn't want to go to another country and preach. He tried to run away and hide; but of course, God saw him.

ANDY: **Who was that?**

INTERVIEWER: Jonah.

ANDY: **I know about him. He swallowed a whale.**

INTERVIEWER: Andy!

ANDY: **Uh—I mean the whale swallowed Jonah. How come?**

INTERVIEWER: God sent the great fish to stop Jonah, so he'd go back and be a missionary. You see, God told Jonah to preach to the wicked people of a great city, Ninevah. Jonah disobeyed and went the other way. Do you know what he traveled on?

ANDY: **A jet plane?**

INTERVIEWER: No. He got on a boat.

ANDY: **I'd have gone on a plane. It's much faster.**

INTERVIEWER: But no matter what a person gets on, God sees and knows all about it. The best thing to do would be to obey God and go where He says in the first place.

ANDY: **I guess Jonah would rather have been in Ninevah than in that fish's stomach.**

INTERVIEWER: Oh, yes. He prayed to God for three days and nights down in that fish. After that, when the fish spit him up on land, he was willing to be a missionary.

ANDY: **Why does God want missionaries?**

INTERVIEWER: Because lots of people have never heard about being saved.

ANDY: **Never heard? Where do they live?**

INTERVIEWER: Oh, in Africa, Japan, China, and all around the world. Why, even in America many have never heard the gospel.

ANDY: **Well, if they've never heard, can't they go to heaven when they die?**

INTERVIEWER: No. No one can go to heaven without being saved.

ANDY: **But it doesn't seem fair not to let them go if they've never heard.**

Interviewer: You see, those people have sinned just as much as we have. They need the blood of Jesus to wash their sins away, just as we do. It's the only way to be saved.

ANDY: **Why doesn't Jesus tell them?**

INTERVIEWER: The Bible tells us that God wants Christians to tell them. We are God's hands, feet, and mouth to be used by Him to take the good news to people, telling them that Jesus died and then came back to life to save them.

ANDY: **Then it's every Christian's responsibility for those people to hear?**

INTERVIEWER: That's right.

ANDY: **But these kids are young. How can they go and tell someone about Jesus?**

INTERVIEWER: Oh, that's simple: They can tell Mom and Dad, aunts and uncles, friends and teachers.

ANDY: **Oh, yeah, why didn't I think of that!**

INTERVIEWER: Well, maybe because you don't have a mom or dad or aunts and uncles. And I'm your teacher.

ANDY: **Ha! Of course! I'm such a dummy!** *(Pauses.)* **But what about telling people way across the sea? The kids can't go there.**

INTERVIEWER: No, they can't. Not yet. But older people can go, and children can give their money to help send them.

ANDY: **Well, I can't give. I don't have very much money.**

INTERVIEWER: You always seem to have enough money to buy candy and bubble gum and pop.

ANDY: **You mean give up my treats? Now, let's don't go overboard!**

INTERVIEWER: You could give up many things and be better off, and you'd have money for missionaries, too. And you can volunteer to do whatever you can. Even though you're a puppet, you can be used to sing and talk about Jesus. These children can do many things for the Lord. They can even give themselves as missionaries when they're grown, if God wants them to do that.

ANDY: **I guess there's nothing more important in the whole world than introducing people to Jesus so they can go live with Him in heaven.**

INTERVIEWER: That's right!

ANDY: **Then I'm not going to hide when I'm needed to tell others about Jesus. That's something I can do. Next time I'm going to be right up front as a volunteer.**

NOW IS THE TIME

Scripture References: 2 Corinthians 6:2; James 4:14; Revelation 22:10-12

Lesson Theme: Now is the time to be saved.

Puppet Used: Any puppet.

Preparation: The puppet must wear a watch, either a real one or a toy.

INTERVIEWER: Hello, Sunshine. How are you today?

SUNSHINE: **Fine.**

INTERVIEWER: I see you have on a new watch.

SUNSHINE: **I sure do. Isn't it pretty?**

INTERVIEWER: Yes.

SUNSHINE: **I weighed my watch this morning.**

INTERVIEWER: Why did you do that?

SUNSHINE: **To see if it was GAINING time.**

INTERVIEWER: Sunshine, I think "gaining time" means your watch runs fast.

SUNSHINE: **But my watch doesn't RUN at all. It just sits here on my arm.**

INTERVIEWER: Well, never mind. Tell you what . . . I'll look at my watch, and you look at yours. Now, what time does it tell you?

SUNSHINE: **It's not TELLING me any time. I'll have to tell you.**

INTERVIEWER: Okay, okay. What time is it, Sunshine? What does your watch say?

SUNSHINE: **Uh, just "Tick-tock. Tick-tock."** (*She giggles.*)

INTERVIEWER: I give up!

SUNSHINE: **Hey, did you know my uncle worked in a watch factory?**

INTERVIEWER: Really? What did he do?

SUNSHINE: **He sat around making FACES. . . . Did you know I sleep with my watch under my pillow?**

INTERVIEWER: You do? Why?

SUNSHINE: **So I'll wake up ON TIME. You know, last night I woke up with a funny feeling my watch was gone, so I looked under my pillow for it.**

INTERVIEWER: Was it gone?

SUNSHINE: **No, but it was GOING!**

INTERVIEWER: Sunshine, what time is it?

SUNSHINE: **I don't know, but it's not twelve yet.**

INTERVIEWER: How do you know?

SUNSHINE: **'Cause Mom said I must be home at twelve, and I'm not home yet.**

INTERVIEWER: You know, Sunshine, a lot of folks think they have plenty of time to give their hearts and lives to Jesus; but God's Word tells them they may not have much time.

SUNSHINE: **Why not?**

INTERVIEWER: We must be saved before we die or before Jesus comes back for the believers, and we don't know when either will happen.

SUNSHINE: **Couldn't they get saved AFTER Jesus comes?**

INTERVIEWER: No, it's too late then. When do you think the boys and girls are old enough to understand that they need Jesus?

SUNSHINE: **Pretty quick?**

INTERVIEWER: The Bible says, "I tell you that the 'right time' is now. The 'day of salvation' is now."*

SUNSHINE: **Oh, I understand. People can be sure they have a chance now, but they can't be sure of having another chance later.** (*Looks at her watch.*) **Well, I see by my watch that I'd better be going.**

INTERVIEWER: Oh, really? What do you see by your watch?

SUNSHINE: **That it's GOING—and I gotta go with it. Bye!**

*2 Corinthians 6:2, *International Children's Bible.*

THE INFLUENCE OF SUNDAY SCHOOL

References: Matthew 5:13-16; Luke 17:1,2; Romans 14:7,13

Lesson Theme: Sunday school is a good place to learn to do the right things. Then the child can be a good influence on others.

Puppet Used: Any puppet.

INTERVIEWER: Sunshine, I'd like to talk about Sunday school. Do you go to Sunday school?

SUNSHINE: Every Sunday.

INTERVIEWER: That's good. Do you like your teacher?

SUNSHINE: Oh, yes!

INTERVIEWER: What does she look like? Is she a tall woman?

SUNSHINE: No.

INTERVIEWER: Is she a short woman?

SUNSHINE: No.

INTERVIEWER: Is she an average-sized woman?

SUNSHINE: No.

INTERVIEWER: I don't understand. If she's not tall, average, or short, what is she?

SUNSHINE: A MAN!

INTERVIEWER: Oh . . . Well, since you go to Sunday school you should be able to answer some Bible questions. Do you remember the story of the three men who were put in the fiery furnace because they wouldn't bow to the image of gold?

SUNSHINE: Sure.

INTERVIEWER: What were their names?

SUNSHINE: Shadrach, Meshach, and a billy goat.

INTERVIEWER: No. Abednego.

SUNSHINE: A-bed we go? Why do we have to go to bed?

INTERVIEWER: The men were Shadrach, Meshach, and Abednego. Do you know who Ezekiel was?

SUNSHINE: I never heard of him.

INTERVIEWER: Who was Joshua?

SUNSHINE: I'm not sure.

INTERVIEWER: Don't you know any Bible characters? Who was Job?

SUNSHINE: I don't know. Give me an easy one.

INTERVIEWER: All right. Who was Peter?

SUNSHINE: He was a BUNNY RABBIT. Ha, Ha! Just kidding!

INTERVIEWER: Be serious. Haven't you learned anything in Sunday school?

SUNSHINE: We've been learning about how God made the world.

INTERVIEWER: That's good.

SUNSHINE: The other day the teacher asked, "Kids, who made you?" And no one raised a hand. So he asked again, "Kids, who made you?" Still no one raised a hand. So he asked one more time, "Kids, who made you?"

INTERVIEWER: Couldn't any one answer him?

SUNSHINE: Yes. A little girl raised her hand and said, "Teacher, GOD made me."

INTERVIEWER: I'm glad someone knew the answer.

SUNSHINE: Well, the next Sunday the teacher asked again, "Kids, who made you?" And no one raised a hand. So he asked again, "Kids, who made you?" but this time I raised my hand.

INTERVEIWER: And what did you say?

SUNSHINE: I said, "Teacher, the little girl that God made isn't here today."

INTERVIEWER: I'm afraid you haven't learned much in Sunday school. But I'm sure it's had a good influence on you.

SUNSHINE: No, it didn't either. I NEVER got INFLUENZA from Sunday school.

INTERVIEWER: Not "influenza." "INFLUENCE."

SUNSHINE: What's that?

INTERVIEWER: Well, suppose that over here (points to the floor on the right) are some sheep on a mountaintop.

SUNSHINE: I don't see sheep.

INTERVIEWER: We PRETEND there are some sheep there on the mountaintop.

SUNSHINE: That's the FLOOR.

INTERVIEWER: We pretend it's a MOUNTAINTOP. And over there is a high cliff (points to the floor on the left).

SUNSHINE: That's the FLOOR again.

INTERVIEWER: SUPPOSE it's a high cliff. And suppose one sheep walks over toward the edge of the cliff.

SUNSHINE: CLOMP, CLOMP, CLOMP!

INTERVIEWER: He keeps going until he drops off the cliff and is killed.

SUNSHINE: And all the other sheep cry.

INTERVIEWER: No. The way sheep act, they would probably ALL follow the first sheep, drop off the cliff, and die. Sheep are like that.

SUNSHINE: Like what?

INTERVIEWER: They don't think for themselves. They follow a leader, even if he's going wrong. So we say the first sheep INFLUENCED the other sheep. Now do you know what "influence" is?

SUNSHINE: Yes. It's a lot of DEAD SHEEP at the foot of a mountain.

INTERVIEWER: No. To influence others is to cause them to think or act in a certain way—either good or bad.

SUNSHINE: Then Sunday school has had a good INFLUENZA on me.

INTERVIEWER: You mean INFLUENCE.

SUNSHINE: Oh, yes. In Sunday school I learn how to be good.

INTERVIEWER: Sunday school is one of the best places boys and girls can go. There they can learn from God's Word how He wants them to act.

SUNSHINE: Hey, I just thought about something. Influenza and influence are sort of alike.

INTERVIEWER: How's that?

SUNSHINE: Well, you catch influenza and then KA-CHOO! KA-CHOO! you PASS IT ON to someone else. Right?

INTERVIEWER: That's true.

SUNSHINE: Okay. If you go to Sunday school and are influenced to do right, you'll PASS THAT ON to someone else, too.

INTERVIEWER: Right! YOU are influenced to do right, and then YOU influence SOMEONE ELSE.

SUNSHINE: And that person influences someone else, and that person influences someone else, and that person—

INTERVIEWER: We get the idea.

SUNSHINE: I'm going to Sunday school every Sunday and learn what's right and catch a good case of influence!

KNOW THE BIBLE TO GROW

Scripture References: Psalm 119:9-11; Hebrews 5:11-18; 1 Peter 2:2; 2 Peter 3:18

Lesson Theme: To grow as Christians we must learn God's Word.

Puppets Used: Any two puppets can be used, preferably a boy and a girl.

INTERVIEWER: Andy, there are sixty-six books in the Bible. Can you say their names?

ANDY: Sure. THEIR NAMES.

INTERVIEWER: What?

ANDY: Their names. You asked if I could say "their names."

INTERVIEWER: I mean, can you repeat the names of the books of the Bible?

ANDY: Sure.

INTERVIEWER: Let's hear them.

ANDY: Here? In front of all these people?

INTERVIEWER: Yes.

ANDY: I guess I don't know them.

INTERVIEWER: Well, Sunshine, can you say them?

SUNSHINE: I'll try. First, there's Genesis, then Exit Dust.

ANDY: EXIT DUST?

INTERVIEWER: She means Exodus.

SUNSHINE: Exodus, Loretta cuss.

INTERVIEWER: That's Leviticus.

SUNSHINE: Oh, yeah. And the next is Numbers, and then Deuter-omity.

INTERVIEWER: That's not quite right. Can one of you children tell her what it is? . . . Yes. It's Deuteronomy.

SUNSHINE: What's next?

INTERVIEWER: Try to remember.

SUNSHINE: I can't. Please help me.

INTERVIEWER: Well, what comes before Judges?

ANDY: I can answer that one: BAD GUYS come before judges.

INTERVIEWER: No, no. It's Joshua, Judges, Ruth.

ANDY: Why did Joshua judge Ruth? Was she bad?

INTERVIEWER: Oh, you two are quite a pair! You must both work on learning the books of the Bible. It's God's Word to us. It's important for us to know as much of it as we can. There are many miracles recorded in the Bible. Do you know what a miracle is?

ANDY: Sure. A miracle is something no one really believes could happen—like when my mother tells me to wash my hands and face, and I wash behind my ears, too. That's a MIRACLE!

INTERVIEWER: The Bible says we should worship God. Do you know what the word "worship" means?

SUNSHINE: Sure. I hear it every day. Mama says, "Andy, go to the bathroom and WORSH UP."

INTERVIEWER: We worship God when we think about Him, love Him, praise Him, and—

SUNSHINE: And pray to Him, right?

INTERVIEWER: Right. Sunshine, Andy, can you say the Lord's Prayer?

ANDY: Sure. "Now I lay me down to sleep, I pray the Lord my soul to keep."

SUNSHINE: Wow! You do know it!

INTERVIEWER: I'm afraid that isn't the Lord's Prayer. Neither of you know the Bible very well. Say, do you like to get letters in the mail?

ANDY: I sure do.

SUNSHINE: Me, too.

INTERVIEWER: What do you do with your letters?

ANDY: I read them, of course.

SUNSHINE: Me, too.

INTERVIEWER: The Bible is God's letter to people. How do you think God feels when the boys and girls fail to read His letter to them?

SUNSHINE: I guess He's sad.

INTERVIEWER: Yes. He's given us His Word so we will know how to live right and please Him. We can't GROW unless we know God's Word.

SUNSHINE: It's lots easier to DO right when you KNOW what is right and wrong.

INTERVIEWER: Yes. And when we read and study the Bible, the Holy Spirit helps us understand it, and He talks to us about obeying it.

ANDY: Is the Bible kind of like food? You have to eat good food to grow big and strong in your body.

INTERVIEWER: That's exactly right.

SUNSHINE: I learned a verse about that. It says, "As newborn babies want milk, you should want the pure and simple teaching. By it you can grow up and be saved.*

INTERVIEWER: Very good, Sunshine! I see you really have been learning something from the Bible after all.

ANDY: I learned a little rhyme in Sunday school: If you want help along your way, / Read your Bible every day.

SUNSHINE: Say, kids, will you try to remember to read the Bible each day this week? Raise your hands if you will. Good! Next week we'll check to see who remembered. Bye, now!

*1 Peter 2:2, *International Children's Bible.*

THE STORY OF THE FIRST SIN

Scripture References: Genesis 1 to 3; John 3:16; Romans 3:23

Lesson Theme: Adam and Eve sinned, so all human beings were born sinners. Jesus never sinned; He died for all sinners.

Puppet Used: A girl puppet should be used.

SUNSHINE: **Hi, everyone! Let's get acquainted. My name is—ummm . . .**

INTERVIEWER: Come on. Tell them your name.

SUNSHINE: **Oh, my name! Well, it's . . . ummm . . . uh—**

INTERVIEWER: Hurry up. What's your name?

SUNSHINE: **Don't rush me. I'm working on it.**

INTERVIEWER: Why can't you say your name?

SUNSHINE: **Because I forgot it.**

INTERVIEWER: How could you forget your own name?

SUNSHINE: **It wasn't easy.**

INTERVIEWER: Well, friends, this young lady's name is—

SUNSHINE: **Sunshine! I knew it all the time. Ha, ha, ha!**

INTERVIEWER: Okay, let's see what else you know: Who was the first man?

SUNSHINE: **George Washington.**

INTERVIEWER: GEORGE WASHINGTON?

SUNSHINE: **Yes. He was the FATHER of our country.**

INTERVIEWER: Uh, well, that's not quite what I had in mind. Who was the first man ever to have LIVED? It's in the Bible.

SUNSHINE: **Oh, if you're going to count foreigners, it was Adam.**

INTERVIEWER: Okay. The first man was Adam.

SUNSHINE: **Did you know he was the FASTEST RUNNER in the world, too?**

INTERVIEWER: Adam was the fastest RUNNER?

SUNSHINE: **Yes. He was first in the human RACE.**

INTERVIEWER: Ah, I see. Well, do you remember what God made Adam from?

SUNSHINE: **No, I guess I forgot.**

INTERVIEWER: God made him from the dust. Adam came from dust; and when he died, he returned to dust.

SUNSHINE: **He came from dust and returned to dust?**

INTERVEIWER: That's right.

SUNSHINE: **Well then, I know where Adam is.**

INTERVIEWER: You do? Where?

SUNSHINE: **Under my BED . . . But I don't know if he's COMING or GOING.**

INTERVIEWER: Let's get back to the story. After God made Adam, He made Eve by taking a rib from Adam.

SUNSHINE: **I know why God made Adam FIRST.**

INTERVIEWER: Why?

SUNSHINE: **So Adam would have a chance to rest before he got a HONEY-DO list.**

INTERVIEWER: Oh, you mean "Honey, do this" and "Honey, do that"? Actually, the Bible indicates they worked pretty closely together. . . . Have you ever thought about how wonderful it must have been, living in the Garden of Eden? Just think how good the food must have been!

SUNSHINE: **If Adam and Eve had all that good food, why do you suppose they ate those apples that God said not to eat?**

INTERVIEWER: It wasn't apples.

SUNSHINE: **Oh, was it peaches?**

INTERVIEWER: No.

SUNSHINE: **Pears?**

INTERVIEWER: No.

SUNSHINE: **I know—watermelon!**

INTERVIEWER: No.

SUNSHINE: **Okay. I give up! What kind of fruit was it?**

INTERVIEWER: The fruit on the tree of knowledge of good and evil.

SUNSHINE: **Boy, that doesn't sound all that good.**

INTERVIEWER: Well, the Bible says Eve saw that the tree was beautiful and its fruit was good to eat. It's just that God said not to eat it. . . . Do you think it made God happy or sad when Adam and Eve disobeyed Him?

SUNSHINE: **Very sad, huh?**

INTERVIEWER: Yes, and because of that, God had to punish them.

SUNSHINE: **Like you do when I'm naughty?**

INTERVIEWER: Yes. Their punishment meant they had to leave the beautiful garden. And then Adam had to work hard to make a living, and there was pain and sickness and death in the world. Also, when children were born, they were born sinners—just like their parents.

SUNSHINE: **What do you mean?**

INTERVIEWER: Children are born like their parents. For instance, think of the animals. If cats have little ones, what do they have?

SUNSHINE: **Kittens.**

INTERVIEWER: What kind of little ones do sheep have?

SUNSHINE: **Lambs.**

INTERVIEWER: What do dogs have?

SUNSHINE: **FLEAS!**

INTERVIEWER: Well, they do have fleas, but not quite in the same way they have puppies. All animals have babies like themselves. So Adam and Eve became sinners, and all people born since then were born sinners.

SUNSHINE: **And they get shorter all the time.**

INTERVIEWER: Shorter? What do you mean?

SUNSHINE: **The Bible says "All have sinned and come SHORT of the glory of God."**

INTERVIEWER: Ah, that's true, but that doesn't mean people get shorter. It means we all fail to measure up. We come short of being what God wants us to be.

SUNSHINE: **So everybody's born a sinner. But that's just who Jesus died for—sinners.** (She sings the following verse to the tune of "Jesus Loves the Little Children.") **"Jesus died for all the sinners, / All the sinners of the world; Red and yellow, black and white, / They are precious in His sight; / Jesus died for all the sinners of the world."** (Perhaps have the children sing along the second time with the puppet.)

REAPING WHAT WE SOW: THE PRODIGAL SON

Scripture References: Luke 15:11-32; Galatians 6:6-9

Lesson Theme: We reap what we sow.

Puppet Used: Any puppet.

Preparation: The puppet has a big bandage on his forehead.

INTERVIEWER: Why, Andy, you've been hurt. What happened?

ANDY: I got hit in the head.

INTERVIEWER: Who hit you?

ANDY: Not WHO—WHAT.

INTERVIEWER: All right. WHAT hit you?

ANDY: A TIN CAN.

INTERVIEWER: How could a tin can hurt you?

ANDY: It was full of BEANS.

INTERVIEWER: Did someone throw the can at you?

ANDY: No. It was on a high shelf, and it fell on me when I reached up to get some COOKIES.

INTERVIEWER: Why didn't you ask your mother to get the cookies down?

ANDY: Because she told me NOT to eat any cookies.

INTERVIEWER: So the real reason you got hit is that you disobeyed.

ANDY: Yeah, I guess so.

INTERVIEWER: You know, Andy, sometimes we think we're going to have something good; but if we do wrong to get it, the outcome is BAD—not good. Like the story Jesus told about the Prodigal Son.

ANDY: Protical Sun? Is that the opposite of a tropical sun?

INTERVIEWER: That's s-o-n. He was a young man who left home. So let's just call him the son who left home.

ANDY: I ran away from home one time.

INTERVIEWER: You did? How far did you go?

ANDY: To the end of our block.

INTERVIEWER: Only to the end of the block?

ANDY: Well, I would have gone farther, but I wasn't allowed to cross the street.

INTERVIEWER: Why did you leave home?

ANDY: On account of bubble gum.

INTERVIEWER: BUBBLE GUM?

ANDY: Yeah. I got punished for spending all my money for bubble gum when my mother said not to.

INTERVIEWER: In the story Jesus told, the young man wanted to leave home so he could live as he pleased. He asked his father for what was coming to him.

ANDY: Oooh, that's not smart! I got what was coming to me once. But I'd never ask for that on purpose.

INTERVIEWER: No, he asked for his INHERITANCE, his share of what the father owned and was going to leave to him and his brother when the father died.

ANDY: Oh, you mean like borrowing on your allowance.

INTERVIEWER: Kind of.

ANDY: Well, I get fifty cents, but I don't think that's enough to leave home—except when I spend it all on bubble gum—then it's too much.

INTERVIEWER: Uh, I think we're getting a little confused here. The allowance Jesus was talking about was supposed to be for the son when he got married and started his own family. But do you know what he did? Jesus said he spent all his money in wild living. Do you know what that means?

ANDY: Like spending all your allowance for bubble gum?

INTERVIEWER: Worse. He spent his money on parties, and drinking, and bad friends—until the money was all gone . . . and his "friends" too.

ANDY: Uh-oh! What did he do then? Did he starve?

INTERVIEWER: Almost. He started looking for work, but all he could find was a job feeding pigs.

ANDY: YUK! That wasn't much fun. Did he get something to eat?

INTERVIEWER: No. He became very hungry. He wished he could eat the corn husks that he fed the pigs.

ANDY: I met a man like that once. He was begging for food on the street. He said he hadn't had a bite in two days.

INTERVIEWER: What did you do?

ANDY: I BIT him.

INTERVIEWER: ANDY!

ANDY: Just kidding. What did this runaway do?

INTERVIEWER: He said to himself, "Why don't I go home? Even the servants there have plenty to eat. I could be my father's servant."

ANDY: Did his father let him come back?

INTERVIEWER: He was waiting for him. He ran to meet him and fell on his neck.

ANDY: I'm sorry the father got hurt.

INTERVIEWER: What?

ANDY: You said he ran and FELL ON HIS NECK.

INTERVIEWER: No, no. That means he HUGGED his son's neck and KISSED him. He prepared a feast, and put a robe on him, shoes on his feet, and a ring on his finger. He threw a welcome-home party.

ANDY: WHAT! He wasn't grounded! his television privileges taken away from him!

INTERVIEWER: No.

REAPING WHAT WE SOW: THE PRODIGAL SON *(continued)*

ANDY: Boy, with THAT kind of father and all that GOOD stuff, why did he EVER want to leave?

INTERVIEWER: I guess he thought he was missing out on some good times.

ANDY: Yeah, I guess I feel that way too sometimes.

INTERVIEWER: We probably all do, Andy. But we should remember that we ALWAYS harvest what we plant. Just like a gardener. If he plants pumpkin seeds, he'll harvest pumpkins; if he plants tomato seeds, he'll get tomatoes. The Bible says, "A person harvests only what he plants. If he plants to satisfy his sinful self, his sinful self will bring him eternal death. But if he plants to please the Spirit, he will receive eternal life from the Spirit."*

ANDY: Oh, that's like a poem I learned:
I plowed the ground and watered it;
I put in little seeds;
I wanted corn, but I got grass,
For I had planted weeds.

INTERVIEWER: That's the idea. If you plant bad actions, or deeds, in your life, you'll get a crop of trouble.

ANDY: But if you plant good actions, or deeds, you'll get a crop of good in your life.

INTERVIEWER: Yes.

ANDY: Kids, here's something easy to remember: Plant bad—harvest bad. Plant good—harvest good. Let's all get started making a good harvest! 'Bye.

*Galatians 6:7-8, *International Children's Bible.*

FROGS IN THE BUTTER

Scripture References: Exodus 8:1-15; Hebrews 12:5-11

Lesson Theme: Obeying God brings His favor. Disobeying Him causes suffering.

Puppet Used: Croaker frog. See Part 2, chapter 10, for instructions on making this special mouth puppet, or use any frog puppet.

INTERVIEWER: Hello, everyone. Here is Croaker—my friend, the frog . . . warts and all.

CROAKER: **Burrup! Not nice. Burrup!**

INTERVIEWER: You're right, Croaker. I'm sorry.

CROAKER: **Burrup! I guess you're wondering about this old frog showin' up in church. Well, I want you to know that frogs—burrup—should have a place in church . . . at least in the lessons you learn. We're in the Bible, you know.**

INTERVIEWER: Well, sure they are: God created them.

CROAKER: **Well, yes, that's true, but God also used us frogs—burrup—to work out some of His plans.**

INTERVIEWER: Tell us about it—burrup—Croaker.

(Croaker eyes the interviewer.)

INTERVIEWER: Uh, sorry again, Croaker. It's kind of catching.

CROAKER: **This happened to some of my family of long ago. They lived in the ponds and rivers of Egypt. God's people, the Israelites, lived in Egypt, too.**

INTERVIEWER: Oh, yes. I remember: The Israelites started off as guests of Egypt and ended up as slaves—for around four hundred years.

CROAKER: **One day God sent Moses to lead the people of Israel out of Egypt. He wanted them to go back to their own land, where they could worship and serve Him.**

INTERVIEWER: But the ruler of Egypt, Pharaoh, didn't want to let them go, did he?

CROAKER: **No. So Moses told him, "The Lord has said, 'Let my people go to serve Me in the wilderness. If you don't, I will turn all the water in Egypt to blood.'"**

INTERVIEWER: Yuk! And Pharaoh wouldn't let Israel go.

CROAKER: **That's right. So all the water turned to blood. There was no water to drink. But Pharaoh wouldn't let the people of Israel go. Then Moses said, "This time there will be frogs everywhere." And Aaron lifted up his rod, and frogs came up from the ponds and the rivers. They went in the houses, in the food, and in the beds.**
(Croaker begins to move from side to side as he chants the following.)

There were
Frogs in the butter,
Frogs in the bed,
Frogs even sitting
On Pharaoh's head.

INTERVIEWER: Oh, how awful!

CROAKER: **Excuse me?**

INTERVIEWER: Oh, my, I did it again. I really didn't mean to offend you, Croaker. Some of my best friends are frogs. Like you, Croaker! It's just that I don't think the proper place for frogs is in a person's bed . . . or his food.

CROAKER: **Well, the Egyptians didn't think so either. They probably came to Pharaoh and said, "You must do something about these frogs. They're everywhere.** *(As Croaker chants the following and moves from side to side, the interviewer nods his head in rhythm.)*

"There are
Frogs in the butter,
Frogs in the bed,
Frogs even sitting
Upon your head."

INTERVIEWER: I guess the people couldn't even walk without squashing frogs.

CROAKER: **No, like they say, it's not easy being green. . . . Can't you imagine what old Pharaoh's wife must have said? I can hear her now, "Pharaoh, you do something about these frogs.** *(Interviewer joins in.)*

"There are
Frogs in the butter,
Frogs in the bed,
Frogs even sitting
Upon your head."

INTERVIEWER: So what did Pharaoh do?

CROAKER: **Well, he probably said to himself, "I must do something about these frogs. There are—"**

INTERVIEWER: Croaker!

CROAKER: **Uh, yeah, well, anyway, he called Moses and said, "Ask the Lord to take away the frogs, and I will let your people go."**

INTERVIEWER: So the Lord caused the frogs to die.

CROAKER: **Yeah, we croaked, so to speak.**

INTERVIEWER: Did Pharaoh let Israel go?

CROAKER: **No. He was a stubborn cuss and wouldn't keep his promise.**

INTERVIEWER: What happened next?

CROAKER: **God sent more troubles to Egypt. Not one, not two, not three, not four—**

INTERVIEWER: Croaker!

CROAKER: **TEN. God sent ten plagues on Egypt. Then Pharaoh let Israel go.**

FROGS IN THE BUTTER *(continued)*

INTERVIEWER: Slow learner.

CROAKER: The SLOWEST!

INTERVIEWER: Pharaoh shouldn't have disobeyed God in the first place. He'd have saved himself and his country lots of troubles. All of us, too, should remember that obeying God brings many blessings, but disobeying Him just brings hard times, sooner or later.

CROAKER: You bet. If you disobey, you might have

> **Frogs in the butter,**
> **Frogs in the bed,**
> **Frogs even sitting**
> **Upon your head.**

INTERVIEWER: Well, we probably wouldn't have trouble with frogs. But there are worse things than frogs.

CROAKER: Yeah, like cats.

INTERVIEWER: Well, let's just listen to the Bible: "No discipline seems pleasing at the time, but painful. Later on, however, it produces a harvest of righteousness and peace for those who have been trained by it."* . . . Thank you for your story, Croaker. I hope it has been a reminder to us that it always pays to do what God says.

CROAKER: I know when God says, "Froggie, jump," I say, "How high?" Or I might have Frogs in the butter—

INTERVIEWER: Croaker!

CROAKER: Burrup! Back to the pond, boys and girls.

*Hebrews 12:11

BIBLE SERPENTS

Scripture References: Genesis 3; Numbers 21:4-9; John 3:14-17

Lesson Theme: Use this dialogue to present the gospel. Because the interviewer's speeches are long, be sure to keep them lively and full of expression. At the conclusion, hold up some drawings or pictures and give the following thoughts:

1. A serpent, crawling on the ground. (Sin brings punishment to the sinner.)

2. The serpent on the pole and a picture of Jesus on the Cross. (God has provided us a remedy for sin. Just as the serpent of brass had done no harm, so Jesus never sinned. Yet He was lifted up on a cross and made to be sin for us.)

3. A child praying. (Look to Jesus for salvation.)

Puppet Used: S-s-s-sissel S-s-s-serpent. See Part 2, chapter 10, for instructions to make this special mouth puppet. The serpent hisses in his speeches, especially when using the "s." Use the first few speeches of this dialogue as a pattern for how to do this throughout.

Developing Dialogues for S-s-s-sissel: Other Scriptures from which you could develop dialogues for the serpent puppet would be
Genesis 3—Adam and Eve in the garden
Exodus 4—Moses' rod turned into a serpent
Acts 28:1-6—Paul bitten by a viper (in this connection, see Mark 16:18)
Proverbs 23:32—the results of drinking alcohol

INTERVIEWER: How many of you like snakes? . . . Well, I guess it's not unanimous. Some of you like them, and many do not—especially among the girls. I hope you will like my snake. His name is S-s-s-sissel S-s-s-serpent.

SISSEL: S-s-s-some of you don't like s-s-s-snakes? Oh, I know a few s-s-s-snakes are very dangerous-s-s-s. But most aren't, and I'm certainly not. I'm your friend. Pleas-s-s-se like me. It's a pretty hard life, being a s-s-s-snake and crawling on the ground.

INTERVIEWER: Do you know why snakes crawl on their bellies?

SISSEL: No.

INTERVIEWER: There is a story in the Bible about it. Long ago, in the Garden of Eden, there lived the first two people in the world—Adam and Eve. All the animals lived there, too.

SISSEL: Including snakes?

INTERVIEWER: Yes. Snakes—another word for "snake" is "serpent"—were there. How they got around before this, we don't know. Maybe they lived in trees all the time.

SISSEL: What happened to change that?

INTERVIEWER: Sin entered the beautiful garden. You see, God wanted people to obey Him in all things. He told them, "You may eat fruit from every tree in the garden but one. Don't eat the fruit from the tree of knowledge of good and evil."

SISSEL: That seems reasonable.

INTERVIEWER: Yes. But Satan himself came into the garden. He hates God and His creation, so he decided to trick Adam and Eve into disobeying God. Using the disguise of a snake, he tempted Eve.

SISSEL: Oh no! The SHAME of it!

INTERVIEWER: Yes. It's quite likely that Eve was used to seeing the snake, so she listened when he questioned God by asking her, "Did God really say that you must not eat fruit from any tree in the garden?"

SISSEL: GOD didn't say that, did He?

INTERVIEWER: No, He didn't, and Eve told him so.

SISSEL: So the snake left—right? The end, and they lived happily ever after!

INTERVIEWER: I'm afraid not, Sissel.

SISSEL (hangs his head): I was afraid of that.

INTERVIEWER: Eve said, "We must not eat fruit from the tree that is in the middle of the garden, or we will die."

SISSEL: What did the serpent say?

INTERVIEWER: He said, "You won't die. God knows that if you eat that fruit, you'll be like gods, knowing good and evil."

SISSEL: Why, that LOWDOWN snake-in-the-grass! He was TRICKY, wasn't he? But Eve saw right through him, and shook her finger in his face, and said...

INTERVIEWER (shaking his head): She fell for it. Both of them, Adam and Eve, fell for it. They ATE the fruit God told them NOT to. (Sissel moans and again hangs his head.)

INTERVIEWER: Sorry, Sissel.

SISSEL: So then what happened?

INTERVIEWER: This disobedience brought trouble and pain and sickness and death into the world. But God promised He would punish Satan for what he had done.

SISSEL: Good! Uh, but what happened to the snake?

INTERVIEWER: DOWN to the ground.

SISSEL: You mean like, "EAT MY DUST" time?

INTERVIEWER: Like, forever after.

SISSEL: Oh, to have such a skeleton in my closet! I'm so ashamed that an ancestor of mine was used by the devil like that.

INTERVIEWER: Well, suppose I tell you a story of how GOD used snakes for good?

SISSEL: Oh, yeah, that's more like it!

INTERVIEWER: It happened when the Israelites were traveling through the wilderness. God had given them manna to eat and water from a rock to drink. But they spoke against God and Moses, and said, "We hate this terrible food!"

SISSEL: They didn't like the food GOD gave them?

BIBLE SERPENTS *(continued)*

INTERVIEWER: No. They were tired of it. They wanted some other kind of food and they talked like they couldn't trust God to provide any more water for them. That was bad, very bad—to complain like that when God had freed them from slavery and then taken care of them as He led them back to their own country.

SISSEL: **So God said okay, I'll give you back to Pharaoh and you can be his slaves again and make bricks—**

INTERVIEWER: Not quite. He really didn't want to give up on the people. But He had to correct and discipline them. Otherwise, they would never learn their lesson of believing and obeying Him. He sent poisonous snakes among them, and they bit the people, and many died.

SISSEL: **Oh, God used snakes to straighten them out. So did they learn their lesson?**

INTERVIEWER: Yes. They said to Moses, "We have sinned by speaking against God. Pray to Him to take away these serpents." God told Moses to make a serpent of brass and put it on a pole. Anyone who had been bitten could look at the snake and he would be healed.

SISSEL: **Wow . . . you think if sick people looked at ME,** *(striking a pose)* **they would get well?**

INTERVIEWER: No.

SISSEL: **Why not?**

INTERVIEWER: Because that was then, and this is now.

SISSEL *(doing a double take)*: **Huh?**

INTERVIEWER *(laughing)*: That was a special, one-time situation that served as a kind of example about Jesus.

SISSEL: **Really?**

Interviewer: Really. Jesus told Nicodemas, "Moses lifted up the snake in the desert. It is the same with the Son of Man. The Son of Man must be lifted up too. Then everyone who believes in him can have eternal life."

SISSEL: **So people look to JESUS now?**

INTERVIEWER: That's right. Just as that brass snake was lifted up on a pole, so Jesus was lifted up on a cross. And whoever believes on Him will have everlasting life. So you see, S-s-s-sissel S-s-s-serpent, snakes played a part in the time when sin first came into the world. But they also were used by God to show us that sin brings punishment and that Jesus died to take away that punishment if we'll believe in Him.

SISSEL: **If I could, I would let God—not Satan—use me. Do you suppose the boys and girls will do that?**

INTERVIEWER: We hope all of them will. And we also hope that children who have not asked Jesus into their lives will look to Him who died on the Cross and trust Him as Savior today.

SISSEL: **Well, kids, I learned something from Bible serpents. Did you? . . . So long.**

A POOR, LOWLY WORM

Scripture References: 1 Corinthians 1:26-31; Ephesians 2:10; 1 Peter 5:5-6; Revelation 4:11

Lesson Theme: No matter who we are, God has a plan for us. We can obey Christ and be useful and content, or we can let the devil discourage us and sin ruin us.

Puppet Used: Wiggly Worm. See Part 2, chapter 10, for instructions for making this special mouth puppet. Hide your arm by resting him on the stage ledge or a tabletop. Or set him on the edge of a box in which your arm has been inserted.

Preparation: As the various worms are mentioned in this dialogue, hold up pictures or printed names of them: silkworm, earthworm, measuring worm, flatworm.

WIGGLY: Oh, WOE is me; oh, WOE is me! A lowly worm am I; nobody ever cares for me; I think I want to die. *(Hangs his head way down.)*

INTERVIEWER: Why, Wiggly Worm, why are you so sad? Please don't talk of dying.

WIGGLY: NOBODY loves a WORM. We CRAWL on the ground, and we WIGGLE and SQUIGGLE and SQUIRM. We're OOEY and GOOEY and SQUISHY and SLIMY. Boys like to throw us on girls, and then the girls scream. Worms are NO GOOD.

INTERVIEWER: Oh, Wiggly, you mustn't say that. GOD made worms and has a purpose for EACH ONE.

WIGGLY *(raising his head in surprise)***: GOD has a PURPOSE for worms?**

INTERVIEWER: Yes, indeed. He has a purpose for all His creation. We people can learn many things from you worms.

WIGGLY: Uh, right!

INTERVIEWER: Take the silkworm, for example.

WIGGLY: Great! My distant, uptown Chinese cousin. I'm not even sure HE would claim me.

INTERVIEWER: Now I know they eventually get wings and you don't, but you've got to admit, they are at least wormlike. Go along with me on this, okay?

WIGGLY: Okay . . . but it makes me squirm.

INTERVIEWER: The usefulness of silkworms in making silk cloth was first discovered in China long ago. But today these worms can be found in many parts of the world, weaving their wonderful cocoons of silk thread.

WIGGLY: DOODAH!

INTERVIEWER: Now, Wiggly.

WIGGLY: Okay, okay.

INTERVIEWER: One silkworm can spin a cocoon that contains from five hundred to thirteen hundred yards of fiber. Silk is one of the finest and most expensive materials in the world.

WIGGLY: So a SILKWORM is pretty valuable.

INTERVIEWER: Aw, Wiggly, I didn't mean to make you feel worse. I meant to make you feel better.

WIGGLY: Yeah, well, you picked the wrong example. Besides, what can anybody learn from a silkworm?

INTERVIEWER: The silkworm spends its life making something beautiful for others. Christians shouldn't seek a life of just pleasing THEMSELVES; they should find what God wants them to do for OTHERS.

WIGGLY: Well, that is a pretty good lesson, but, like I said, the silkworm's a distant cousin, VERY distant.

INTERVIEWER: Oh, there are other worms that are valuable. For instance, do you know about the earthworm?

WIGGLY: Boy, you go from one extreme to the other! YUK! What good is HE?

INTERVIEWER: The way he digs around in the ground. He's the gardener's friend. He leaves air holes in the soil, making it more porous and able to hold air and moisture. He makes topsoil more fertile.

WIGGLY: So?

INTERVIEWER: So even though the earthworm's home is in the dirt, with very little light and air, he goes about doing the job he's been given to do, and he is a blessing. No matter where Christians live, no matter what opportunites they have, they can live their lives to please God and help others.

WIGGLY: Hmm, well maybe you have a point about worms being useful.

INTERVIEWER: And what about how the earthworm gives himself for our pleasure in fishing?

WIGGLY: YIKES! *(He ducks out of sight.)*

INTERVIEWER: Now, Wiggly, come on back. We're not going to do anything like that to YOU.

WIGGLY *(pokes his head up cautiously)***: Promise?**

INTERVIEWER: Promise. . . . But you know, Christians are supposed to give of themselves.

WIGGLY: They are?

INTERVIEWER: Yes. In fact, Jesus said we are to be fishers of men. So just as fishworms lure fish to be caught for food, Christians should attract sinners to Christ.

WIGGLY: I didn't know that.

INTERVIEWER: And how about this—I saw a measuring worm the other day, and he gave me another lesson for Christians. You know, he crawls along by looping his body: He brings his hind feet up to his forefeet and then stretches his forefeet out again, just as if he were measuring the ground.

WIGGLY: Yeah. I got a LOOPY friend like that. His name is Stretch.

INTERVIEWER: Well, Christians should measure their steps, that is, be careful about the kind of lives they live. In Proverbs we are told, "Watch your step. Stick to the path and be safe."*

WIGGLY: So you should measure your steps, like Stretch?

INTERVIEWER: Yes. And the Bible helps us do that. Psalm 119:133 says, "Guide my steps as you promised."†

*Proverbs 4:26, *The Living Bible.*
†*International Children's Bible.*

A POOR, LOWLY WORM *(continued)*

WIGGLY: **I never knew worms were so valuable.** *(Holds his head up high.)* **I'm proud to be a worm now. We ARE helpful.**

INTERVIEWER: Not all worms are helpful. Some are very HARMFUL. They weren't like that in the beginning when they were first made by God, but sin changed many good things to bad in this world. Sin does the same with people. We can let sin RUIN us, or we can let Christ make something WONDERFUL out of us.

WIGGLY: **Well, I'M just a worm puppet, but I'll try to be the BEST worm puppet in the WHOLE world. And kids, YOU try to be just what Jesus wants YOU to be. Then your life will be beautiful—no matter WHO you are.**

INTERVIEWER: And if you get discouraged along the way when things go wrong or someone tries to keep you from doing right, remember the flatworm.

WIGGLY: **Why?**

INTERVIEWER: Even though it may get cut in two, each part will grow into a new worm. It doesn't let ANYTHING discourage it.

WIGGLY: **I get the idea. The flatworm doesn't give up when things go wrong. It keeps going . . . and going . . . and going. I'm not going to be upset anymore about being a worm. I'll keep on doing the best I can—no matter WHAT! Kids, how about you?**

BETCHACAN BE KIND

Scripture References: Matthew 6:14-15; 10:21-22; Ephesians 4:32; Philippians 4:13; 1 Peter 2:21-24

Lesson Theme: Be kind and forgiving, for Christ has set us an example of true forgiveness.

Puppets Used: Betchacan Bee and a boy person puppet. See Part 2, chapter 10, for instructions for making the special mouth bee puppet.

You can place a sign that says "Be Kind" on a stick and fasten it to the bee's hand.

You can develop other dialogues with Betchacan Bee from some of these Bible "be's."

Be:
steadfast, unmovable—1 Corinthians 15:58
imitators of God—Ephesians 5:1
an example in speech, in life, in love, in faith, and in purity—1 Timothy 4:12
strong in grace—2 Timothy 2:1
ready to do whatever is good—Titus 3:1
peaceable and considerate—Titus 3:2
careful to devote themselves to doing what is good— Titus 3:8
doers of the Word of God—James 1:22
patient until the Lord's coming—James 5:7
holy because God is holy—1 Peter 1:16
sympathetic—1 Peter 3:8
compassionate and humble—1 Peter 3:8
self-controlled and alert—1 Peter 5:8
faithful, even to the point of death—Revelation 2:10

Be not:
afraid—Mark 5:36
yoked together with unbelievers—2 Corinthians 6:14
deceived—Galatians 6:7
foolish, but understand what the Lord's will is— Ephesians 5:17
anxious (worried) about anything—Philippians 4:6
tired of doing what is right—2 Thessalonians 3:13
arrogant—1 Timothy 6:17

INTERVIEWER (to audience): Has someone ever done a bad thing to you? How did you feel? Did you want to get even? Our puppet is going to play the part of a real boy who is a Christian, Jimmy by name. Here he is.

JIMMY: I am SO mad I could chew nails. I am MAD, MAD, MAD!

INTERVIEWER: Why, Jimmy, I'm surprised at you. What's wrong?

JIMMY: My mean old sister, Judy—SHE'S what's wrong. I am SO MAD at her.

INTERVIEWER: What did she do?

JIMMY: She broke the model plane I was building. I TOLD her not to touch it. But she THREW it to see if it would fly. Oh, I'll get even with her, if it's the LAST thing I do.

INTERVIEWER: What are you going to do?

JIMMY: Burn up all her dolls. That will teach her a lesson.

INTERVIEWER: I think you'd better learn a lesson. And I know just the guy to teach you—Betchacan Bee.

JIMMY: WHO?

INTERVIEWER: Betchacan Bee. Come out, Betchacan. *(Bee appears.)*

BEE: Bzzz, bzzz. Hello, Jimmy.

JIMMY: YIKES! Get out of here! I don't want to get stung.

BEE: I won't hurt you. I'm a Bible bee.

JIMMY: A Bible bee?

BEE: Yes. There are many "be's" in the Bible. And there's one you need today. "Be kind and loving to each other. Forgive each other just as God forgave you in Christ."*

JIMMY: You mean I have to be kind and forgiving to my mean old sister? NO WAY—not if she asked me a million trillion times to forgive her.

BEE: Jesus said, "If you don't forgive the wrongs of others, then your Father in heaven will not forgive the wrong things you do."†

JIMMY: Oh, I WANT God to forgive me when I do wrong. Do I really HAVE to forgive others, or HE won't forgive me?

BEE: Yes. Remember, you're to forgive "as God forgave you in Christ." God's love for you was so great that Jesus came to earth and took the punishment for all your sins. Surely you can forgive one little wrong done to you.

JIMMY: Yes, I guess I should. But I get SO MAD when I think about my plane. It's HARD to forgive. I-I just can't do it.

BEE: Betchacan. You see, a Christian has help in doing hard things—GOD'S help. The Bible says, "I can do all things through Christ, because he gives me strength."‡

JIMMY: Oh, JESUS will give me strength? I didn't think of that. Thanks, Betchacan Bee. I'll pray, and then with Jesus' help, I'll be kind and forgiving to Judy.

BEE *(sings the following verse to the tune of "London Bridge Is Falling Down")*: Betchacan be what God wants, What God wants, what God wants; / Betchacan be what God wants, For He will help you. Bzzz, bzzz! Good-bye, Jimmy. *(He exits.)*

JIMMY: Now to find Judy. Jesus loved me enough to die for my sins. I can sure love and forgive my sister. Betcha I can—with God's help.

*Ephesians 4:32, *International Children's Bible*

†Matthew 6:15, *International Children's Bible*

‡Philippians 4:13, *International Children's Bible*

THE GREAT ADVENTURE

Scripture References: Proverbs 1:8; 15:20; Ephesians 6:1-3; Colossians 3:20

Lesson Theme: Obedience to parents

Puppet Used: Buffy Bunny or any rabbit puppet. See Part 2, chapter 10, for instructions for making this special mouth puppet.

INTERVIEWER: I brought a special friend with me today. Her name is Buffy Bunny.

BUNNY: Hi!

INTERVIEWER: Where do you live, Buffy?

BUNNY: In Green Forest, down Pine Tree Trail in Little Bunny Burrow.

INTERVIEWER: Do you live there all by yourself?

BUNNY: No. I live with my daddy. He's Daddy Bunny. And I live with my mommy. She's Mommy Bunny. And I have a sister, Fluffy, and a brother, Tuffy.

INTERVIEWER: Buffy, Fluffy, and Tuffy—what a nice family! Do you ever have any adventures in Green Forest?

BUNNY: Is that something to eat? If it is, I don't have any. I've just got carrots.

INTERVIEWER: No. An adventure is an exciting happening.

BUNNY: Then I did have one just the other day.

INTERVIEWER: Tell us what happened.

BUNNY: I was playing with my best friend, Sally Squirrel. We were cutting out carrot curls, but we got tired of doing that and we just couldn't think of anything to do.

INTERVIEWER: That doesn't sound like an adventure.

BUNNY: That was before the adventure. We decided to go swimming.

INTERVIEWER: Do you have a nice place to swim in Green Forest?

BUNNY: We have Round Lake. But Daddy always says, "Don't swim in Round Lake."

INTERVIEWER: Why not?

BUNNY: Daddy says Alvin the Alligator lives there. But I said to Sally, "I don't think there's any 'gator in the lake."

INTERVIEWER: Buffy! Shame on you for not believing your father!

BUNNY: Well, see—I wanted to go swimming so much. And Sally said, "Even if the 'gator is in the lake, I'm not scared. I can swim faster than any old 'gator."

INTERVIEWER: Did you really go to Round Lake?

BUNNY: Yep. We started out, hippity-hoppity, hippity-hoppity. At last we got to Round Lake, and WHOOSH, we jumped in.

INTERVIEWER: I'm sorry to hear you disobeyed your father.

BUNNY: We were having lots of fun. Splishy-splashy, splishy-splashy! Fun, fun, fun! Then we saw him!

INTERVIEWER: Who? Alvin the Alligator?

BUNNY: Yep. He was swimming right toward us, and I saw his long, white teeth. I sure did believe a 'gator was in Round Lake then!

INTERVIEWER: What did you do?

BUNNY: Sally swam fast, fast to the shore and jumped on the bank. Then she ranned away.

INTERVIEWER: What did you do?

BUNNY: I was so scared I couldn't move. And that old 'gator kept coming closer . . . and closer . . . and closer. I turned around and tried to swim away; but I heard him getting closer . . . and closer . . . and then CHOMP he got hold of me.

INTERVIEWER: Where?

BUNNY: He just missed my tail, but he caught my dress in his teeth. I tried to pull loose, but I couldn't. I pulled . . . and pulled . . . and pulled. Then I started yelling, "Help, help!" And I heard somebody coming.

INTERVIEWER: Who was it?

BUNNY: Sally Squirrel. When I didn't follow her, she came back. And you know what she did? She jumped right in and grabbed my paw.

INTERVIEWER: That was very brave, especially when she was already safe. Did you escape?

BUNNY: Well, she PULLED . . . and PULLED . . . and PULLED 'til she got me loose.

INTERVIEWER: So you got away?

BUNNY: All but the back side of my new dress. I left it in the 'gator's mouth. We swam fast to the shore and jumped on the bank. Then we ranned away.

INTERVIEWER: Buffy, I hope you learned your lesson. You got into a lot of trouble for disobeying your father.

BUNNY: I sure did. I got scared to death, my pretty new dress got tored, and when I got home Daddy gave me something.

INTERVIEWER: What was that?

BUNNY: You can guess. He gave it to me right back where the dress was missing. From now on I'm gonna do what my daddy tells me.

INTERVIEWER: That's good. You see, he loves you, and he does his best to take care of you. He didn't tell you to stay out of Round Lake to keep you from having a good time, but to protect you. If you'd listened to him—

BUNNY: I know. I would've stayed out of trouble.

INTERVIEWER: Yes. That's one reason God tells boys and girls to obey their parents.

BUNNY: Hey, kids, you do what your daddy and mommy say. Okay? I wish I had.

BUFFY IS RESCUED

Scripture References: John 8:36; Romans 5:6-9; 6:23

Lesson Theme: Jesus died to set us free from sin and death.

Puppet Used: Buffy Bunny or another rabbit puppet. See Part 2, chapter 10, for instructions for making this special mouth puppet.

Preparation: Bandage one of Buffy's feet before bringing her out. If she is used in a stage, either have her sit on the ledge for the interview, or bandage her "hand" instead and change the wording slightly.

INTERVIEWER: Here she is again—Buffy Bunny.

Bunny: Hi!

INTERVIEWER: Why, your foot is bandaged up, Buffy! What happened to you?

BUNNY: I got hurted real bad.

INTERVIEWER: How did that happen?

BUNNY: It's a long story.

INTERVIEWER: Oh, I'm sure we'd all like to hear it.

BUNNY: Well, you know I live in Green Forest.

INTERVIEWER: Yes.

BUNNY: Some bad men came into Green Forest and set traps to catch us animals.

INTERVIEWER: Traps? Oh, that's terrible. I think that's against the law.

BUNNY: I guess they didn't care. Traps were hidden all around, and some animals were getting caught.

INTERVIEWER: I guess you had to be very careful.

BUNNY: Uh-huh. Daddy told me never to go off the path, or I might get caught.

INTERVIEWER: I suppose the traps were hidden in the bushes.

BUNNY: Well, one day Sally Squirrel and I went down the path—hippity-hoppity, hippity-hoppity—and throwing a pine cone to each other.

INTERVIEWER: That sounds like fun.

BUNNY: I missed a catch and the cone went into the bushes.

INTERVIEWER: You didn't go in after it, did you?

BUNNY: I forgot, and I ranned into the bush.

INTERVIEWER: Oh, Buffy!

BUNNY: Sally hollered, "STOP! There might he a trap in there!" So I stopped still.

INTERVIEWER: Could you see if there was a trap?

BUNNY: It was too dark in there. So I started tiptoeing out very carefully—tip, tip, tip, tip . . . Then SNAP! I was CAUGHT!

INTERVIEWER: Oh, a trap did catch you?

BUNNY: Yes. And it hurted something awful in my foot.

INTERVIEWER: What did you do?

BUNNY: Sally tried to pull me out. She PULLED . . . and PULLED and PULLED . . . But nothing happened. Then she ranned to tell Daddy.

INTERVIEWER: I guess you were afraid that the hunters would come and get you.

BUNNY: Yes, ma'am. I was so afraid I just shook all over. I just knew I was going to die. And—oh!—I hurt so bad!

INTERVIEWER: We're all so sorry, Buffy. Did your daddy come soon?

BUNNY: No. I waited . . . and waited . . . and waited. And I waited . . . and waited some more. Then I heard someone coming.

INTERVIEWER: Your daddy?

BUNNY: No. It was BIG FEET—TROMP! TROMP! TROMP!

INTERVIEWER: Uh-oh! A hunter?

BUNNY: I thought so. I was so scared! And then I saw a face poked in the bushes.

INTERVIEWER: A HUNTER!

BUNNY: It was a boy. He said, "Oh, poor little bunny! I've been finding the traps and springing them. I'll get you loose."

INTERVIEWER: What a fine thing to do! Did he set you free?

BUNNY: He had a hard time, but at last he did. He was scared the hunters would see him and beat him up.

INTERVIEWER: What a brave boy!

BUNNY: He bandaged my foot and carried me home.

INTERVIEWER: And now you'll be all right.

BUNNY: Soon I will. I sure love that boy who rescued me!

POOR LITTLE KITTY

Scripture References: Matthew 7:9-11; John 1:21-24; Galatians 3:26; 1 John 3:1

Lesson Theme: Becoming God's children and receiving the spiritual gifts He has for us.

Puppet Used: Catastrophe Cat or any other small animal puppet. See Part 2, chapter 10, for instructions for making this special mouth puppet.

INTERVIEWER: Look, everyone! See what I found on my doorstep—a sweet little kitty cat.

CAT *(trembling)*: **You're not gonna beat me, are you?**

Interviewer: Of course not. Who are you? Do you have a name?

CAT: **Yes, ma'am. I call myself Catastrophe, because bad stuff always happens to me.**

Interviewer: Why were you on my doorstep? You should be home.

CAT: **I don't have a home.**

Interviewer: You don't? Where did you come from?

CAT: **Somewhere a long ways off. I don't 'xactly know where, cause I'm lost.**

INTERVIEWER: How did you get here?

CAT: **A bad man stole me from my mommy and poppy and he beat me, and he yelled at me, and he cussed me. So I ranned away.**

INTERVIEWER *(hugging him)*: Oh, you poor little thing!

CAT: **Nobody loves me. I tried to get some other folks to take me after I ranned away, but nobody would have me. They said I was ugly.**

INTERVIEWER: You're not very pretty, but I love you, anyhow, Catastrophe.

CAT *(surprised)*: **You do?**

INTERVIEWER: Oh, yes. Do you want to live with me?

CAT: **Oh, yes! Uh-huh! Sure 'nuff! Yes, I do. Yes, ma'am!**

INTERVIEWER: All right. Then I'll adopt you as my very own little kitty cat.

CAT: **Oh, goody, goody!** *(Pauses and then pleads.)* **I'm hungry. Can your little 'dopted kitty have something to eat? All that bad man would gimme me was some dry old bones.**

INTERVIEWER: Yes, I'll give you some nice food right away. How did you happen to get stolen, Catastrophe?

CAT: **Well, that bad man, he told me he'd gimme lots of food and toys and yummy candy. So I snuck away with him, and I didn't tell my mommy and poppy. Then when we were far away, he grabbed me tight and wouldn't let go.**

INTERVIEWER: No one should ever go off like that with someone they don't know. Bad things can happen.

CAT: **They sure can! He didn't gimme nothin' but bones. And he kicked me. He said he was gonna sell me to a lab—whatever that is.**

INTERVIEWER: How did you get away from him?

CAT: **He went to sleep, but I didn't. So I snuck out of the house and ranned away. But I got all losted, and I didn't know how to get home.**

INTERVIEWER: You're safe now, Catastrophe. I'll feed you and take good care of you.

CAT: **Could you gimme some eggs?**

INTERVIEWER: Sure. How many eggs can you eat on an empty stomach?

CAT: **One.**

INTERVIEWER: Only one?

CAT: **Yes ma'am. After the first one my stomach's not empty any more—I wanna whole bunch of eggs and some steak and some biscuits and—**

INTERVIEWER: Wait. I think that's enough.

CAT: **But I'm on a see-food diet.**

INTERVIEWER: I'm not sure I have any seafood.

CAT: **Oh, just show me what you have. When I SEE FOOD, I eat it. How about milk? Can I have a bowl of milk?**

INTERVIEWER: MAY I have a bowl of milk.

CAT: **I asked you first.**

INTERVIEWER: I was correcting your English.

CAT: **I'm not English. I'm a good old American cat.**

INTERVIEWER: You know, Catastrophe, you remind me of some Bible teachings. First, you were tempted by the bad man to run away with him. Then he held you tight and wouldn't let you go.

CAT: **Uh-huh. And he didn't keep his promise, either.**

INTERVIEWER: In the same way, Satan has tempted people, like these boys and girls here; and we've all listened to him, and we've sinned.

CAT: **Does he give you good things—or bad?**

INTERVIEWER: At first it might seem like good, but really he only gets us into trouble.

CAT: **Will anyone 'dopt you, like you did me?**

INTERVIEWER: Yes. God will, if we'll let Him. We must believe in Jesus, who died for our sins and rose from the dead. We tell Him we're sorry and ask for His forgiveness. Then we ask Him to be a part of our lives. God will take us in and make us His very own children.

CAT: **Does God give you lotsa good food?**

INTERVIEWER: He gives us spiritual food—His Word—that feeds our souls.

CAT: **I sure love you for 'dopting me.**

INTERVIEWER: And we love God so much for making us His children. We should show our love by getting all the spiritual food we can. His gifts come to us as we pray for them and as we read His Word and obey it.

CAT: **Well, if you'll just lead me to some food, I'll show you how much I love it. I'll gobble up anything you'll give me. I sure am ready for my SEE-FOOD diet! YUM! YUM!**

SUGAR BEAR'S WEAKNESS

Scripture References: Romans 13:14; Ephesians 4:27; 6:10-18; James 1:14-15; 4:7

Lesson Theme: Avoid the places and ways where you could easily fall into temptation. Resist temptation and do right.

Puppet Used: Sugar Bear or any bear puppet. See Part 2, chapter 10, for instructions for making this special mouth puppet.

INTERVIEWER (*speaking to the audience*): I have a special friend for you to meet at this time. (*Looks at the Bear.*) Will you introduce yourself?

BEAR: Hi, folks! My name is Sugar Bear.

INTERVIEWER: Sugar Bear, who gave you your name?

BEAR: I did.

INTERVIEWER: Why?

BEAR: 'Cause I LOVE sugar. It's YUMMY, YUMMY in the TUMMY! I love all kinds of sweets—sugar and candy and honey and cake and cookies and 'lasses.

INTERVIEWER: Don't you mean MOlasses?

BEAR: Sure I like mo' 'lasses—the mo' 'lasses the better! Good old sweet stuff—it's yummikins for the tummikins.

INTERVIEWER: Don't all those sweets ever make you sick?

BEAR: I sure had a tummyache the other day.

INTERVIEWER: I'll bet you ate too much sweets.

BEAR: Oh, no. I never have too much sweets.

INTERVIEWER: What did you eat?

BEAR: Ice cream.

INTERVIEWER: Ice cream shouldn't hurt you. How much did you eat?

BEAR: Eight gallons.

INTERVIEWER (*horrified*): Eight gallons! You better not eat so much ice cream again.

BEAR: Maybe it wasn't the ice cream. Maybe it was those six candy bars I et after the ice cream.

INTERVIEWER: Oh, my! Six candy bars, too! But you shouldn't say "et." You should say "ate."

BEAR: Maybe it WAS eight candy bars I et.

INTERVIEWER: No. I ATE six candy bars.

BEAR: Oh, YOU et six candy bars, too? No wonder you're so fat.

INTERVIEWER: I'm not fat.

BEAR: Oh, YEAH? (*Looks at the audience.*) He/she stepped on some scales the other day, and this little card came out that said, "One at a time, please—one at a time.

INTERVIEWER: Sugar Bear, doesn't your conscience bother you when you say things like that?

BEAR: My what?

INTERVIEWER: Your conscience.

BEAR: I didn't know I had one. What is it?

INTERVIEWER: Your conscience is a little voice inside you that says, "Don't do that." Have you ever heard that little voice?

BEAR: Sure.

INTERVIEWER: When?

BEAR: When I was at the candy store the other day. I was so hungry, but I didn't have any money. And I saw some yummy chocolate bars.

INTERVIEWER: Oh, I hope you didn't steal one.

BEAR: I started to, but this little voice inside said, "Don't take that chocolate bar."

INTERVIEWER: So you didn't take it?

BEAR (*loudly*): No, I didn't take the CHOCOLATE BAR.

INTERVIEWER (*relieved*): Oh, I'm so glad! I'm proud of you for listening to your conscience.

BEAR: Yeah. It said not to take the chocolate bar, so I didn't. I took two SUCKERS instead.

INTERVIEWER: Oh, I'm so sorry to hear that you yielded to temptation like that. You must learn to say no. By the way, I've been meaning to ask you about that pudding I asked you to take to Mrs. Jones the other day.

BEAR: Oh, I took it right over to her.

INTERVIEWER: But I gave you a whole bowl of it to take to her. She said the bowl was half empty when you gave it to her.

BEAR: It wasn't half EMPTY. It was half FULL.

INTERVIEWER: But it was ALL full when I gave it to you. What happened to half of the pudding?

BEAR: Uh . . . it evaporated?

INTERVIEWER: No. Someone ate it. Was it you?

BEAR: Well, I did eat just a little.

INTERVIEWER: Oh, Sugar Bear, why did you do that?

BEAR: Well, I was very hungry, and it looked so good, and I just love sweets, and—well—I was tempted, and I can resist anything but temptation, so I took it.

INTERVIEWER: But how did you manage to eat the pudding out of the bowl? You couldn't eat it with your paws.

BEAR: I thought I might be tempted, so I took along a spoon.

INTERVIEWER: Never, never give yourself a chance to be tempted like that again. Taking the spoon made it almost a sure thing you'd yield to temptation. You must learn to say no when you're tempted.

BEAR: It's hard for me to refuse food—especially sweets.

INTERVIEWER: That's your weakness. We should all realize where our weaknesses are—the ways in which it's easiest for us to give in to something wrong. Then we should stay away from such things.

BEAR: Oh, no! You mean I have to stay away from food?

INTERVIEWER: Not always—just at times you're not supposed to eat.

BEAR: Yeah. And don't carry along a spoon when I take pudding to Mrs. Jones. Hey, all this talk about food has made me very HUNGRY. Can your little dummikins have some yummikins for his tummikins?

YOU CAN'T HIDE FROM GOD

Scripture References: Proverbs 15:3; Jonah 1 to 3; Mark 4:22; Hebrews 4:12-13

Lesson Theme: We should obey God, for He always sees us.

Puppets Used: Jonah and the Big Fish. See Part 2, chapter 10, for instructions for making this special mouth puppet.

Preparation: As you begin this dialogue, put Jonah on your right hand and insert him inside the fish as far as the back of its mouth. Keep Jonah's face flat against the tongue so it won't be seen. Place your left index finger in the loop under the fish's mouth.

BIG FISH: Oh, I am very wonderful, / As special as can be; / You know why I am different? / 'Cause God created me.

INTERVIEWER: Why, Big Fish, God made all fish. What makes you think you're special?

BIG FISH: I'm one of a kind. God made me to do a special job, so He gave me a very big tummy. Want to hear my story?

INTERVIEWER: Oh, yes!

BIG FISH: It began on a beautiful day in the Great Sea. As I swam along, a ship sailed nearby.

INTERVIEWER: Is this a Bible story?

BIG FISH: Yes.

INTERVIEWER: Then it's a true story.

BIG FISH: Of course. Suddenly there was a great storm. WINDS! THUNDER! LIGHTNING! RAIN! It was AWFUL.

INTERVIEWER: A storm at sea can be very dangerous.

BIG FISH: Yes. I started to dive into deep water. Then I saw a man sinking in the sea nearby.

INTERVIEWER: What did you do?

BIG FISH: I ATE him.

INTERVIEWER: You ATE him!

BIG FISH: Well, more like I swallowed him whole.

INTERVIEWER: Why, I know who it was you swallowed—Jonah.

BIG FISH: I didn't ask him his name. Whoever he is, he's giving me a whale of a tummyache.

INTERVIEWER (surprised): He's still in your stomach?

BIG FISH: Yes. Hoo, hoo! Hold still, Jonah. You're tickling my innards!

INTERVIEWER: How long has he been inside you?

BIG FISH: Three days and three nights. I think God wants me to get rid of him now.

INTERVIEWER: This is a good place. You're by the land.

BIG FISH: Okay. Here goes—u-u-u-lp! *(Remove the finger of your left hand from the loop under the fish's mouth. Place*

your fingers at the opening in the stomach and pull the stomach toward you. At the same time push Jonah forward through the fish's mouth as far as his waist.)

JONAH: Oh, my! There's something fishy going on here!

INTERVIEWER: That's right, Jonah. You've been in that fish's stomach for three days and three nights.

JONAH: Which way is Ninevah? I must go there at once.

INTERVIEWER: Have you learned your lesson, Jonah?

JONAH: Oh, yes. Disobeying God got me into a WHALE of a lot of trouble. I want to obey Him now.

INTERVIEWER: Tell us what happened to you.

JONAH: God told me to preach to the wicked city of Ninevah, but I didn't want to go.

INTERVIEWER: Where did you go?

JONAH: The other direction. I got on a boat and began sailing far away from Ninevah.

INTERVIEWER: You weren't afraid of disobeying God?

JONAH: No. I thought maybe I could leave God back in Judah. I went to sleep in the boat.

INTERVIEWER: But God was right there. And He sent a storm—a very bad storm, didn't He?

JONAH: It was awful. The sailors were very scared of the storm. They woke me and said, "Call on your God to deliver us."

INTERVIEWER: What did you say?

JONAH: I told them God was punishing us all for my sin. I said, "Throw me in the sea, or you'll drown."

INTERVIEWER: That was pretty brave. So they tossed you overboard?

JONAH: Yes. I started sinking down, down, DOWN! Then this fish swallowed me.

INTERVIEWER: So he told us.

JONAH: I slid down his great, big tongue and kept sliding down his huge throat and KERPLUNK! I landed in his stomach. Talk about SCARED! I shook so much the fish got the hiccups.

INTERVIEWER: What did you do then?

JONAH: I prayed to God, "O, Lord, save me! I'll go and preach in Ninevah." *(He pauses.)* So here I am.

INTERVIEWER: Headed for Ninevah.

JONAH: Yes. Right away. I've learned my lesson. *(Faces audience and chants following.)* You cannot hide From God;/ He sees you ev'rywhere;/ Your ev'ry thought and word and deed are known to Him up there./ Don't try to run and hide,/ or cover up your sin;/ But turn around and face the Lord/ and let His will begin.

YOU'LL GET HOOKED, FILBERT

Scripture References: Psalm 119:13; Proverbs 20:1; 23:29-32; 1 Corinthians 6:12,19-20

Lesson Theme: The addictiveness of tobacco, alcohol, and illegal drugs.

Puppets Used: Croaker Frog and Filbert Fish. See Part 2, chapter 10, for instructions for making these special mouth puppets.

Preparation: This dialogue must be done in a stage. The interviewer stands outside the stage. Use a backdrop of sky and water—see the backdrop drawing in Part 2, chapter 7. For Croaker's rock, cut two round pieces of cloth and sew them together, leaving an opening for stuffing with cotton or fiber. Tape the rock to the stage, extending it a little over the right bottom ledge of the proscenium. Tape some blue scallops on the inside, extending above the bottom ledge, to look like water. The inside of the stage is the lake. When Filbert Fish is on stage, be sure he's not raised so high that the puppeteer's arm can be seen. As the interviewer tells the story, the fish and frog act it out.

INTERVIEWER: Somewhere—not very far from here—is a beautiful little round lake with sparkling water and white, sandy beaches. Tall trees grow right up to its edge, and flower bushes drop their petals into its water. Here and there lily pads float on its surface. Under a giant oak a smooth, gray rock juts out over the water. Sometimes, if you look carefully, you may see Croaker the frog sitting there, dozing peacefully. Many fish swim in the cool, clear water below Croaker's rock. He likes to drop in and swim with them awhile and then climb atop a lily pad to watch for an unsuspecting fly. *(Curtain is raised. Croaker enters, climbs on his rock, and goes to sleep.)* One day Croaker was snoozing as usual on his rock when suddenly a splash in the water nearby awakened him with a start. A fish poked his head out of the water. It was Filbert, Croaker's best friend.

CROAKER: Oh, it's you, Filbert. You woke me up.

FILBERT: **It's much too beautiful a day to spend it sleeping!** *(He dives into the water and back up again.)*

CROAKER: Hey, you sure are getting to be a big fish! Do you know how much you weigh?

FILBERT: **Sure I do. I always know how much I weigh. You see, I carry my SCALES with me. Ha, ha! I weigh nine and a half pounds now.**

CROAKER: Ribit! You are big. You'd better be looking out for the fishermen around here. They'll try to catch a big fellow like you for sure.

FILBERT: **Oh, I've seen their bait, and I've eaten some, too. You see, I'm so fast that I pull off the bait before they can hook me.** *(He dives into the water and disappears.)*

INTERVIEWER: Later that evening two boys with long fishing poles and a bucket of worms walked up to the edge of the lake and stood near Croaker's rock. *(Croaker looks toward the left as though seeing the boys.)* With their hands shading their eyes, they looked down into the water a long time. Then Croaker heard them speak. "There he is," cried one. "Do you see him? Ain't he a beauty?"

"Wow! He is big!" exclaimed the second boy. "I hope we can catch him."

"Well," said the first boy, "I've had him steal the worms off my hook lotsa times. He's too fast for me. But I've got a plan. If it works, we'll be eating him for supper one of these days."

Croaker listened in amazement as he heard what the boys planned to do. Then with a hop and a plop he landed in the water and swam to find Filbert. *(After a pause, Croaker reappears and climbs on his rock. Filbert lifts his head above the "water.")*

CROAKER: Filbert, you must not eat any more worms that those fishermen put in the water for you. I heard them talk, and they're going to tie the worms on their strings, with no hook.

FILBERT: **Really? Why would they do that?**

CROAKER: They think that after you've been getting worms so easily as that for awhile, you'll become careless. And one day they'll have a worm on a hook. But you'll pay no attention, and they'll snag you and pull you in.

FILBERT: **Me, pay no attention? No way! They won't catch me.**

CROAKER: They said they plan to eat you for supper real soon.

FILBERT: **Ha, ha, ha! They'll never do it. I'll eat their worms, but I'll never get hooked.**

CROAKER: Yes, you will, Filbert. Stay away from those worms. Don't touch any of them!

FILBERT: **Cool Filbert, the fish, / Will never be cooked; I'll eat all their worms— / But I will not get hooked.** *(He dives into the "water.")*

INTERVIEWER: Soon Filbert was eating every worm the boys tied on their lines. Day by day the boys came back and fed Filbert, and he was getting fat and lazy. When he would see Croaker on his rock he would lift his head out of the water and shout:

FILBERT: **Cool Filbert, the fish, / Will never be cooked; I'll eat all their worms— / But I will not get hooked.**

INTERVIEWER: Again and again Croaker warned him.

CROAKER: You'd better quit eating those worms, Filbert. You will get hooked. *(Filbert disappears. Croaker looks toward left rear.)*

INTERVIEWER: One day Croaker noticed the boys laughing quietly as they threw in their baited lines.

CROAKER: Uh-oh! They look very suspicious. I'll bet there are hooks on those lines.

YOU'LL GET HOOKED, FILBERT *(continued)*

INTERVIEWER: Before Croaker could warn Filbert about it, there was churning and splashing in the water. Then a beautiful fish was hauled in to the shore. It was Filbert. "Didn't I tell you we'd get him?" said one boy, holding up Filbert for the other to see. The big fish's scales gleamed in the sunlight, and he whipped his tail around as he gasped for breath. Then the boys pulled the hook from his mouth, dropped him in a big bucket, and closed the lid. "We'll have a great supper tonight," the boys said as they walked away. And Croaker shook his head sadly.

CROAKER: **I warned him, but he wouldn't listen. I told him he'd get hooked.**

**Cool Filbert, the fish, / Is going to be cooked;
He ate all their worms— / And then he got hooked.**

(Croaker hops off his rock. Curtain closes. The spiritual meaning of this puppet show may be obscure to most boys and girls without some explanation. Be sure to follow it up with a discussion about the use of tobacco, alcohol, and illegal drugs, something like the following.)

Boys and girls, you have probably been warned many times about using tobacco, alcohol, and drugs. All of these are harmful to us. They can make people sick, and they often eventually kill those who use them. Each of them has something in it that causes your body to want more and more. We call that "addiction." You know you're being harmed, but you can't stop. You're hooked. If Filbert had only listened to Croaker and not taken the first worm, he'd never have been hooked. But he kept on taking worms, even when he was warned. He kept saying, "I won't get hooked." But soon he got careless and lazy. And before he knew it, he was hooked. How can you be sure you will never get hooked on tobacco, alcohol, or illegal drugs? By never taking the first taste. Promise the Lord that with His help you'll never take the first puff on a cigarette, taste the first sip of an alcoholic drink, or try illegal drugs even once. Keep your promise, and you'll never get hooked.

QUIET AS A CHURCH MOUSE

Scripture References: 1 Chronicles 16:29; Habakkuk 2:20; 1 Timothy 3:15

Lesson Theme: Reasons for behaving at church

Puppet Used: Chucky Church Mouse. See Part 2, chapter 10, for instructions for making this special mouth puppet.

Preparation: Chucky has a large wad of cotton attached to the inside of each ear with double-sided tape. Inform the children that Chucky will not appear if they are noisy. Wait until all are quiet. Then after the first speech the ventriloquist brings him out or he pops up in the stage.

INTERVIEWER *(to children)*: Thank you for being quiet. That's how Chucky Church Mouse likes it. Now, here he is!

CHUCKY: **Hi, everybody! I hope you're being quiet.**

INTERVIEWER: They are quiet. Don't you know that?

CHUCKY: **Huh? What did you say?**

INTERVIEWER: I said that the children are quiet.

CHUCKY: **I can't hear you.**

INTERVIEWER: What's the matter with you?

CHUCKY *(loudly)*: **What?**

INTERVIEWER *(louder)*: What's the matter with you? *(Looks at Chucky and sees the cotton.)* Why, you have cotton in your ears! *(Removes the cotton balls.)* No wonder you couldn't hear. Chucky, why did you put cotton in your ears?

CHUCKY: **'Cause all this noise hurts my ears.**

INTERVIEWER: But there isn't any noise.

CHUCKY *(pauses, listening)*: **Oh, isn't that nice?**

INTERVIEWER: Why do you think children should be quiet in church, Chucky?

CHUCKY: **'Cause if they're noisy it hurts our ears.**

INTERVIEWER: That's not the real reason for being quiet in church.

CHUCKY: **It's not? Oh, I know the reason: so we can all go to sleep.** *(Yawns.)* **I'm so sleepy.** *(Lays his head down on the front ledge of the stage or on the ventriloquist's arm, with his eyes hidden.)*

INTERVIEWER *(to audience)*: Is that why we should be quiet in church—so we can sleep? No, of course not. Wake up, Chucky! Church is not the place to sleep.

CHUCKY *(raising his head slightly)*: **Huh? What?**

INTERVIEWER: Wake up. We're in church.

CHUCKY: **Oh.** *(Looks at the children.)* **Thanks for being quiet so I can sleep.** *(He lays his head down again.)*

INTERVIEWER: But you're not supposed to sleep in church. Wake up! WAKE UP!

CHUCKY *(mumbling)*: **I'm sleepy.** *(Repeat this several times.)*

INTERVIEWER: Now, Chucky, you must stay awake.

CHUCKY *(raising up)*: **Okay.**

INTERVIEWER: We aren't quiet in church so we can sleep. But why should the children be quiet?

CHUCKY: **'Cause I'll give a prize to the one that's quietest.**

INTERVIEWER: What if they're all perfectly quiet? Are you going to give a prize to everyone?

CHUCKY: **No, no. I can't do that. I'm not a millionaire.**

INTERVIEWER: Hoping to get a prize is not the best reason for being quiet, anyway.

CHUCKY: **Well . . . I know.** *(Speaks to children.)* **Be quiet so the teacher won't yell at you.**

INTERVIEWER: Respecting and obeying the teacher is very important. But that's still not the real reason for being quiet.

CHUCKY: **Oh, I thought of a good reason. You should be quiet so you can hear me sing.** *(He sings a short chorus.)*

INTERVIEWER: You're getting closer. We should be quiet so we can hear what's going on.

CHUCKY: **Like hearing how good I can sing.**

INTERVIEWER: No. To understand the message of the songs. And when the teacher gives the lesson, why should the students be quiet?

CHUCKY: **To learn something?**

INTERVIEWER: Yes. Learning God's Word is a very important reason for being quiet. And there's one more. Do you know where God is?

CHUCKY: **Sure. He's right here. Hey, I know the best reason of all! Be quiet so you can think about God.**

INTERVIEWER: Yes. The most important reason of all for being quiet in church is so you can truly worship God.

CHUCKY: **I'll sneak away so you can do that now. Shhhh!** *(He disappears.)*

LET YOUR LIGHT SHINE

Scripture References: 1 Kings 2:1-11; 19:1-18; Matthew 5:14-16; Philippians 2:15-16

Lesson Theme: Shining for Jesus however and wherever He wants you

Puppet Used: 'Lijah Light Bulb. See Part 2, chapter 10, for instructions to make this special mouth puppet.

INTERVIEWER: At this time I'd like to introduce to you 'Lijah Light Bulb.

'LIJAH: Hi! I want you to know I'm the brightest puppet in the world.

INTERVIEWER: Oh, you are?

'LIJAH: Yes siree, and I'll prove it. I can count. Listen: 1-2-3-7-10-6.

INTERVIEWER: You think that proves you're bright?

'LIJAH: Sure. And I can say the alphabet: A-B-C-F-K-M-Q.

INTERVIEWER: No. No. That's not right.

'LIJAH: It's not? Well, listen to me spell then. Candy: K-A-N-D-E, candy. Cat: K-A-T-T, cat. Dog: D-O-G-G, dog.

INTERVIEWER: Wrong—all wrong.

'LIJAH *(surprised)*: **You mean I got everything wrong?**

INTERVIEWER: Yes.

'LIJAH: I just don't understand it. I'm a light bulb. I'm supposed to be bright.

INTERVIEWER: You're not supposed to be bright, meaning smart. You should be SHINING bright.

'LIJAH: I can't do that. I try and try to shine. But when it gets dark, no one can even see me. I don't shine at all.

INTERVIEWER: Then something's wrong with you. You're supposed to shine.

'LIJAH: I think I'll hang around with the other light bulbs. Maybe some of their shine will rub off on me.

INTERVIEWER: That won't work at all.

'LIJAH: Well, then, I'll just tell everyone I'm shining. Maybe they won't notice I'm not.

INTERVIEWER: Kind of like the emperor and his new clothes? Someone's bound to notice.

'LIJAH: What can I do? Do you know how I can begin to shine?

INTERVIEWER: You need to go to the source of light. You need to be plugged into the electricity.

'LIJAH: Oh. I've never been plugged into electricity.

INTERVIEWER: You are just like sinners who try to fool people into thinking they're really Christians. They think that by being with Christians, they'll be called Christians. Or they suppose that just saying so will make it so.

'LIJAH: Just like me—it won't work, huh?

INTERVIEWER: No, it won't work. They need to get the Light of the World in their hearts—the Lord Jesus Christ.

'LIJAH: Hey, I want to start shining. Where can I get plugged into the electricity?

INTERVIEWER: We need a light in the attic. I think I'll put you up there.

'LIJAH: In the attic? Please don't put me there. No one will see me. I want to be in the chandelier in the living room.

INTERVIEWER: 'Lijah, that's just like some Christians. They say they'll let their light shine for Jesus, but they want to be in some important place or they won't shine.

'LIJAH: What kind of place?

INTERVIEWER: Let's suppose a little girl is asked to sing a song in children's church. She likes to show off her talent, so she gladly gets up front and sings. Then she is asked to go and sing for a sick old man who is lonely. But she refuses to do that.

'LIJAH: Well, I would go shine in the attic, but it's so dark and scary-looking. I'm afraid to be there.

INTERVIEWER: Of course it's dark. That's why you're needed there. Lights are meant for dark places.

'LIJAH: Oh. I knew that. But I'm still scared of the attic.

INTERVIEWER: You're named after Elijah, a prophet in Old Testament times. He was a very brave preacher of God's message. But the queen threatened to kill him. Elijah was afraid and ran far away.

'LIJAH: Did he get killed?

INTERVIEWER: No. God told him to go back and keep on serving Him. Elijah obeyed, and he bravely preached God's Word.

'LIJAH: Then was he killed?

INTERVIEWER: Not at all. God took care of Elijah until he had finished all the work God wanted him to do. Then God took him to heaven in a chariot of fire. The brave prophet didn't die at all.

'LIJAH: Hey, you say you need me in the attic? Okay. I'll go there and shine the best I can.

INTERVIEWER: That's the way! And Christians should shine brightly for Jesus wherever He puts them.

'LIJAH: Well, good-bye, everybody. I'm headed for the attic. I'll get plugged into the electricity, and then I'll shine and shine and shine!

HOORAY FOR JESUS

Scripture References: 1 Corinthians 9:24-27; 1 Timothy 4:7-8; 2 Timothy 2:5; Hebrews 12:1-2

Lesson Theme: Put Jesus first in all of life.

Puppet Used: Hooray! Football. See Part 2, chapter 10, for instructions for making this special mouth puppet. Give him a beanie and a banner in the colors of your church team, if any, or of the team of the school where most of your class attend. You may wish to give him a name which fits the team. This dialogue is best for older children and teens.

FOOTBALL: Hooray for our team! Hooray! Hooray!

INTERVIEWER: Folks, here is Hooray! Football. What is your team, Hooray?

FOOTBALL: Why, the team of (name of school or church), **of course. That's the best team. I want them to make me the mascot.**

INTERVIEWER: We all like that team. (Football gives two or three yells that are usually given by the local cheerleaders and a new one—if possible.)

INTERVIEWER: A football game can be very exciting.

FOOTBALL: Football season is the most important time of the year.

INTERVIEWER: Wait a minute. There are many things that are far more important than football.

FOOTBALL: Wash your mouth out with soap! Don't tell me you think baseball is more important than football. Or maybe basketball is. For shame!

INTERVIEWER: No. I mean there are things that are far more important in life than any kind of sport.

FOOTBALL: I can't believe what I'm hearing! Sports help keep your body in shape, they bring about a good school spirit, and they help people relax and enjoy themselves.

INTERVIEWER: Participating in sports, especially if you're actually involved and getting exercise, is VERY good for you. But the inside of a person is much more important than the outside.

FOOTBALL: Oh, well, every good sportsman knows you have to eat right to be strong.

INTERVIEWER: That's not the inside I'm talking about. That's the stomach, which is still part of the body. I'm talking about the soul and spirit. Paul says in the Bible, "Training your body helps you in SOME ways, but serving God helps you in EVERY WAY. Serving God brings you blessings in this life and in the future life, too."*

FOOTBALL: I hadn't ever thought of that. Exercise and sports don't help you get ready for eternity.

INTERVIEWER: No, they don't. Taking part in good, clean sports is a fine way to get the exercise our bodies need; and watching games is a fun way to relax. But sports should not have first place in our lives.

FOOTBALL: What should have first place, then?

INTERVIEWER: Not "what" but "who." Jesus should have first place. Games and sports must not keep us from being our best for Him. We must make sure we've given time to reading our Bibles, praying, going to church, and letting people know about Jesus. We should put Jesus first when we're playing games, too. Do you know how that can be done?

FOOTBALL: I think so. Play fair and don't get mad and things like that?

INTERVIEWER: Exactly. And just as an athlete in the Olympics must follow the rules to win a medal, so a Christian must follow God's rules to win a crown in heaven. Paul said "If an athlete is running a race, he must obey all the rules in order to win."†

FOOTBALL: I guess getting a crown in heaven is more important than winning the gold at the Olympics.

INTERVIEWER: Right. Paul talked about runners in the first Olympics in Greece long ago. And he said, "All those who compete in the games use strict training. They do this so that they can win a crown. That crown is an earthly thing that lasts only a short time. But our crown will continue forever."‡ Running a good race in the Christian life gains us rewards in heaven that last forever.

FOOTBALL: Hooray for games
And hooray for fun—
If Jesus is first
In all that is done.
Hooray for Jesus!

*1 Timothy 4:8, *International Children's Bible.*

†2 Timothy 2:5, *International Children's Bible.*

‡1Corinthians 9:25, *International Children's Bible.*

FOOD FOR THE BODY & FOOD FOR THE SOUL

Scripture References: Job 23:12; Psalm 119:20; Colossians 1:10-11; 1 Peter 2:2

Lesson Theme: God's Word will strengthen us if we'll read it.

Puppet Used: Forgetful Fojo, or other clown puppet. See Part 2, chapter 10, for making Fojo.

Preparation: When Fojo is brought out he has four notes sticking in various places on his body and clothes: in his hair, behind his ear, in his pockets, protruding from his sleeves. Number the notes and remove them in order.

INTERVIEWER: How are you, Fojo?

FOJO: **I'm SO hungry. I wish I had something to eat.**

INTERVIEWER: Hungry? Didn't you eat your breakfast?

FOJO: **I don't think so.**

INTERVIEWER: Why not?

FOJO: **I forgot to eat. Oh, I'm real weak!**

INTERVIEWER: Why, that's terrible! Did you read your notes? Maybe they were to remind you to eat.

FOJO: **I forgot to read them.**

INTERVIEWER: Let's read them right now. *(Removes note no. 1 and puts it before Fojo.)*

FOJO *(reading)*: **"Wash the dishes." Oh, I can't do that. They're already clean. I didn't use them.**

INTERVIEWER *(removing note no. 2 and showing it to Fojo)*: What does this say?

FOJO *(reading)*: **"Eat breakfast." Well, I couldn't eat it, because I forgot to cook any food. Oh, I sure feel weak!**

INTERVIEWER: Of course you're weak. Next time you must remember to cook your food and eat it.

FOJO: **I'll write that on a note.**

INTERVIEWER: You probably already did. *(Removes note no. 3 and reads it.)* "Cook breakfast." You see, Fojo, the words were there, but you forgot to read them. You know, some Christians are like you in spiritual things. They're weak Christians because they forget to read God's Word.

FOJO: **Does it tell them what to do?**

INTERVIEWER: Yes. Like your notes, it tells them the things they should do. God inspired the writing of the Bible, and all Christians need to read it every day to learn how He wants them to live. When we read it and obey it, we become strong spiritually. Oh, look, Fojo, here's one more note. *(Removes note, placing it before Fojo.)* What does this say?

FOJO *(reading)*: **"Read your Bible every day."**

INTERVIEWER: Why, Fojo! You knew about Bible reading all the time, didn't you?

FOJO: **Sure I did. I may forget to do things, but I've got sense enough to know I need to read the Bible. I'm no dummy!**

CORNPONE, THE FARMER BOY

Scripture References: Deuteronomy 30:1; Joshua 24:15; Matthew 7:13-14; John 3:18,36

Lesson Theme: Choosing to be saved or to remain unsaved—to have life or death, heaven or hell.

Puppet Used: Cornpone D. Nutt. See Part 2, chapter 10, for instructions for making this special mouth puppet.

CORNPONE: **Howdy do.**

INTERVIEWER: Folks, I'd like for you to meet this young man. His name is—

CORNPONE: **Now jest hold yer horses. I'll tell 'em who I am. My name is Cornpone D. Nutt.**

INTERVIEWER: Tell us a little about yourself, Cornpone. Where were you born?

CORNPONE: **In Georgia.**

INTERVIEWER: What part?

CORNPONE: **All of me, of course. Cain't part of me be born in Georgia and part in Florida. Guess you think my foot was born in Florida and my head was born in Georgia.**

INTERVIEWER: Aren't you from the farm?

CORNPONE: **Yep, I shore am. My dad's a farmer, but it's awful hard to make a living on the farm.**

INTERVIEWER: Does your father plant potatoes on his farm?

CORNPONE: **He planted 'taters one time. When they growed up, I ran a steamroller over them.**

INTERVIEWER: Why did you run a steamroller over your potatoes?

CORNPONE: **So's I could get instant mashed 'taters. Hey, hey, hey! Dad don't plant 'taters no more.**

INTERVIEWER: Why not?

CORNPONE: **He's scairt 'tater bugs will eat 'em.**

INTERVIEWER: Does he plant corn?

CORNPONE: **Nope. Don't plant no corn.**

INTERVIEWER: Why not?

CORNPONE: **He's scairt it won't rain on the corn.**

INTERVIEWER: Does he plant tomatoes?

Cornpone: **Nope. Don't plant no 'maters.**

INTERVIEWER: Why not?

CORNPONE: **He's scairt it'll rain too much on the 'maters.**

INTERVIEWER: Well, what does he plant?

CORNPONE: **Nothin'. He jest plays it safe.**

INTERVIEWER: Cornpone, I don't think you know anything about farming.

CORNPONE: **Why, shore I do. I know more'n you do, and I'm D. Nutt around here.**

INTERVIEWER: Let's check that out. See if you can ask me any questions about the farm that I can't answer.

CORNPONE: **Okay. Tell me this: What has one horn and gives milk?**

INTERVIEWER: One horn and gives milk? Let's see—a cow or a goat? No, they have two horns. I don't think there is anything that has one horn and gives milk.

CORNPONE: **Yep, there is. It's a milk truck. Hey, hey, hey!**

INTERVIEWER: That's not fair. Ask me a real farm question.

CORNPONE: **Is something about chickens a good farm question?**

INTERVIEWER: Yes, I suppose so.

CORNPONE: **Well, on which side does a chicken have the most feathers?**

INTERVIEWER: Nobody knows that.

CORNPONE: **I do.**

INTERVIEWER: No, you don't.

CORNPONE: **I do so.**

INTERVIEWER: All right. Tell me which side of the chicken has the most feathers.

CORNPONE: **The outside. Hey, hey, hey!**

INTERVIEWER: You're impossible.

CORNPONE: **No, I'm Cornpone D. Nutt. Say, if a rooster laid an egg on top of a hill, which side of the hill would the egg roll down?**

INTERVIEWER: Of course I don't know that. Do you?

CORNPONE: **Neither side. A rooster cain't lay eggs. Hey, hey, hey! And something else—betcha cain't tell me how to keep a rooster from crowing on Sunday morning.**

INTERVIEWER: Hmm . . . No, I guess I can't.

CORNPONE: **Cook him Satruday night. Hey, hey, hey! Why is a rooster on a fence like a penny?**

INTERVIEWER: I guess I don't know that either.

CORNPONE: **Because his head is on one side and his tail is on the other.**

CORNPONE, THE FARMER BOY  *(continued)*

INTERVIEWER: Well, Cornpone, I may not know the answer to your corny jokes. But I know one thing—people can't be on the fence about salvation.

CORNPONE: **What do you mean?**

INTERVIEWER: Either they're saved or they're not saved. There's no place in between.

CORNPONE: **But what if they jest haven't decided yet?**

INTERVIEWER: Until they decide to get saved, it means that they've decided to stay unsaved.

CORNPONE: **So they need to climb over the fence from being unsaved to being saved.**

INTERVIEWER: God places us on the side of salvation when we trust Jesus as Savior. But those who won't trust Him are headed for hell.

CORNPONE: **Hey, everybody—you'd better git on the side of salvation.**

INTERVIEWER: That's true. You know, Cornpone, you said your father just played it safe and did nothing about farming. That's why he can't make a living. Persons who think they can play it safe and do nothing about salvation will some day find that's the most unsafe thing they could do.

CORNPONE: **I ain't got much sense, but I know that the ones that are on the wrong side of the fence better get saved now when they can. They cain't play it safe by doing nothing.**

INTERVIEWER: That's right. The Bible says, "Now is the day of salvation." You know, this proves you're pretty smart, Cornpone!

CORNPONE: **Shore. I ain't sech a nut after all.**

CORNPONE AND THE COW

Scripture References: Romans 6:13; 12:1-2

Lesson Theme: Our lives grow more useful to God as we give ourselves to Him.

Puppet Used: Cornpone D. Nutt.

INTERVIEWER: Here's our friend from the farm, Cornpone D. Nutt.

CORNPONE: **Howdy, y'all. Have you heard the story about** (*names a woman who is present or is well-known*)**?**

INTERVIEWER: I guess we haven't. What about her?

CORNPONE: **She took a ride out in the country with her husband the other day, and they saw a cow and a calf rubbin' noses.**

INTERVIEWER: What about it?

CORNPONE: **She said to her husband, "Oh, Sugar, I wish we could do that." And he said, "You go ahead, dear. I'm sure the cow won't mind." Hey, hey, hey!**

INTERVIEWER: You live on a farm, don't you, Cornpone?

CORNPONE: **Yep, I shore do.**

INTERVIEWER: Are there any cows on your farm?

CORNPONE: **Yep—a whole bunch of cows.**

INTERVIEWER: Not "bunch"— "herd."

CORNPONE: **Heard what?**

INTERVIEWER: Herd of cows.

CORNPONE: **Course I've heard of cows.**

INTERVIEWER: No. A cow herd.

CORNPONE: **I don't care if a cow heard. I don't have any secrets.**

INTERVIEWER: I don't think you know anything about cows. I'll bet you don't even know which side a cow is milked from.

CORNPONE: **I do too.**

INTERVIEWER: All right. What side is the cow milked from?

CORNPONE: **The UTTER side.**

INTERVIEWER (*shaking his head*): The "UTTER" side! . . . So the cows on your farm give milk?

CORNPONE: **Nope.**

INTERVIEWER: Why, surely, some of them must give milk.

CORNPONE: **Nope. Cows don't give milk.**

INTERVIEWER: Oh, yes, they do—You see, you don't know about cows.

CORNPONE: **I shore do. Cows don't GIVE milk. You gotta SQUEEZE it out of 'em.**

INTERVIEWER: Well, then, why when you milked a cow the other day did you take the bucket of milk and let the cow drink it?

CORNPONE: **The milk looked sorta weak, so I was runnin' it back through again. Hey, hey, hey! Say, did you know we have cows on our farm that we get buttermilk from?**

INTERVIEWER: Buttermilk? How can that be?

CORNPONE: **Well, did you ever hear of a cow that you got anything from BUT HER milk? Hey, hey, hey!**

INTERVIEWER: Well, did you realize cows can be useful for things besides milk? You know where leather comes from, don't you?

CORNPONE: **No. You tell me.**

INTERVIEWER: Hide.

CORNPONE: **What?**

INTERVIEWER: Hide! hide! the cow's outside.

CORNPONE: **I don't care if she's outside. I don't need to hide. I'm not scairt of a cow.**

INTERVIEWER: You still don't understand. The HIDE is the cow's SKIN. Didn't you ever see the skin of a cow?

CORNPONE: **Sure.**

INTERVIEWER: Where?

CORNPONE: **On the cow.**

INTERVIEWER: Well, now do you know what the cow's hide is used for?

CORNPONE: **Yep. It holds the cow together. Hey, hey, hey!**

INTERVIEWER: You know, Cornpone, almost every part of a cow can be useful. The cow is a great help to mankind.

CORNPONE: **Yeah, well, the other day we couldn't git nothin' from our cows. They ran away.**

INTERVIEWER: Yes, the farmer must have the cow's cooperation. She must stay in the pasture and eat grass and then come to the barn and let someone milk her. And some cows have to die so we can use their meat or hide.

CORNPONE: **Cain't give much more'n that.**

INTERVIEWER: That's true. . . And Christian's ought to be more like the cow.

CORNPONE: **Huh?**

INTERVIEWER: We can do great things for God, but we must let Him take charge of our lives. We can't be useful to Him if we refuse to be under His control.

CORNPONE: **Like a cow that won't let down her milk.**

INTERVIEWER: Exactly. What you and I are doing is a good example of what I mean. You see, you would be totally useless by yourself. (*Puppet collapses. Cornpone makes muffled noises.*)

INTERVIEWER: What? I can't understand you?

CORNPONE (*comes erect*): **Whew! I said, "I cain't do nothin' by myself."**

INTERVIEWER: But when you're in my hands, you can be greatly used to give the gospel. I just open your mouth.

CORNPONE: **And I let you fill it. Well, I need to go now. I'm goin' to the farm and perform a miracle.**

INTERVIEWER: Perform a miracle?

CORNPONE: **Yep. I'm going to let the cows out of the barn so's they can eat GREEN grass, give WHITE milk, from which I'll make YELLOW butter. 'Bye, y'all.**

NOBODY LOVES ME

Scripture References: Matthew 7:12; 1 John 4:10 to 5:2

Lesson Theme: We should show love to others, for Christ loved us and gave himself for us.

Puppet Used: Honey Dew. See Part 2, chapter 9, for instructions for making this a puppet that can have a human hand inserted for the puppet's hand. A regular puppet may be used for this and the next dialogue, but you must place the telephone to the puppet's ear yourself and dial the phone. Also in this dialogue you will need to put a handkerchief to the puppet's nose.

Preparation: Prerecord on audio tape some sounds for blowing a nose and for the ring of a telephone. Then when these sound effects are needed, press a foot pedal connected to the tape recorder or have someone else ready to turn on the recorder at the right times. Place a real or toy phone and handkerchief within reach.

INTERVIEWER: Hello, everyone. I would like for you to meet this young woman. Her name is Honey Dew.

HONEY DEW *(crying)*: **Ohhh, BOOHOO, 'HOO!** *(Places handkerchief to nose and blows.)*

INTERVIEWER: What's going on here? Why are you crying, Honey Dew?

HONEY DEW: **Because I'm not laughing.** *(Cries.)* **OHHH!** *(Blows nose.)*

INTERVIEWER: I mean, what have you been crying ABOUT?

HONEY DEW: **About half an hour.** *(Cries.)* **OHHH!** *(Blows nose.)*

INTERVIEWER: Please don't cry like that.

HONEY DEW: **I don't know how to cry any other way.** *(Cries.)* **OHHH! BOOHOO, 'HOO!** *(Blows nose.)*

INTERVIEWER: Has someone hurt your feelings?

HONEY DEW: **Yes. BOOHOO, 'HOO!** *(Blows nose.)*

INTERVIEWER: Who has hurt your feelings?

HONEY DEW: **Lots of kids. I asked them to come to my party, but no one came. I feel so bad.**

INTERVIEWER: Please don't cry any more. When was your party?

HONEY DEW: **Today.**

INTERVIEWER: And no one came?

HONEY DEW: **Not a SINGLE, SOLITARY person.**

INTERVIEWER: Did anybody tell you why?

HONEY DEW: **No. I stayed by the phone and WAITED and WAITED, but it never rang. See? It just sits there and never rings.** *(Phone rings.)* **YIKES! That scared me.**

INTERVIEWER: Well, answer the phone.

HONEY DEW: **Oh, yeah.** *(Picks up the phone.)* **Hello. No. Goodbye.** *(Slams down receiver.)*

INTERVIEWER: Who was that?

HONEY DEW: **Wrong number. I told you, nobody loves me. I think I'll call up my boyfriend and see why he didn't come.**

INTERVIEWER: Who's your boyfriend?

HONEY DEW: **Herkimer.** *(Dials phone.)* **Hello—Oooh, it's his answering machine. I hate answering machines, especially at a time like this. . . . Why aren't you home to answer your phone—no, better yet, why aren't you here at my birthday party? Don't you love me any more? Well, good-BYE!** *(Slams down receiver.)* **Ohhh! I told you NO ONE loves me. Now I don't even have a boyfriend.**

INTERVIEWER: Why don't you pick one out here?

HONEY DEW *(Looking at audience)*: **Well, I just might do that. I know! I choose** *(a boy who can take a joke)*. **No . . . not him. He chews his nails.**

INTERVIEWER: That's not so bad. Lots of people chew their nails.

HONEY DEW: **Toenails? . . . Oh, nobody loves me. Everybody HATES me.**

INTERVIEWER: Someone loves you very much.

HONEY DEW: **Really? Who?**

INTERVIEWER: I do. *(Looking at audience.)* Who else loves Honey Dew? *(Have a show of hands.)* You see, Honey Dew, lots of people love you. You know, sometimes we all get to feeling that we are unloved. But there are always other people who love us.

HONEY DEW: **And best of all, you've got Jesus to love you.**

INTERVIEWER: Yes. He loved all the people in the world so much that He died for them, even though we all have sinned.

HONEY DEW: **And He'll take you to heaven, if you'll believe in Him, won't He?**

INTERVIEWER: That's right. God loves us very much. And you know one way we can show our love for Him?

HONEY DEW: **By sending Him valentines?**

INTERVIEWER: Not exactly. By the way we love each other. The Bible says, "Since God loved us . . . we surely ought to love each other too."*

HONEY DEW: **That's hard to do when people don't treat you right.**

INTERVIEWER: True. But Jesus said that whatever you want others to do for you, that's what you should do for them.

HONEY DEW: **Then I should love my friends and be nice to them just the way I want them to be to me. I'm going to try real hard to do that.** *(Phone rings. She picks it up.)* **Hello. . . . Oh, hello, Judy . . . What? You say you're coming to my party NEXT week? But it was supposed to be TODAY! . . . My letter says NEXT Tuesday!—No wonder no one showed up. Thanks for calling, Judy.** *(Hangs up.)* **Oh, I put the wrong date in the letter. My friends DO love me after all!—** *(gasps)* **Oh, I gotta call Herkimer back and leave a different message. . . . Ain't love grand?** *(She sighs as she dials the phone.)*

*1 John 4:11, *The Living Bible*.

HONEY DEW'S TONGUE

Scripture References: Psalm 15:1-3; 119:171-172; Proverbs 25:9-10; 1 Timothy 5:13; James 3:3-12

Lesson Theme: We should use our tongues (and telephones) to spread the gospel—not gossip. This dialogue is best for an adult audience, or one of mixed ages. The puppet has a very long speech, but it is broken somewhat by the pauses.

Puppet Used: Honey Dew. See Chapter 9 for instructions for making this puppet. Also see the introduction to the previous dialogue. Have a real or toy telephone nearby.

INTERVIEWER: Have you met my friend? I'll let her tell you her name.

HONEY DEW: **Well, when I was born, they called me Theophilus.**

INTERVIEWER: Theophilus? But that's a boy's name. Why did they call you that?

HONEY DEW: **Well, I'm not sure, but I think my uncle looked at me and said, "That's Theophilus kid I ever saw."**

INTERVIEWER: Ooh . . . I'm sorry.

HONEY DEW: **Oh, he's a cut up. He didn't mean it. Besides, I have a better name now.**

INTERVIEWER: You do? What is it?

HONEY DEW: **Honey Dew.**

INTERVIEWER: Ahh, that's a pretty name. How did you get that name?

HONEY DEW: **Well, someone is always saying to me, "Honey, do this! Honey, do that!" So I call myself Honey Dew.** (Phone rings.) **Excuse me, folks.** (She picks up phone.) **Hello . . . How are you, Sister All-Ears? . . . Have you heard any juicy gos—** (glances at audience) **Uh, I mean, have you heard any news today? . . . Well, yes, I have heard some news. Brother Henpecked gave his wife a new dress. It will never go out of style. . . . Really, it will look just as ridiculous next year as it does this year. . . . Yeah, that woman looks like a million—every year of it. She'll never live to be as old as she looks, either. Of course her mind has stayed quite young. That's because she uses it so little! . . . Oh, someone's at your door? I'll call you sometime when I've got some juicy gos— I mean, news. 'Bye.** (Hangs up the phone.)

INTERVIEWER: Honey Dew, I'm surprised at you. Why, you're a gossip.

HONEY DEW: **I consider myself to be more like a news anchorwoman.**

INTERVIEWER: You're a rumormonger. Don't you know that gossip is seldom true; and if it is true to start with, it soon becomes lies if it's repeated often enough? People have a way of changing the facts as they pass stories along.

HONEY DEW: **Not me. I'm strictly a truth-teller.** (Phone rings. She picks it up.) **Hello. . . . Hello Sister Ima Gossip. . . . What? You RAN into the preacher today? Did you HURT him? . . . Oh, you mean you SAW him. How'd he look? . . . Sorta TIRED? . . . What? It's hard to tell with his DARK eyes? Well, thanks for calling. Good-bye.** (Hangs up.) **It's beginning to look like a good day for me. I think I'll call Sister Tattle-It.** (Picks up phone and dials, singing) **Glory, glory, hallelujah, the truth goes marching on. Hello, is this Sister Tattle-It? . . . This is Honey Dew. . . . I heard that the preacher looks SICK, and he has DARK eyes. . . . I'll keep one ear close to the phone in case I hear anything. Good-bye, Sister Tattle-It.** (Hangs up.) **Yes, it's a fine day. Glory, glory, hallelujah, the truth goes marching on.** (Phone rings. She picks it up.) **Hello. . . . Oh hello, Brother Fork-ed Tongue. . . . Have I heard anything about the preacher? Well, I did hear a little. What did YOU hear? . . . What? You say he looks half-DEAD, and some one gave him a BLACK eye? . . . Do you s'pose he was in a fight? That must be it! Oh, the shame of it! . . . Why, of course, you know me, Brother. I won't tell a soul. Good-bye.** (Hangs up.) **Except of course I must talk to Sister Carrie Tales.** (Dials phone, singing) **Glory, glory, hallelujah, the truth goes marching on. Hello, Sister Carrie Tales. This is Honey Dew. Do you know what I heard today? The preacher had a TERRIBLE fight. He's most dead. . . . Yeah, and they say you should see his TWO black eyes! Some woman, I think. . . . Nearly killed him. . . . I think it was a DEACON'S wife. Now don't tell a soul, Sister Carrie Tales. You know, we've been real nice to our preacher. We treat him just like a kitty cat. The first year we said, "Nice kitty." Last year we said, "Poor kitty." And now I think we'd better say, "Scat!"**

INTERVIEWER: Honey Dew, hang up that phone.

HONEY DEW: **But I'm not through gossip— I mean, talking yet.**

INTERVIEWER: Hang it up. WE need to talk.

HONEY DEW (hanging up phone): **Aw, you're spoiling my fun.** (Phone rings.) **I have to answer the phone.**

INTERVIEWER: Leave it. (They look back and forth at each other and then at the phone until it stops ringing.)

INTERVIEWER: No more phoning, at least not until you change the way you use your telephone. The tongue is a powerful tool that can be used either to destroy or to help. The things you and your friends are spreading will destroy. (Honey Dew hangs her head.)

INTERVIEWER: You know, Honey Dew, that phone could be used to talk about Jesus and the Bible. Just think of all the good that could be accomplished if people used their phones only for the Lord's glory.

HONEY DEW: **I'm sorry. I just didn't think. From now I'll try to think about what I'm saying and how it will affect people.**

JUST AN OLD SOCK

Scripture References: Ecclesiastes 9:10; 1 Corinthians 12; Colossians 3:23-25

Lesson Theme: Serve joyfully and well in whatever place God assigns to you.

Puppets Used: Sockem and Sockette. See Part 2, chapter 9, for instructions for making these puppets.

SOCKEM: **Hi, folks. My name is Sockem, and my friend here is Sockette—the sweetest little sock you ever put your foot into.**

SOCKETTE: Hello.

SOCKEM: **Say, would you like to play a game, Sockette?**

SOCKETTE: What kind of game?

SOCKEM: **I'll ask you five questions. If you get two right, I'll give you a prize.**

SOCKETTE: Oh, goody. Ask me the questions. But what's the prize?

SOCKEM: **The prize is a surprise. I'll tell you if you win. Here's the first question. What president wore the largest size shoe?**

SOCKETTE: How should I know that? I'll bet you don't know, either.

SOCKEM: **Yes, I do. The president who wore the biggest shoe was the one with the biggest feet. Ha, ha, ha!**

SOCKETTE: That's not fair. That was a trick question.

SOCKEM: **Now here's the next question: Why was the little shoe sad?**

SOCKETTE: I don't have any idea.

SOCKEM: **'Cause his father was a sneaker and his mother was a loafer. Hey, hey!**

SOCKETTE *(disgustedly):* That's dumb!

SOCKEM: **Third question: What did the elephant do when he broke his toe?**

SOCKETTE: Oh, oh, I know that one! He called a tow truck.... Now if I get one more right, I can get the prize, right?

SOCKEM: **Yep. Here's number four: What's the difference between a tight shoe and an oak tree?**

SOCKETTE: I—I guess I don't know.

SOCKEM: **A tight shoe makes corns ache. An oak tree makes acorns. Last question coming up.**

SOCKETTE: Make it easy. I want the prize.

SOCKEM: **Okay. Why does everyone always put on the left sock last?**

SOCKETTE: I know that! I know that! When they put one sock on, the other one is always LEFT. Now I answered the two questions, give me the prize.

SOCKEM: **You want it right now?**

SOCKETTE: Yes. What is it?

SOCKEM: **A sock.**

SOCKETTE: A sock? But I AM a sock.

SOCKEM: **This will be . . . a sock in the NOSE.**

SOCKETTE *(moving as far away as possible)*: Get away from me! (name of interviewer) help! He's going to hit me! That wasn't fair, Sockem.

INTERVIEWER: Yes, Sockem, that wasn't fair. You should give her a nice prize.

SOCKEM: **Well, what do you want, Sockette?**

SOCKETTE: What I want more than anything is to be something else instead of a sock.

INTERVIEWER: Why don't you like being a sock?

SOCKETTE: For one thing, socks always get stepped on.

SOCKEM: **Yeah, and we get shoved into dark, smelly shoes. It stinks in there!**

SOCKETTE: And when we come out of the shoes, everyone holds their noses. And no one ever notices us.

INTERVIEWER: What would you prefer to be instead of a sock?

SOCKETTE: A pretty hat—right up on top for all to see.

SOCKEM: **Or a glove, so we could shake hands and make friends.**

INTERVIEWER: But our feet need socks to keep them warm and dry and from getting blisters. You are very useful, even if you don't get much honor and respect.

SOCKEM: **Let someone else be the sock. That's what I say.**

INTERVIEWER: But you were made for that reason—to be a good covering for feet. You should be thankful you have a job to do, and then you should do your job the very best you can.

SOCKEM: **I guess we would look kinda funny on top of a head.**

INTERVIEWER: In a way, people are like you. God made each person to do a special job for Him. We should pray and ask Him to show us what it is. Then we should do the best job we can in whatever He leads us to do—whether other folks notice us or not.

SOCKETTE: I'm glad I'm a sock, 'cause everyone needs socks. I'll be the best sock I can.

SOCKEM *(facing audience):*
I'm nothing but a sock;
But that I wouldn't knock,
For I was made to live in a shoe.
Now you should take your place
And wear a happy face,
Doing what the Lord has said to do.

MAKING THE GRADE

Scripture References: Proverbs 1:2-9; 2:1-6; Ecclesiastes 9:10; 2 Timothy 2:15

Lesson Theme: Study hard and do good schoolwork now in order to give to God the best that you can be. This dialogue works well in a Christian school setting but is an important message for children at any time.

Puppets Used: Sockem and Sockette. See the instructions in Part 2, chapter 9, for how to prepare and use these puppets. Any boy and girl puppets could be used in this dialogue by changing the first few sentences slightly.

Ventriloquist: Hide puppets behind your back until they are introduced.

Puppeteer: Bring the puppets on stage as they are introduced.

INTERVIEWER *(to audience)*: When you pull off your socks at night, do they ever talk to you? No, I suppose not. I, however, do have a pair of socks that can talk. Do you want to meet them? Here is Sockem. *(He appears and bows.)* And here is Sockette. *(She appears and bows.)*

SOCKEM: Sure we can talk, 'cause we're smart.

INTERVIEWER: Show us how smart you are.

SOCKETTE: I can't do that. My brains are sealed in my head.

INTERVIEWER: But can you use your brains? I'm going to ask you some questions.

SOCKEM: Great! Then you can learn something.

INTERVIEWER: How much is two and two?

SOCKEM: Easy question! Two and two is twenty-two.

INTERVIEWER: No, no. What is two and two? Two and Two?

SOCKEM: A train whistle! TOO-TOO! TOO-TOO!

INTERVIEWER: Silly! How much is two PLUS two?

SOCKEM: Why didn't you say so? Two plus two is four.

INTERVIEWER: Excellent! For that correct answer, I'll give you four chocolates.

SOCKEM: If I'd known you were giving away chocolates, I'da said ten.

SOCKETTE: I wish I had someone to help me with my homework.

SOCKEM: I'll help you.

SOCKETTE: Oh, no thanks. I can get it wrong by myself.

INTERVIEWER: How are your grades in school, Sockette?

SOCKETTE: Oh, they're under water.

INTERVIEWER: Under water?

SOCKETTE: Yeah. They're below C level.

INTERVIEWER: Maybe I'd better help you with your schoolwork. I'll give you some words to spell. How do you spell "geography"?

SOCKETTE: Geography. G-e-e-o-g-r-a-f-f-e-e. Geography.

SOCKEM: WRONG!

SOCKETTE: Oh, yeah? You spell everything wrong. I'll bet you can't even spell "mouse."

SOCKEM: M-O-U-S. Mouse.

SOCKETTE: Ha, ha! That's not right. I told you so. You can't spell "mouse."

SOCKEM: Yes, I can. M-O-U-S.

SOCKETTE: You've got to give it an end.

SOCKEM: Why? It's already got a tail.

SOCKETTE *(proudly)*: I learned how to spell "banana" today. B-A-N-A-N-A-N-A-N—

INTERVIEWER: Stop! That's too many letters.

SOCKETTE: Well, I know how to spell it. I just don't know when to quit.

SOCKEM: I can spell it.

SOCKETTE: Betcha can't.

SOCKEM: Can so.

SOCKETTE: All right. Spell it.

SOCKEM: I-T, it.

INTERVIEWER: Who can spell the word "needle"?

SOCKETTE: I can. N-I-D-L-E, needle.

INTERVIEWER: There's no "I" in needle.

SOCKETTE: There's not? Then how do you thread it?

INTERVIEWER: Sockem, are you good at mathematics?

SOCKEM: Sure.

INTERVIEWER: Well, if you had five dollars in one pocket and two dollars in the other pocket, what would you have?

SOCKEM: Someone else's pants.

SOCKETTE: I need someone to help me with my math. Will you do it, (name of interviewer)?

INTERVIEWER: I'm sorry; I'm not really that good at math.

SOCKETTE: Well, I'll just have to ask God to give me the answers.

INTERVIEWER: I don't think that will work, not if you haven't studied.

SOCKETTE: Why? Isn't God any good at math either?

MAKING THE GRADE *(continued)*

INTERVIEWER: God's very good at math. But He won't help you or me or anyone with their schoolwork if they don't study. They must store facts in their brains. Then when they need them, they can ask God to help them recall those facts.

SOCKEM: But doesn't God care if the kids make good or bad grades?

INTERVIEWER: Yes. It pleases Him for them to make the best grades they are capable of making.

SOCKETTE: Why?

INTERVIEWER: For one thing, they need to learn all they can when they're young so they can be the very best at whatever they do when they're grown.

SOCKETTE: I guess now's the time they're getting themselves ready to be somebody special when they're grown.

INTERVIEWER: Well, they're somebody special right now. But someday they will take up their life's work and they'll want to be the best that they can be to give God glory. He gave them their brains, their abilities, their health—that's His gift to them. What they make of those things is their gift to God.

SOCKEM: So if they want to give the best gift to God they can, then it's even more important to study, isn't it?

INTERVIEWER: Yes. For one thing, such study will make it easier for them to read, understand, and live out what the Bible teaches.

SOCKETTE: I'm going to study hard from now on. I hope all the boys and girls will, too.

SOCKEM: Me, too. (Name of interviewer), I want to tell you something, but you won't believe me.

INTERVIEWER: I'll believe you.

SOCKEM: No, you won't believe me.

INTERVIEWER: Yes, I will.

SOCKEM: No, you won't.

INTERVIEWER: I will, too. What do you want to tell me?

SOCKEM: I made all A's on my report card.

INTERVIEWER: I don't believe you.

SOCKEM: I told you so. Well, I didn't make ALL A's, but I'm going to try to do it from now on.

SOCKETTE: Me, too. Let's go do our homework now, Sockem.

TWO OFFERINGS

Scripture References: Haggai 1:6; Malachi 3:10; Matthew 6:33; 1 Corinthians 16:1-2

Lesson Theme: Tithing and giving. This dialogue is better for adults than for children. Use it at a stewardship banquet or similar affair.

Puppets Used: Two Offering Envelopes (Sack Puppets). See Part 2, chapter 9, for instructions for making these puppets.

Ventriloquist: Place two offering plates side by side on a lectern and put some offering envelopes and dollar bills in them. With puppets on your hands put one elbow in one plate and one in the other.

Puppeteer: Bring puppets to front of the stage.

NARRATOR'S INTRODUCTION: It is Sunday morning. The offering has just been taken at church, and among the money and envelopes are two offering envelopes who greet each other.

No. 26: Why, hello, No. 3. How nice to see you at church!

No. 3: It's good to be here, No. 26. I thought I'd NEVER get out of my owner's offering box.

No. 26: I'm here on the very Sunday I should be. My owner has brought one of my brothers every Sunday. It's halfway through the year, so now it's my turn—No. 26.

No. 3 *(sighing)*: It would be good to have an owner that really loves the Lord. How much money is in you?

No. 26: Well, there's my owner's tithe, his mission offering, and some money for the building fund. And oh, yes—at the last minute he put in some more: "a love gift," he said.

No. 3 *(sadly)*: There are only two dollars in me.

No. 26 *(surprised)*: Why, No. 3, how can that be? Is your owner out of work?

No. 3: Oh, no. He makes good money.

No. 26: Then he doesn't tithe?

No. 3: No. He doesn't believe in tithing. He says, "Tithing's under the law, and I'm under grace. I'll take care of my bills and family first. Then, if there's anything left, I'll give it to the church."

No. 26: "Seek first his kingdom and his righteousness . . ."

No. 3: My owner thinks it says, "Seek first your own interests and pleasures."

No. 26: I guess he has a lot of this world's goods.

No. 3: Yes—and a lot of unpaid bills. And something's always going wrong for him.

No. 26: Such as?

No. 3: Last week his wife wrecked his Cadillac, and he'd forgotten to pay his car insurance.

No. 26: "You earn wages, only to put them in a purse with holes in it"—Haggai, chapter one, verse six.

No. 3: Yep, that's the way it is with my owner. He says he can never get ahead. Does your owner grumble when he puts money in you?

No. 26: Never. As he filled me he was humming, "Praise God from Whom All Blessings Flow."

No. 3: Mine cried a little over me, and he sang, "God Be with You Till We Meet Again." Does your owner ever have any money troubles?

No. 26: Sometimes. But I've heard him say to his family, "Isn't it great to see how God supplies our needs just in time?"

No. 3 *(wistfully)*: Your family sounds so happy.

No. 26: Yes, they are. Isn't yours?

No. 3: No. They fuss and fight a lot, and they're never satisfied with what they have.

No. 26: Do you know what I think is wrong, No. 3? My owner loves the Lord—

No. 3: And mine doesn't. Well, here comes a deacon to count the money.

No. 26: Wonderful! I'm on my way to be a great blessing.

No. 3: And I have just enough in me to keep someone in chewing gum.

FOJO'S ANNOUNCEMENTS

Puppet Used: Forgetful Fojo, or other clown puppet. See Part 2, chapter 10, for making Fojo.

Use Fojo to help make announcements of coming events or to remind children of things to do.

Preparation: When Fojo is brought out he has six notes sticking in various places on his body and clothes: in his hair behind his ears, in his pockets, protruding from his sleeves. Number the notes and remove them in order. Put Fojo's glasses on top of his head.

INTERVIEWER: Look, kids, we have a clown with us today.

FOJO: **Thank you kindly. Howdy, everyone!**

INTERVIEWER: What's your name?

FOJO: **Uh. . . . Well, let me see. . . . My name is . . . I'm sorry. I forgot it.**

INTERVIEWER: You forgot your own name? How could you do that?

FOJO: **It wasn't easy.**

INTERVIEWER: I see you have lots of notes here. What are they for?

FOJO: **Um . . . I forget.**

INTERVIEWER (removing note no. 1 and reading it aloud): Why, this note says, "My name is Forgetful Fojo."

FOJO: **Oh, your name is Forgetful Fojo? I thought your name was—I forget what I thought it was.**

INTERVIEWER: My name is ___. YOUR name is Forgetful Fojo.

FOJO: **Oh, yes. I thought the name seemed familiar. Yes, that's it. My name is Forgetful Fojo.**

INTERVIEWER: I brought you out here to make an important announcement for me. Do you remember what it is?

FOJO: **No.**

INTERVIEWER (removing note no. 2): Maybe this note has it written down. (Places note in front of Fojo.) Will you please read it?

FOJO: **I can't see it. I don't know where I put my glasses. Where can they be?** (Looks all around, giving audience time to call out the location of the glasses.)

INTERVIEWER (pulling glasses down over Fojo's eyes): Now, what does the note say?

FOJO (reading): **"Put out the cat." Oh, me, oh, my! I put SOMETHING outside this morning. I'm afraid I put out the bird and fed seeds to the cat.**

INTERVIEWER: Well, where is my announcement? (Removes note no. 3 and places it before Fojo.) Read this, Fojo.

FOJO (reading): **"Brush my false teeth." I would've done that, but I couldn't find my teeth.**

INTERVIEWER: Did you write a note about my announcement or not?

FOJO: **I forget.**

INTERVIEWER: Let's see what this says. (Removes note no. 4.)

FOJO (reading): **"Don't forget to write an announcement note."**

INTERVIEWER: Fojo, did you write that note?

FOJO: **I don't remember.**

INTERVIEWER: This is getting ridiculous. I see only one more note. It had better be my announcement. (Places note no. 5 before Fojo.)

FOJO (reading): **"Don't forget to read the note." How can I read it? Where is it?**

INTERVIEWER: Oh, Fojo, that's all the notes I see. After all this, you forgot to write the note, didn't you?

FOJO: **I don't remember.**

INTERVIEWER: (looking more carefully and then finding a note behind Fojo's back) Oh, here's another note. (Places it before Fojo. He reads the announcement.)

FOJO HELPS TEACH BIBLE VERSES

There are a number of ways for using Forgetful Fojo to help with memory work.

➤ Have part of the verse or other memory work missing from Fojo's notes. The children must supply the missing words.

➤ Fojo has pieces of paper but none have words on them. Pass these to some children to work together to print one right word on each note for Fojo.

➤ Each of Fojo's notes has only the first letter of the word on it. Children must tell him what the words are. These notes should be numbered and removed in order.

➤ Put each word of the memory verse on a separate slip of paper, which is then put in a balloon. Tie the balloons with strings, which are attached to Fojo. Each of the children who have done the best job of memorizing may choose a balloon, pop it, and retrieve the note. The children then read the words in order.

Scrambled Words

Puppet Used: Forgetful Fojo.

Preparation: Print each word of the memory verse and its reference on separate notes. Place the notes on Fojo's clothes and body. Do not number these notes. The memory verse will either be one the class has just learned or one you are reviewing from a former class time.

INTERVIEWER: It's time to review our Bible verse. Forgetful Fojo, do you remember it?

FOJO: **Oh, I love Bible verses, and I want to say it. But I seem to have forgotten it.**

INTERVIEWER: Maybe it's written on your notes.

FOJO: **Hmm, I think maybe I did write the verse on my notes, but I'm not sure. May I see them, please?**

INTERVIEWER (*removing one note*): Why, there is only one word here!

FOJO: **I didn't put the whole verse on the note?**

INTERVIEWER: No. Let's see another note. Oh, it's one other word from the verse. Each note must have one word, and they're not in order.

FOJO: **Well, how am I going to know how the verse goes if the words are all mixed up? Do you think the children would help me?**

INTERVIEWER: I'm sure they would. I'll give these notes to two children to hold, and we'll get the rest of the notes for other children. Then let's see if they can unscramble the verse. (*Takes all the notes off Fojo and gives them to different children. Have the children try to stand in order of the words in the verse. Then have Fojo "read" the verse.*)

FOJO (*after reading the verse*): **Oh, yes. Now I remember. Let's all say the verse together, shall we?**

ERLENE EARLY BIRD WELCOMES CHILDREN

Puppet Used: Any bird puppet.

Uses for Erlene Early Bird

➤ You may want to set an alarm clock to ring when class should begin. When it rings, Erlene pops up, bright and cheerful.

➤ Some Sunday if the class is not too large, Erlene can meet the children as they enter the room. She can ask the name of each one and then try to repeat it. She gets it all wrong, but finally gets it right after the child corrects her several times. She can ask questions, such as: "Did you ride a helicopter to church this morning? You didn't? How did you get here?" "Did you have some nice, fresh, yummy worms for breakfast? Well, I did." "Who helped you look so pretty today? Your mother? I had to get this pretty all by myself."

➤ Another Sunday Erlene could call the roll as a teacher marks the book. Of course she will mispronounce some names. She will be very pleased every time a child answers "present." (After several have said "present," she could ask where her present is.) When a child is absent, she could have someone look under the chairs or in a closet for the person, and she could be very disappointed when it's evident that the child is really absent.

➤ Use Erlene to welcome visitors, introducing them to the class and showing much pleasure in their being there.

➤ Also use Erlene to honor those with birthdays and to give special attention to the ones who bring visitors. Sometimes she could praise those who are on time. (After all, she is Erlene Early Bird!) If you have both Erlene Early Bird and Booster Rooster puppets, use them together sometimes to make announcements or to welcome the children to church. They could have some friendly arguments (which end peacefully) over who makes the announcements.

Good Morning to You

ERLENE *(sings following verse to the tune of "Happy Birthday to You")*: **Good morning to you, / good morning to you, / Good morning, ev'rybody, / We're glad to see you.**

INTERVIEWER: Good morning, Erlene. You're certainly cheerful today.

ERLENE: **Why shouldn't I be? This is the best place in the world to be on Sunday morning: church. What are you going to do today?**

INTERVIEWER: There will be singing.

ERLENE: **Oh, I LOVE singing, especially in church. Are you going to sing about Jesus?**

INTERVIEWER: Yes.

ERLENE: **Good! I'll be back in my nest listening. I hope the children sing VERY WELL so I can hear them. What else will you do?**

INTERVIEWER: We'll have a Bible lesson.

ERLENE: **The Bible is the best Book in the whole world. Who's going to listen very, very well?** *(Show of hands.)* **What else will you do?**

INTERVIEWER: We'll learn a Bible verse.

ERLENE: **When you are finished, see who can say it better—the children, or ME—okay?** *(Add in other activities you plan to have.)* **With all those wonderful things planned for you to do, I'd better go so you can get started. 'Bye.**

This Is the Way We Go to Church

ERLENE: **Oh, what a BEAUTIFUL morning! I LOVE Sunday mornings. Boys and girls, what is it we do on Sunday mornings? Right! We go to church.** *(To interviewer)* **Show them how to do the motions for "This is the Way We Go to Church." When you're ready, I'll lead the singing, and the kids can follow you in the motions.**

(Sing the following verses to the tune of "Here We Go 'Round the Mulberry Bush." The children begin by pretending to be asleep and are awakened by the alarm clock. Do appropriate motions for each activity.)

This is the way we get out of bed, / get out of bed, / get out of bed. / This is the way we get out of bed, / Every Sunday morning.

(Other verses could include: This is the way we wash our face, brush our teeth, put on our clothes, comb our hair, eat our food, go to church, hear God's Word.)

ERLENE: **Wasn't that fun? Don't forget to come to church next Sunday. I'll have some jelly bean eggs from my nest for everyone who's here.**

SOMETHING TO CROW ABOUT

Puppet Used: Any rooster puppet.

The Official Announcer

Preparation: Make a badge with the words "Official Announcer" on it to be attached to the rooster's chest.

ROOSTER: COCK-A-DOODLE-DOO! COCK-A-DOODLE-DOO! Wake up, wake up, you sleepy heads. It's time to get out of bed. COCK-A-DOODLE-DOO! Wake up! Get out of bed. COCK-A-DOODLE-DOO! COCK-A—

INTERVIEWER (*interrupting*): That's enough, Booster Rooster. We heard you. But we're already out of bed.

ROOSTER: Ohhh. . . but its my job to wake folks. Now I don't have anything to do.

INTERVIEWER: Oh, yes, you have something to do. You're the official announcer around here.

ROOSTER: I am? Really?

INTERVIEWER: Yes.

ROOSTER: COCK-A-DOODLE-DOO! COCK-A-DOODLE-DOO! I am now an offish—offish—offish. A what?

INTERVIEWER (slowly): An official announcer.

ROOSTER: I am an O-fish-ial announcer. (*Struts around.*) I am an o-fish-ial announcer. I am an o-fish-ial announcer. Uh—what is an o-fish-ial announcer?

INTERVIEWER: Well, you've always announced the coming of a new day. Now you'll announce something else—important happenings here at our church. That is, of course, if you'll accept the job.

ROOSTER: Accept? I was born for such a job as this.

INTERVIEWER: Then here is your official announcer badge. (*Puts badge on rooster.*)

ROOSTER: Oh, thank you, thank you. (*Struts around some more.*) Look at ME! Look at ME!

INTERVIEWER: An official announcer doesn't call attention to himself. He gets everyone to pay attention to the announcements. You will be very good at that with your loud crowing.

ROOSTER: Oh. Hey, I do have a good crower, don't I? Okay, here goes! COCK-A-DOODLE-DOO! COCK-A-DOODLE-DOO! I wish to make an of-fish-ial announcement . . . Uh . . . I don't know what the announcement is.

INTERVIEWER: Oh, here it is. (*Holds a note so rooster can read.*)

ROOSTER: COCK-A-DOODLE-DOO! COCK-A-DOODLE-DOO! Ladies and gentlemen here's the announcement: (*Reads it.*)

Good News

ROOSTER: COCK-A-DOODLE-DOO! COCK-A-DOODLE-DOO! I come before you today as your o-fish-ial announcer. And I have superduper, get-out-your-whooper, do-a-loop-the-looper, publish-the-scooper news. It is . . . (*clears his throat*)—uh . . . (*He begins again.*) COCK-A-DOODLE-DOO! COCK-A-DOODLE-DOO! I have superduper, get-out-your-whooper, do-a-loop-the-looper, publish-the-scooper news. It is . . . uh . . . COCK-A-DOODLE-DOO! COCK-A-DOODLE-DOO! Ladies and gentlemen, I have superduper, get-out-your-whooper, do-a-loop-the-looper, publish-the-scooper news. It is . . . uh . . .

INTERVIEWER: Booster Rooster, what's the announcement?

ROOSTER (*hanging head*): I forgot it.

INTERVIEWER: Forgot it? But you remembered all those words describing your announcement. How could you forget the announcement?

ROOSTER: I guess that's all the words my remembery will hold. I'm sorry I let you down. Now I guess you'll take away my o-fish-ial announcer badge.

INTERVIEWER: No. I'll remind you of the announcement.

ROOSTER: You will! Oh, thank you, thank you. I'll listen. (*Interviewer whispers in rooster's ear.*)

ROOSTER: Ladies and gentlemen, I have superduper, get-out-your-whooper, do-a-loop-the-looper, publish-the- scooper news for you. It is . . . (*Makes the announcement.*)

Where's My Crower?

ROOSTER (*very weakly begins to crow.*): Cock-a . . . Cock-a . . . Cock . . . Oh, dear me! Oh, dear me! What has happened? I can't crow. Cock . . . a . . . It's no use. My crower won't crow. NOW what am I going to do? Why, I believe my crower is lost. How can I be an o-fish-ial announcer without a crower? Has anyone out there seen my crower? (*He begins to look up and down and all around.*) It has simply vanished. Where can my crower be?

INTERVIEWER: Oh, you must have your crower. We have a very important announcement to make today.

ROOSTER: Please everybody look under your chairs. Is my crower there? No? Did one of you eat it for breakfast?

INTERVIEWER: When was the last time you used it, Booster?

ROOSTER: Yesterday morning, when I crowed to wake up the world.

INTERVIEWER: You didn't wake up the world today?

ROOSTER: No. I overslept. Hey, I know where my crower is! I left it under my pillow. Quick! Let me get it! (*He exits, going behind the stage or out of sight elsewhere. When he returns he can crow.*) COCK-A-DOODLE-DOO! COCK-A-DOODLE-DOO! COCK-A-DOODLE-DOO! COCK-A—

INTERVIEWER: That's enough. Let's get on with the announcement, Booster. (*He makes the announcement.*)

SUGAR BEAR & THE SWEET SHOP CONTEST

Puppet Used: Any bear puppet.

Contest Goal: To earn tokens that will allow children to "buy" items in the Sweet Shop.

Contest Rules: The children earn tokens (something like play money or checkers) for performing the assigned tasks—one token for each visitor brought, each verse learned, etc. At the close of each service, they bring their tokens to the Sweet Shop (consisting of small wrapped candies and gum, cookies, little boxes of sweetened cereal, or other sweets) and exchange them for their choice of sweets. If you wish, keep a record of all the tokens each child earns and at the end of the contest give the sweets which remain in the Sweet Shop to the child who has earned the most tokens.

Use Sugar Bear to promote the contest each service with the following dialogues.

Day One

INTERVIEWER: Here's Sugar Bear, our friend who loves sweets.

BEAR: **I love candy—it's so neat; I love anything that is sweet.**

INTERVIEWER: The children like sweets, too, so we're giving them a chance to buy things in the Sweet Shop, such as *(names items)*.

BEAR *(very excited)*: **WOW! Lots of sweets! Yummy, yummy in the tummy! Where is it? I want to go to the Sweet Shop right NOW!** *(Suddenly stops.)* **But you say you BUY things there? Then I can't go, 'cause I don't have any money.** *(Looks at children.)* **Oh, please, please, will somebody gimme some money?**

INTERVIEWER: Oh, you don't need money to buy things in the Sweet Shop. You need TOKENS, and you have to EARN them.

BEAR: **Well, tell me quick how to earn some. I just gotta go today.**

INTERVIEWER: No one goes today. The contest starts next week. When the children bring visitors and learn Bible verses they earn tokens to buy sweets.

BEAR: **And Sugar Bear can he be in the contest, too, huh? PLEASE?**

INTERVIEWER: Yes.

BEAR: **Oh, goody! I'll earn the mostest tokens of all, 'cause I love candy—it's so neat; I love anything that is sweet.**

Day Two

BEAR: **Oh, JOY, JOY, JOY! This is the day the Sweet Shop opens. I will go and get my treat; I'll choose anything that is sweet.**

INTERVIEWER: How many tokens did you earn, Sugar Bear?

BEAR: **Tokens? Oh, you mean those things you get for bringing visitors and learning verses?**

INTERVIEWER: Yes. Did you earn some tokens?

BEAR: **Well, I was gonna do it, but—uh—I guess I didn't. I was too busy. Yes, that's it. I was too busy.**

INTERVIEWER: What were you doing all the time?

BEAR: **Playing ball and hide-and-go-seek and watching the man at the candy store—sometimes he lets me have the lickin's. And I was extra sleepy, so I slept a lot.**

INTERVIEWER: Okay, Sugar Bear. You goofed off all week, so now you can't go to the Sweet Shop.

BEAR: **Oh, I'm so sorry! It won't happen again. Please lemme go today!**

INTERVIEWER: You know the rules, Sugar Bear: no tokens—no Sweet Shop. Next time you work harder.

BEAR: **I will. Eating sweets is the best thing in the world.**

INTERVIEWER: I know something better. In Psalm 19:9 and 10 we are told that God's Word is "sweeter also than honey and the honeycomb." It should mean more to us than anything sweet for our tummies. Let's all learn those verses this week and bring others to hear God's Word.

Day Three

INTERVIEWER: Sugar Bear, have you worked hard this week to earn some tokens? Will you be able to go to the Sweet Shop?

BEAR: **Yes, yes! Please gimme two tokens.**

INTERVIEWER: Oh, I'm so proud of you! I guess, then, you're ready to say the Bible verse for us?

BEAR: **Yes.**

INTERVIEWER: All right. Let's hear it.

BEAR: **Humpty-Dumpty sat on a wall; / Humpty-Dumpty had a great fall; / All the king's horses and all the king's men / Couldn't put Humpty back together again.**

INTERVIEWER *(shocked)*: Sugar Bear! That's not a Bible verse.

BEAR: **It's not?**

INTERVIEWER: You know it's not. Why didn't you learn the memory verse?

BEAR: **It was too hard. I didn't think you'd ask me to say the verse out loud. I just thought I could say I knew it.**

INTERVIEWER: Oh, no. We have to hear you say it. Did you bring a visitor? You said you earned two tokens.

BEAR: **Yep. I asked** *(any other puppet present)*.

INTERVIEWER: When did you ask him?

BEAR: **Uh—after I got here this morning.**

INTERVIEWER: Then he can't be your visitor. He was already here at church. A visitor is one who comes because of your invitation during the week.

BEAR: **Well, next time I'm gonna have me some tokens, and I'm going to the Sweet Shop.** *(Looks at children.)* **If you'll earn some tokens, too, raise your hands. Wow! Look at all those hands! Don't too many of**

SUGAR BEAR & THE SWEET SHOP CONTEST *(continued)*

you do it, or there won't be any sweets for me.

INTERVIEWER: No danger of that. There'll be plenty for all.

BEAR: **Oh, goody, goody! There'll be lots and lots of sweets; so we all can have some treats.**

Day Four

Preparation: Fill a small bag with buttons of various sizes and tape it to Sugar Bear's hand before he comes out.

BEAR *(very excited)*: **I DID it! I DID it this time! I got some tokens.**

INTERVIEWER: Good for you! Are they in that bag?

BEAR: **Yessum. Now lemme go to the Sweet Shop.**

INTERVIEWER: Wait a minute. How many tokens do you have?

BEAR: **Fifty-'leven.**

INTERVIEWER: I think we'd better look at your tokens. *(Takes bag and pours buttons out on a table.)* Why, Sugar Bear! What have you done here? These are buttons—not tokens.

BEAR: **Well, they look a little bit like the tokens. Please, won't they do?**

INTERVIEWER: Of course not. This is cheating, Sugar Bear. Why do you do things like this?

BEAR: **'Cause I want some sweets.**

INTERVIEWER: If you really want them, you'll work for them. Tell me again what you must do to earn tokens.

BEAR: **Learn Bible verses and bring visitors. And don't bring buttons.**

INTERVIEWER: Right. How many of you children really did earn tokens? That's great! You see, Sugar Bear, it CAN be done.

BEAR: **I'll do it next time, I betcha.**

Day Five

Preparation: Dress Sugar Bear in a wig, a dress or shawl, and colored glasses.

BEAR *(in a squeaky, disguised voice)*: **Hello, folks. My name is Honey Bear. I'm Sugar Bear's visitor. He couldn't come today, but I'm s'posed to get his sweets for him.**

INTERVIEWER: Oh my, you look very much like Sugar Bear.

BEAR: **But I'm not. I'm his sister, Honey Bear.**

INTERVIEWER: Why couldn't Sugar Bear come today?

BEAR: **Uh—well, he's—uh—sick. Yes, that's it. He's sick.**

INTERVIEWER: That's too bad. But if he's sick, I don't think he should have any sweets. So I won't send him any.

BEAR: **Oh, he's not THAT sick. Sweets will make him feel LOTS better. So just GIVE 'em to me.**

INTERVIEWER: No. I'm glad Sugar Bear invited you to be his visitor, but he'll have to get his sweets when he's here himself.

BEAR *(in real voice)*: **But I AM myself. You can give ME the sweets now! Ulp—I mean—** *(resumes disguised*

voice) **I, Honey Bear, would be glad to take the sweets to Sugar Bear, PLEASE.**

INTERVIEWER: Just as I thought all along. You ARE Sugar Bear. You tried to trick me again. If you'd work half as hard at inviting visitors and learning verses as you do at ways to trick me, you'd have gone to the Sweet Shop by now. But at least I'm sure the children will work hard this week, won't you? Remember, the one who earns the most tokens in the whole contest will get to take home everything that's left in the Sweet Shop.

BEAR: **It'll be ME. I'm gonna start working hard. I'll beat everybody. You just wait and see!**

Day Six

Preparation: In this dialogue Sugar Bear brings a note with him. In order for all the children to see the words, use a large piece of paper or cardboard and make the letters uneven, the way a child would print. Sugar Bear can bring the note under his arm, or it can be on a nearby table. See the script for the words to write on the note.

INTERVIEWER: Hello, Sugar Bear. I hope you're going to get some tokens today. Did you bring a visitor and learn the memory verse?

BEAR: **I tried, but I couldn't. But I think it's gonna be all right, 'cause I brought a note from my mama. Here it is.** *(Indicates note under his arm or on the table.)*

INTERVIEWER: A note from your mother? How will that help? Let's see what the note says. *(Gets note and holds it up for audience to see while reading.)* Deer Teecjer: Sugar Bear wurked reel hard to git a vissuter, but nobuddy wood cum. He cain't lurn no vers. Theys 2 hard. Pleez, pleez, pleez, let him have sum sweets. Mama.

BEAR: **Now, you'll give me some tokens, won't you? 'Cause Mama said to do it.**

INTERVIEWER: Sugar Bear, your mother didn't write this note.

BEAR: **How did you know? I mean, what makes you think she didn't write it?**

INTERVIEWER: There are too many mistakes. And she wouldn't sign her name "Mama" when writing to me. I'm not her daughter/son.

BEAR: **Uh-oh.**

INTERVIEWER: This is another one of your tricks, Sugar Bear. When are you going to start doing the right thing?

BEAR: **You mean, like really working at bringing visitors and learning verses?**

INTERVIEWER: Yes. The contest is almost over, you know.

BEAR: **Oh, I'm sorry I've been so bad. I promise I'll work hard this week—truly I will.**

INTERVIEWER: Good. Then maybe you'll be the proud owner of some tokens next time.

BEAR: **I'm getting excited. I think working for the tokens will be lots of fun. Hey, kids, let's all work hard, okay?**

SUGAR BEAR & THE SWEET SHOP CONTEST *(continued)*

Day Seven

Preparation: Bring a puppet as Sugar Bear's visitor, one that has not been used in church during the contest, if possible. A ventriloquist should put one puppet on each hand or the two puppets can appear in the stage.

BEAR *(very excited and happy)*: **Look, look, I did bring a visitor. I did! It wasn't as hard as I thought.**

VISITOR: Thank you, Sugar Bear, for inviting me to church. I like it here very much.

BEAR: You do? That's nice!

VISITOR: I wish you'd asked me a long time ago.

BEAR: Me, too. Say, (name of interviewer), I know the Bible verse, too.

INTERVIEWER: Wonderful! Let's hear it.

BEAR *(repeats verse without a mistake)*: **There. How's that?**

INTERVIEWER: Perfect. Now you'll get two tokens. Earning them the right way wasn't so hard, after all, was it?

BEAR: No, ma'am. Oh, goody, goody! Yummies for the tummy! But you know what's even better than that?

INTERVIEWER: Oh, you really think something's better than eating sweets?

BEAR: Yes. It's the good feeling you get inside for doing the right thing. You try it, kids, you'll see!
(If more days are involved in the contest, let Sugar Bear bring a visitor and say the verse each time, promoting the contest by a good example.)

JACK & JILL CLIMB THE HILL CONTEST

Puppets Used: Any boy and girl puppet.

Contest Goal: To see whether Jack or Jill reaches the top of the hill first. Each moves up the hill if its team earns the most points for the day.

Contest Rules: Divide the children into two teams, boys and girls, or some other division. The Jack and Jill puppets in the following dialogues are team captains. The contest is similar to a World Series in that there is a winner each day, but the overall winner is the team who wins the most times. Points earned one day are counted for that day only and are not accumulated.

Decide what the teams must do to earn points, such as giving one point for each team member who says the memory verse and one point for each visitor brought. Or you could simply find the winning team each day by counting to see which team has the most members present.

Preparation: On a piece of 27- by 36-inch flannel, draw a line from the lower left corner to the upper right corner, depicting a hill. Attach the flannel to a board. Decide how many times a team must win to reach the top of the hill. (If it's five, this could be accomplished in as few as five days or as many as nine.) From left to right across the top of the flannel board write out numbers, beginning with "1" and ending with the number of times you have decided must be won in order to win the contest. (See Figure 50: Jack and Jill.)

From cardboard, cut out two silhouette figures to represent Jack and Jill. Glue pieces of flannel to their backs. Cut them in two at the waist and fasten them together again with brads, so they can be bent. Place the figures at the bottom of the hill.

Moving the Figures on the Hill: If Jack's team wins the first day, the figure of Jack is moved to the number "1" spot on the flannel board. The other figure remains at the bottom. If Jack's team wins the second day, his figure moves to number "2," indicating that his team has won 2 days. If Jill's team wins, her figure moves to the first number with Jack, each team having won 1 day. Each figure continues to move up the hill until one reaches the top.

Contest Chant: The following chant can be said on each day of the contest by the winning team.

> Jack and Jill went up the hill
> To fetch a pail of prizes;
> Jack/Jill fell down and broke his/her crown;
> But look at Jack/Jill as he/she rises.

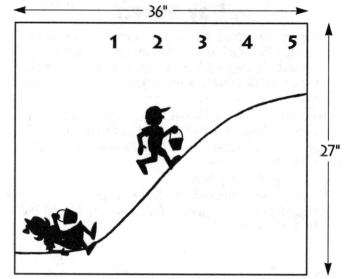

FIGURE 50: JACK & JILL

Introduction

(To be given the day before the contest begins.)

INTERVIEWER: Boys and girls, I have some twins I'd like for you to meet. Their names are Jack—

JACK: Hi! I'm Jack.

INTERVIEWER: —and Jill.

JILL: Hello, I'm Jill.

INTERVIEWER: They're the captains for our new contest: Jack and Jill Climb the Hill.

JACK: I'm the captain of the boys' team (*or if not all boys, he gives his team's name*). **That's the winning team, of course.**

JILL: You made one teensy mistake, Jack. I'm the captain of the winning team. It's the girls (*or gives other name who will win*).

JACK: NO, NO! (*He chants the following.*)

> **Jack and Jill went up the hill**
> **To fetch a pail of prizes,**
> **Jill fell down and broke her crown,**
> **But look at Jack as he rises.**

JILL: Oh, YEAH? You got THAT wrong, too. It goes like this:

> Jack and Jill went up the hill
> To fetch a pail of prizes;
> Jack fell down and broke his crown,
> But look at Jill as she rises.

INTERVIEWER: We won't really know which way it is until we have the contest, will we?

JACK: Oh, I know right now. It will be the BOYS (*or team name*) **every time.**

JILL: No. It will be the GIRLS (*or team name*). (*They exit, each yelling for their team.*)

JACK & JILL CLIMB THE HILL CONTEST *(continued)*

Day One

INTERVIEWER: Here are our team captains again.

JACK: I'm Jack, captain of the winning team. YEA, TEAM!

JILL: No. I'M captain of the winning team. I'm Jill.

JACK: The girls can't win.

JILL: Why not?

JACK: Because their captain isn't strong enough.

JILL: *(Jill pretends to sniff the air and then leans toward Jack's underarm.)* You're right—I'm not as strong as you.

JACK: Hey!

INTERVIEWER: Jack! Jill! Let's keep this a CLEAN contest.

JILL: Well, I'll vote for that, won't you, Jack? Shall we raise our hands . . . HIGH?

JACK: Yes—NO! She's being mean.

INTERVIEWER: Why don't you just forget the whole thing?

JILL: Does that include HIM?

JACK: Oh, yeah? Nobody forgets the GREAT Jack.

JILL: Well, listen, IRVING, let's do keep it clean.

JACK: Huh? IRVING? I'm not Irving! I'm Jack.

JILL: Oh, I'm sorry. I forgot!

INTERVIEWER: Let's have no more of this behavior. Root for your TEAM, and that's all.

JACK: Okay. The BOYS *(or team name)* **will win.**

JILL: No. The GIRLS *(or team name)* will.

Day Two

INTERVIEWER: I think it would be nice if you would sing something today. How about it, Jack?

JACK: I don't want to sing.

JILL: I'll sing.

JACK: Nobody asked you to sing.

JILL: Well, you won't sing, so I will.

JACK: You know what's worse than CAN'T sing and WON'T? Can't sing and WILL!

JILL: I can too sing, and I'm going to do it.

JACK: You couldn't carry a tune if it was in a BUCKET.

JILL: Don't talk about me. You don't know music.

JACK: Oh, yeah? I can pick up anything musical.

JILL: Then let me see you PICK UP an organ.

INTERVIEWER: I think the boys and girls would like to hear BOTH of you sing.

JILL: Okay. *(Sings the following verse to the tune of "London Bridge Is Falling Down.")* All the boys *(or team name)* are falling down, falling down, falling down; / All the boys are falling down, off the hillside.

JACK: Listen to my song. *(Sings the following verse to the tune of "Three Blind Mice.")* **Loser girls, loser girls; / See how they fall: see how they fall! / They tried to climb to the very top; / They huffed and they puffed but they went KERPLOP! / Those loser girls.**

Day Three

JACK: Hi! Remember me? I'm Jack.

JILL: And I'm Jill.

JACK: I'm captain of the boys' team *(or team name)*. **Will all the fellows raise your hands? Kids, you just saw the hands of the WINNING TEAM.**

JILL: Well, I want all the girls to wave at me. You see, there's REAL ACTION. We don't just raise our hands; we wave them. WE'LL be the winners.

JACK: Girls CAN'T win.

JILL: Yes, we CAN. We'll beat the SOCKS off you boys.

JACK: You're not going to take OUR socks off.

JILL: Oh, I mean we'll WIN the contest. We wouldn't really take your socks off, because then it would STINK around here.

JACK: The girls are the ones that—

INTERVIEWER: Now, don't say something naughty, Jack.

JILL: I have two words to say: HOORAY, GIRLS!

JACK: And I have three: BOYS WILL WIN!

Day Four

(In this dialogue the team captain whose team is ahead in the contest is designated No. 1 and the other team's captain is No. 2.)

INTERVIEWER: We're having fun in our contest, aren't we? Both sides must keep working hard. Either one could still win.

No. 1: We're ahead, so WE'LL win. Listen to this: 1—2—3—4—5, we'll skin you boys/girls *(or team name)* **alive.**

No. 2: 6—7—8—9—10, we're going to win again.

No. 1: 10—9—8—7—6, we'll put you in a fix.

No. 2: 5—4—3—2—1, we'll be the team who won.

INTERVIEWER: It's getting exciting. Boys, you work hard for Jack; and girls you help Jill by doing your very best.

JACK: Which is not good enough.

JILL: But it's still better than the boys.

Day Five

(In this dialogue the team captain whose team is ahead in the contest is designated No. 1 and the other team's captain is No. 2.)

No. 1: Do you know why you girls/boys *(or team name)* **fall down so much?**

No. 2: No.

No. 1: You're falling down because you can't fall UP.

No. 2: Well, if all the boys/girls on YOUR team climbed to the top of the hill, which they won't, of course, I could carry them DOWN all by myself.

No. 1: No you couldn't. No way. Impossible.

No. 2: Yes, I could. I'd carry them DOWN all by myself.

No. 1: How?

No. 2: I'd carry them DOWN on a FEATHER.

No. 1: What are you talking about?

JACK & JILL CLIMB THE HILL CONTEST *(continued)*

No. 2: DOWN—that fuzzy stuff on a feather. I'd carry IT to all of you.

No. 1: Oh, go fly a kite.

No. 2: I will—when the boys/girls reach the top of the hill first.

No. 1: You'll never make it. You'll fall down, and we won't need a feather to bring you down.

Day Six

(In this dialogue the captain who is ahead in the contest is designated No. 1 and the other is No. 2.)

No. 1: I have a song I wish to sing today. *(Sing the following verse to the tune of: "Where, Oh, Where Has My Little Dog Gone?")*
Oh, where, oh, where have the weak *(boys/girls or team name)* **gone?**
Oh, where, oh, where can they be?
For we are ahead in the con-test,
And we will win, don't you see?

No. 2: We've just LET you win so you won't be discouraged, but never again. This is our song from now on *(to the tune of "I've Been Working on the Railroad")*:
We are going to win the contest
Ev'ry single day;
As we're climbing ever higher
We'll sing along our way,
We will reach the top before you,
So you be wise.
You had might as well surrender,
For we will get the prize.

No. 1: That's very funny, because it's all WRONG. Ha, ha, ha.

No. 2: You won't laugh next time. You'll CRY.

No. 1: Yeah—all the way to the TOP OF THE HILL!

Day Seven

JILL: Hi, folks! I'm sure you remember this nice guy here. He's my brother, Jack.

JACK: Hi! And this sweet girl is my sister, Jill.

INTERVIEWER: What is this? You two are acting nice to each other and saying sweet things.

JACK: Yeah, I've turned over a new leaf.

INTERVIEWER: Jill, is that true?

JILL: That's because he was going to get turned over someone's knee.

JACK: Uh, huh, and you were going to get grounded.

INTERVIEWER: Well, I'm still impressed. It means you CAN get along.

JACK: Yeah, I guess she's okay.

JILL: And Jack can be a nice brother, really.

JACK: Thank you. You're a nice sister.

JILL: I think you're good looking, Jack.

JACK: And I think you're pretty, Jill.

INTERVIEWER: And I think you both may be carrying this a little far.

JILL: And I even hope that the boys *(or team name)* will win . . .

JACK: All right!

JILL: . . . someday . . . some contest . . .

JACK: What?!

INTERVIEWER: I didn't think it could last at the rate they were going.

JACK: Well, then, I don't want the girls to win, either. I hope you fall down and stay there.

JILL: Your wish will not be granted, for BOYS can't win.

JACK: Oh, yeah? GIRLS can't win.

JILL: Yeah?

JACK: Yeah!

INTERVIEWER: We're back to normal, I see. For a minute I was going to take your temperatures. So who's going to win the contest?

JACK: The BOYS.

JILL: The GIRLS. *(They go off arguing.)*

Day Eight

(Continue some similar dialogues if the contest extends beyond eight days. Use this brief dialogue for the last day, after one team has won. Here the winner is designated No. 1, and the loser, No. 2.)

INTERVIEWER: The contest is over now, Jack and Jill. I think both teams did a good job, didn't they?

No. 1: Especially mine.

No. 2: My team worked hard, too.

INTERVIEWER: Actually, everyone is a winner, because of all the good things that all the children have done.

Jack: Jill and I aren't really mad at each other. We just sound like it sometimes, because we're rooting for our teams.

INTERVIEWER: You need to be careful that you don't hurt each other's feelings.

JILL: Jack and I are really good buddies. I'm glad he's my brother.

JACK: And I'm glad she's my sister. But next time we have a contest, the BOYS *(or team name)* **will win.**

JILL: No, the GIRLS will. *(They go off arguing again.)*

TALKING BIBLE TEACHES ABOUT THE BIBLE

Puppet Used: Talking Bible. See Part 2, chapter 12, for instructions for making the Talking Bible and the Bible bookmarks.

Facts About the Bible

Scripture References: Psalm 119:89,160; Matthew 24:35; 2 Timothy 3:16; 2 Peter 1:21

Lesson Theme: The Bible is the inspired Word of God, recorded by many men over a long period of years.

Preparation: Prepare a list of questions, similar to the ones in this dialogue, to be used with a quiz game at the end of the dialogue.

INTERVIEWER: Mister Bible, we want to learn some facts about you today. First, who wrote you?

BIBLE: God the Holy Spirit wrote me.

INTERVIEWER: Do you mean that God wrote you with His own hand?

BIBLE: He wrote the Ten Commandments with His own hand.

INTERVIEWER: Did He write all of the Bible that way?

BIBLE: No. Peter tells us, "Men led by the Holy Spirit spoke words from God"—2 Peter 1:21.

INTERVIEWER: Oh, men wrote down the words. Did they write just whatever they thought God wanted to say?

BIBLE: No. Paul told Timothy, "All scripture is given by inspiration of God"—2 Timothy 3:16.

INTERVIEWER: What does "inspiration" mean?

BIBLE: God the Holy Spirit guided each man to write the words that God wanted, and He kept them from making mistakes.

INTERVIEWER: How many men did God use to write the Bible?

BIBLE: More than forty.

INTERVIEWER: Did they all sit down together, like a committee, and write the Bible?

BIBLE: No, my first book was written about 1500 years before Christ was born, and the last one, about 90 years after He was born.

INTERVIEWER: Why, that took about 1600 years! . . . So there are forty books in the Bible, right?

BIBLE: No. Sixty-six.

INTERVIEWER: Sixty-six? Oh, so some men wrote more than one book. I see. But that's a lot of books. Is there any way to divide them up, so they can be studied more easily?

BIBLE: I have two main divisions, called the Old Testament and the New Testament. Testament, you know, means "promise," or "agreement."

INTERVIEWER: Oh, I see. So there is an old promise from God and a new promise. Interesting. . . . So how many books are in the Old Promise and how many are in the New?

BIBLE: Thirty-nine in the Old; twenty-seven in the New.

INTERVIEWER: So are there any more breakdowns in the Bible?

BIBLE: Oh, no. All my parts hold up very well.

INTERVIEWER *(laughs)*: Yes, but you know what I mean.

BIBLE: Yes. The Old Testament has books of history, books of prophecy, books of poetry. And the New Testament has books called gospels and letters.

INTERVIEWER: I see. And how much of all that is true and how much of it's pretend?

BIBLE: All true. Each word is true and is God's Word. Psalm 119:160 says, "Your words are true from the start."

INTERVIEWER: You said your first book was written about 1500 before Jesus' birth. That makes you almost 3,500 years old. How much longer do you think you can last?

BIBLE: The Psalmist said, "Lord, your word is everlasting" —Psalm 119:89. Jesus said, "The whole world, earth and sky, will be destroyed, but the words I have said will never be destroyed" —Matthew 24:35.

INTERVIEWER: Mister Bible, you are God's Word. He wrote you, and that makes you the most important Book in the whole world! The whole world should pay attention to you, especially we Christians.

The Talking Bible and Lazybones Christian*

Scripture References: Matthew 4:4; 2 Corinthians 7:1; 1 Timothy 4:8

Lesson Theme: As Christians we can't afford to neglect our Bibles.

Preparation: The interviewer (whether a ventriloquist or one who stands outside a stage and talks to the Bible) will play the part of Lazybones Christian. Sprinkle some powder on the cover of the Talking Bible to represent dust and place some strings on it for cobwebs.

LAZYBONES CHRISTIAN: Hi, folks! I want you to know that I've brought my Bible to church today. *(Holds up Bible, or points to it in the stage, but does not look at it.)*

BIBLE: That's the first time he's noticed me in over a month.

LAZYBONES CHRISTIAN *(startled)*: What? Who said that? *(Continues to look at audience as though trying to discover the speaker.)*

BIBLE: I did—your Bible.

LAZYBONES CHRISTIAN *(looking at the Bible)*: That's ridiculous. BOOKS can't talk.

*Published May/June, 1988, *Evangelizing Today's Child*

TALKING BIBLE TEACHES ABOUT THE BIBLE *(continued)*

BIBLE: **Son, I've been trying to talk to you for a long time, but you won't listen.**

LAZYBONES CHRISTIAN *(astonished)*: It IS talking!

BIBLE: **Yes, and I have a complaint to make.**

LAZYBONES CHRISTIAN: A complaint?

BIBLE: **Yes. Kachoo! Kachoo! All this dust is making me sneeze.**

LAZYBONES CHRISTIAN: You are sort of dusty. I hadn't noticed. How did that happen?

BIBLE: **You've left me on the shelf too long. Kachoo!**

LAZYBONES CHRISTIAN *(whispering)*: Shhh! These folks will think I don't read you.

BIBLE: **Young man, you don't.**

LAZYBONES CHRISTIAN *(defensively)*: Why, I do, too—but just not lately. I've been so busy.

BIBLE: **You should never be too busy for me. Why didn't you have time for me today?**

LAZYBONES CHRISTIAN: Well, I had to eat breakfast.

BIBLE: **Jesus said, in Matthew 4:4, "It is written in the Scriptures, 'A person does not live only by eating bread. But a person lives by everything the Lord says.'"**

LAZYBONES CHRISTIAN: I had to take a bath, and—

BIBLE: **But you have these promises from God. You should make yourself pure—free from anything that makes body or soul unclean—2 Corinthians 7:1.**

LAZYBONES CHRISTIAN: I had to exercise so I can be strong and healthy.

BIBLE: **It's true that training your body helps you in some ways, but serving God helps you in every way. Serving God brings you blessings in this life and in the future life, too—1 Timothy 4:8.**

LAZYBONES CHRISTIAN: I—I didn't think about that.

BIBLE: **You really need me, son, but you don't even know me very well.**

LAZYBONES CHRISTIAN: Oh, I wouldn't say that.

BIBLE: **All right, let's have a little pop quiz: Hezekiah is one of my books. True or false?**

LAZYBONES CHRISTIAN: It's false . . . no—true!

BIBLE: **If you knew me, you would be sure: You would know there is no book of Hezekiah in me.**

LAZYBONES CHRISTIAN *(humbly)*: Yes, sir.

BIBLE: **Tell me, the Book of Hebrews, is it in my New Testament or my Old Testament?**

LAZYBONES CHRISTIAN: Well, I've heard of the three Hebrew children and the fiery furnace. That's in the Old Testament. I bet they're in the Book of Hebrews—the Old Testament.

BIBLE: **Sorry, son. You're thinking is good, but your knowledge is poor. The three Hebrew children are in the Old Testament, but the Book of Hebrews is in the New.**

LAZYBONES CHRISTIAN: Well, uh—I—

BIBLE: **Can you quote any of my verses?**

LAZYBONES CHRISTIAN: Uh, well, probably I can.

BIBLE: **Okay, which ones?**

LAZYBONES CHRISTIAN: Oh, now, you wouldn't ask me to do that here in front of all these people?

BIBLE *(insisting)*: **It's THAT important.**

LAZYBONES CHRISTIAN: Well. Oh, I know one! "Cleanliness is next to godliness."

BIBLE: **That's not a Bible verse.**

LAZYBONES CHRISTIAN: Hmmm. My mother quotes it like it is. . . . Well, how about "Spare the rod and spoil the child"?

BIBLE: **Could you give me chapter and verse for that?**

LAZYBONES CHRISTIAN: Well, no.

BIBLE: **That's because it's not in me. Something similar, but not that. You ought to know exactly what's in me. Otherwise, someone could take you away from my truth and you wouldn't even know it. Son, my truth is intended to light your way, to help you avoid things that would make you trip and fall—to shepherd you along the path of life.**

LAZYBONES CHRISTIAN: But the Lord is my shepherd.

BIBLE: **But how do you learn about the Lord—and what He wants and how He would lead you—unless you read His Word, me?**

LAZYBONES CHRISTIAN: I guess I never thought about it that way.

BIBLE: **You're missing out on a lot.**

LAZYBONES CHRISTIAN: I am?

BIBLE: **Besides giving you knowledge about God—so you know what to believe—I can encourage you when you are down, remind you of what God has done for you and will do for you; I can teach you how to become a grown-up Christian.**

LAZYBONES CHRISTIAN: Really?

BIBLE: **Yes.**

LAZYBONES CHRISTIAN: So the more I read you and study you and memorize you . . . and obey you, the stronger I'll become and the more I'll be like Jesus?

BIBLE: **That's the idea. I'm more important than any other book you'll ever read. Don't neglect me—it's a matter of life and death—spiritual life and death.**

LAZYBONES CHRISTIAN: I'm glad we had this little talk.

BIBLE: **I'll be glad to talk to to you any time; just open me and read. And, one more thing, try not to let me get so dusty.**

LAZYBONES CHRISTIAN: No, sir. I won't.

TALKING BIBLE TEACHES ABOUT THE BIBLE *(continued)*

Faithful Unto Death

Scripture References: Matthew 24:35

Lesson Theme: Many people over the years have given their lives so that we can have the Bible today.

Preparation: You will use both your regular Bible and the Talking Bible puppet for this dialogue.

INTERVIEWER: I brought my Bible with me today. *(Holds up a regular Bible.)* How many of you brought yours? Hold them up high—unless you brought the family Bible—so we can see them. Thank you. You may put them down. I'm glad to see so many Bibles. Have you ever forgotten your Bible? If so, listen carefully to a little history of the Bible and maybe it'll help you realize what a privilege it is to be able to carry a Bible around with you.

BIBLE: **You should all be very glad that you have the freedom to have a Bible, which you can bring to church.**

INTERVIEWER: What do you mean?

BIBLE: **You couldn't have owned one if you had lived in the days of my forefathers.**

INTERVIEWER: Your forefathers? . . . Oh, do you mean earlier translations and versions of the Bible?

BIBLE: **Yes. I was thinking about the Roman Emperor Diocletian and his reign.**

INTERVIEWER: Diocletian was an emperor in Rome about three hundred years after Jesus was here on earth. He ordered that every Bible be destroyed. Many brave Christians were tortured and some were killed for hiding their Bibles from him.

BIBLE: **Tell the children about Timothy and his wife, Maura.***

INTERVIEWER: They were persecuted and then crucified simply because they wouldn't give up their copy of God's Word.

INTERVIEWER: Right. If Diocletian had been able to destroy every copy of the Bible, we wouldn't have any Bibles today.

BIBLE: **And then there was a time in England, when Henry VIII was king.**

INTERVIEWER: Ahh, about the time Christopher Columbus discovered America. Ordinary people weren't supposed to own Bibles then—at least not during the first part of his reign. So what happened if someone secretly owned one?

BIBLE: **If that person was caught, he was punished. Also, the king didn't want the Bible to be printed in English.**

INTERVIEWER: Oh, that's right. The Bible was still using Latin at the time—*E Pluribus Unum, et cetera, et cetera*—the language of the Roman Empire and the Catholic church after the third century.

BIBLE: **Do you remember the story of William Tyndale?**

INTERVIEWER: Yes. An Englishman who wanted the common people to have copies of the Bible in their own English language, so he began to translate it for them.

BIBLE: **But he was killed for doing so.**

INTERVIEWER: Yes. William Tyndale died just because he wanted people to be able to read the Bible for themselves. The man who produced the *Living Bible* named his publishing company after him.

BIBLE: **Because of such brave Christians, I'm still here today.**

INTERVIEWER: God promised to keep His Word safe, didn't He?

BIBLE: **Yes. In Matthew 24:35 Jesus says, "The whole world, earth and sky, will be destroyed, but the words I have said will never be destroyed."**

INTERVIEWER *(to audience)*: We love the Bible, don't we? How could we get along without it? We thank the Lord for the brave Christians who kept His Word safe so we could have our copies.

BIBLE: **So treat your Bible special: Bring it to church, read it—and hide it in your heart—memorize it. That way it can never be taken away from you.**

How Do You Treat Your Bible? [†]

Scripture References: Psalms 19:10; 119:11,72; Jeremiah 15:16; 36; Acts 17:11

Lesson Theme: We should love God's Word and handle our personal copies with care and respect.

Preparation: You will need the following Bibles or drawings of Bibles: (1) The abused Bible—one with torn pages, missing or loose cover, etc. (2) The defaced Bible—one with scribbling and drawings in it. (3) The neglected Bible—new, but dusty. (Powder will give a dusty look.) (4) The lost Bible—not there. (5) The well-worn Bible—good shape, but giving evidence of use. Place your Bibles or drawings on a nearby table. Then bring out the Talking Bible.

INTERVIEWER: I understand you have something special for us today, Bible.

BIBLE: **Yes, I brought some of my relatives with me.**

INTERVIEWER: Your relatives? *(Glances at Bibles on table.)* Oh, you mean these other Bibles? Who owns them?

BIBLE: **Different children.**

INTERVIEWER *(Picking up abused Bible and holding it so children can see it)*: Oh, look at this poor, abused Bible! It's all torn. What happened to it?

BIBLE: **Its owner sat on it, tossed it into the air, and even hit another child on the head with it.**

---

*From *Fox's Book of Martyrs* (Grand Rapids: Zondervan Publishing House, 1978), p. 29.

†Published May/June, 1988, *Evangelizing Today's Child*

TALKING BIBLE TEACHES ABOUT THE BIBLE *(continued)*

INTERVIEWER: I think this Bible's owner must have been very careless in turning the pages, too; many of them are torn. How sad that its owner treats it like this! It's not an ordinary book.

BIBLE: **That's right, for God wrote it.**

INTERVIEWER: I remember a Bible story about the apostle Paul as he was taking the good news about Jesus to the Jews who lived in many of the Roman cities outside of Israel. The Jews in Thessalonica rioted over what he said, without checking their Old Testaments. But the Jews in Berea "were better than the Jews of Thessalonica. They were eager to hear the things Paul and Silas said. These Jews in Berea studied the Scriptures every day to find out if these things were true" —Acts 17:11.

BIBLE: **It makes me feel good to get used like that!**

INTERVIEWER: Yes, I can understand why. We hope all the children will be like the Berean Jews. How should the children feel about their own Bibles?

BIBLE: **The psalmist declared, "Your teachings are worth more to me than thousands of pieces of gold and silver"—Psalm 119:72.**

INTERVIEWER: They will never abuse their Bibles if they really love them. *(Picks up the defaced Bible.)* What's the story about this relative of yours, Mister Bible?

BIBLE: **Look inside on some of the pages.**

INTERVIEWER *(finding a page with scribbling and showing this to class)*: Uh, oh. Look at this, boys and girls. This Bible has scribbling in it, and pictures have been drawn in it. It looks terrible! Should we ever write in a Bible?

BIBLE: **Taking notes is fine.**

INTERVIEWER: Yes. It's good to write down things that will help us remember the meaning of verses. But we should never use the pages of the Bible like an art tablet. A Bible should be very special to us.

BIBLE: **It is "worth more than gold, even the purest gold"—Psalm 19:10.**

INTERVIEWER: Oh, we would take very good care of something made of gold. But God's Word is worth MORE than gold. *(Picks up neglected Bible.)* Here's a nice, new-looking Bible. But look—it's very dusty. *(Blows some dust off cover.)*

BIBLE: **That's my neglected cousin. The child who owns that Bible forgets to read it, and it stays on the shelf until it's all dusty.**

INTERVIEWER: Oh, that's too bad! We need to read God's Word every day.

BIBLE: **Yes. The psalmist wrote, "I have hidden your word in my heart that I might not sin against you" —Psalm 119:11.**

INTERVIEWER: You know, if this child would keep his Bible free from dust by reading it every day, his life would be cleaner, too.

BIBLE: **My next relative is missing.**

INTERVIEWER: Missing?

BIBLE: **Yes, its owner lost it. She always puts it down just any place. Now she can't find it at all.**

INTERVIEWER: She should have had a special place to keep her Bible. Then it would have been right there when she wanted it. . . . What was it that Jeremiah said about you, Mister Bible?

BIBLE: **"Your words came to me, and I listened carefully to them. Your words made me very happy" —Jeremiah 15:16.**

INTERVIEWER: I don't think Jeremiah would have been careless with his copy of God's Word, do you? *(Picks up well-read Bible.)* What's wrong with this cousin of yours, Mister Bible? It looks rather worn.

BIBLE: **Nothing is wrong. Its owner loves it and reads it every day.**

INTERVIEWER: I see. It's been well-cared for, but it's been used a lot. I believe this Bible is really loved.

BIBLE: **I hope these children will love my relatives that they own.**

INTERVIEWER *(laying down Talking Bible)*: Boys and girls, what does your Bible show about your love for God's Word? Which Bible would you like yours to look like? The last one, right? *(Discuss ways the children can show their respect and love for their Bibles.)*

What Is the Bible Like?

Scripture References: Job 23:12; Psalms 119:2,9,105, 130; 126:6; Jeremiah 23:29; Zechariah 7:11-12; Luke 8:11; Ephesians 5:26; 6:17; James 1:23-25; 4:7; 1 Peter 2:2

Lesson Theme: God's Word supplies many of our needs, if we'll read and obey it.

Preparation: Bring to class the following objects or pictures of them: a mirror, a hammer, a glass of water, milk, a plastic sword, a packet of seeds, and a lamp. Ask seven children to hold these objects and line up in front of the class. The children can read their parts without practice, or you can give the children a copy of what they'll say so they can memorize it ahead of time. Practice the dialogue with the children before you present it to the rest of the class.

INTERVIEWER: Today some of our children are going to ask our Talking Bible some questions. *(Name of child)*, what question would you like to ask the Talking Bible?

CHILD NO. 1 *(holding the mirror toward audience)*: Mister Bible, how are you like a mirror?

BIBLE: **James 1:23-24 says, "If you hear [God's] message and don't obey it, you are like people who stare at themselves in a mirror and forget what they look like as soon as they leave. . ." ***

CHILD NO. 1: What is the right way to use you as a mirror, Mister Bible?

*Contemporary English Version

TALKING BIBLE TEACHES ABOUT THE BIBLE *(continued)*

BIBLE: James 1:25 says, "You must never stop looking at the perfect law that sets you free. God will bless you in everything you do, if you listen and obey, and don't just hear and forget."*

CHILD NO. 2 *(holding the hammer)*: Mister Bible, why are you sometimes like a hammer?

BIBLE: Zechariah 7:11-12 says, "They refused to pay attention. They were stubborn and would not listen. They made their hearts as hard as rock. They would not listen to the teachings of the Lord." And Jeremiah 23:29 says, "My message is like a . . . hammer that smashes a rock!"

INTERVIEWER: People can have hearts as hard as rocks. They don't listen and obey God. But God's Word can break their stony hearts and help them to love God.

CHILD NO. 2: How can we keep our hearts from becoming as hard as rock, Mister Bible?

BIBLE: Psalm 119:2 says, "Happy are the people who keep his rules. They ask him for help with their whole heart." †

CHILD NO. 3 *(holding the glass of water)*: Mister Bible, how are you like water?

BIBLE: Ephesians 5:26 says, "Christ used the word to make the church clean by washing it with water."

INTERVIEWER: When we read the Bible and see how we've sinned we can tell God we're sorry. Then Jesus will wash our sins away. Through hearing God's Word and doing what it says, we are made clean.

CHILD NO. 3: How can we use you like water, Mister Bible?

BIBLE: Psalm 119:9 says, "How can a young person live a pure life? He can do it by obeying your word." †

CHILD NO. 4 *(holding milk)*: Mister Bible, why should we think of you as milk?

BIBLE: First Peter 2:2 says, "As newborn babies want milk, you should want [my] pure and simple teaching."

INTERVIEWER: Just as milk helps children grow physically strong, the Bible helps God's children grow spiritually strong.

CHILD NO. 4: Can we like reading your words as much as eating, Mister Bible?

BIBLE: Job 23:12 says, "I have treasured his words more than my food."

CHILD NO. 5 *(holding sword)*: Mister Bible, how are you like a sword?

BIBLE: Ephesians 6:17 says, "Take the sword of the Spirit—that sword is the teaching of God."

INTERVIEWER: God's Word is like a sword we can fight the devil with.

CHILD NO. 5: How can we use you as a sword, Mister Bible?

BIBLE: James 4:7 says, "Stand against the devil, and the devil will run away from you."

INTERVIEWER: If we have memorized verses from the Bible, we can say them when the devil tempts us, just as Jesus did. They help us resist the devil—that is, to say no to him.

CHILD NO. 6 *(holding the seed packet)*: Mister Bible, how are you like seed?

BIBLE: Luke 8:11 says, "The seed is God's teaching."

INTERVIEWER: Jesus told a story of a man who planted seeds. He said the seed was the Word of God. We are to receive God's seed in our hearts and let it grow. Also, we are to give the seed of God's Word to others.

CHILD NO. 7: How can we use you as seed, Bible?

BIBLE: Psalm 126:6 says, "Those who cry as they carry out the seeds will return singing and carrying bundles of grain."

INTERVIEWER: We can tell others about the message of God's love, and some people will become Christians and grow just like a beautiful plant that comes from a small seed. That will make us very happy.

CHILD NO. 7 *(holding the lamp)*: Mister Bible, how are you like a lamp?

BIBLE: Psalm 119:105 says, "Your word is like a lamp for my feet and a light for my way."

CHILD NO. 7: How can we use you as a lamp, Mister Bible?

BIBLE: Psalm 119:130 says, "The unfolding of your words gives light; it gives understanding to the simple."

INTERVIEWER: When we read and study God's Word, it enters into our minds and our lives, helping us to become more like God wants us to be. *(Holds up a Bible.)* Let's pay attention to our Bibles, so we can be growing Christians, pleasing the Lord and attracting others to Him.

The Talking Bible and the Gospel Bookmarks

This is a series of dialogues in which the interviewer asks questions and the Talking Bible quotes verses of Scripture for the answers while bookmarks are held up. See Part 2, chapter 12, for instructions for making the bookmarks.

Preparation: Before presenting a dialogue, place the suggested bookmarks in the middle of a Bible, with the ribbons hanging out. The Bible verses quoted by the ventriloquist must be exact, so have the words plainly visible on a lectern or table.

HEAVEN OR HELL

Scripture References: Matthew 13:42; John 14:2; 20:31; Revelation 20:15; 21:4,15,18,21,27

Lesson Theme: Teaches what heaven and hell are like according to Scripture and how children may be sure their names are written in the Lamb's Book of Life.

*Contemporary English Version

†*International Children's Bible*

TALKING BIBLE TEACHES ABOUT THE BIBLE *(continued)*

Preparation: Put the heaven bookmark and the hell bookmark in the middle of a Bible.

INTERVIEWER: I brought a most unusual Bible with me today. Instead of reading it, we will listen to it, because it will open its mouth and talk to us. First, what does the Bible say about why it was written?

BIBLE: **"So that you can believe that Jesus is the Christ, the Son of God. Then, by believing, you can have life through his name"—John 20:31.**

INTERVIEWER: Oh, look! I see some beautiful bookmarks in this Bible. *(Holds up a copy of the Bible with the bookmarks hanging out.)* Let's take them out and look at them. *(Removes and holds up the heaven bookmark.)* I like this bookmark. This makes us think of heaven. Tell us something about it, Mister Bible.

BIBLE: **"The city [of God] was made of pure gold, as pure as glass. . . . Each gate was made from a single pearl. The street for the city was made of pure gold. The gold was clear as glass"— Revelation 21:18,21.**

INTERVIEWER: Oh, how beautiful that will be! Will this city have homes to live in?

BIBLE: **Jesus said, in John 14:2, "There are many rooms in my Father's house. . . . I am going there to prepare a place for you."**

INTERVIEWER: Will there be any troubles or sadness in heaven?

BIBLE: **"He will wipe away every tear from their eyes. There will be no more death, sadness, crying, or pain"— Revelation 21:4.**

INTERVIEWER: Who will go to heaven?

BIBLE: **"Only those whose names are written in the Lamb's book of life . . ." —Revelation 21:27.**

INTERVIEWER: We hope all of us here have made sure our names are written down. *(Lays down heaven bookmark and removes and holds up hell bookmark.)* We don't like to think of this place, but it's necessary to know about it, so we won't go there. What should we know about hell? What is it like?

BIBLE: **Like a "blazing furnace. There," Jesus said, "people will cry and grind their teeth with pain" —Matthew 13:42.**

INTERVIEWER: Who will be in hell?

BIBLE: **"Anyone [whose] name was not found written in the book of life . . ."—Revelation 20:15.**

Interviewer *(lays down Bible and picks up both bookmarks)*: I want to tell you how you get your name written in the Lamb's Book of Life: You invite Jesus into your heart and life. You tell Him you are sorry for the wrong things you have done and you want His forgiveness. He will come in and your name will be written down in heaven. Then someday you will go to be with Him or He will come to get you. You don't want to miss that.

SIN

Scripture References: 1 Samuel 16:7; Jeremiah 17:9; Romans 3:23; 6:23; Revelation 20:15; 21:27

Lesson Theme: All people sin and deserve the punishment of death. Only because of Jesus can we go to heaven.

Preparation: Put the heaven bookmark, the hell bookmark, and the sinner's heart bookmark in the middle of a Bible.

INTERVIEWER: Let's look at the bookmarks in my Bible. *(Removes and holds up the heaven bookmark.)* We've seen this one before. Tell us again, Mister Bible, who will go to heaven?

BIBLE: **"Only those whose names are written in the Lamb's book of life will enter the city" —Revelation 21:27.**

INTERVIEWER *(removes and holds up hell bookmark)*: And this one reminds us of that awful place, the lake of fire. Who will go there?

BIBLE: **"If anyone's name was not found written in the book of life, he was thrown into the lake of fire" — Revelation 20:15.**

INTERVIEWER: Oh, how important it is to believe on the Lord Jesus as Savior, so your name will be in the Lamb's Book of Life! *(Removes and holds up sinner's heart bookmark.)* Here is a beautiful heart. I guess a person who has a heart like this would surely have his name in God's book.

BIBLE: **"God does not see the same way people see. People look at the outside of a person, but the Lord looks at the heart"— 1 Samuel 16:7.**

INTERVIEWER: Oh, we're looking on the outside! Maybe we'd better see what's inside. *(Turns heart over, revealing the stains.)* This heart is very stained, in spite of its beautiful side. What does this mean?

BIBLE: **"The heart is deceitful above all things, and beyond cure"— Jeremiah 17:9.**

INTERVIEWER: Oh, sin has stained this heart. How many of us have sinned?

BIBLE: **"All people have sinned and are not good enough for God's glory"—Romans 3:23.**

INTERVIEWER: What are the results of sinning?

BIBLE: **"When someone sins, he earns what sin pays— death"—Romans 6:23.**

INTERVIEWER *(puts down bookmark)*: Death is the pay that a sinner receives for sinning. This means to be in hell forever. None of us wants to go there. We want to go here *(holds up heaven bookmark)*, to God's beautiful home, heaven. When we trust Jesus to save us, He washes our sins away with His blood. Then we can know for sure we'll be in heaven some day.

TALKING BIBLE TEACHES ABOUT THE BIBLE *(continued)*

THE CROSS

Scripture References: 1 Corinthians 15:3-4; 2 Corinthians 5:21; 1 John 1:7; Revelation 1:5

Lesson Theme: Christ died on the Cross for the sins of all people and was resurrected and lives today to free people of their sins.

Preparation: Put the sinner's heart and the cross bookmark in the middle of a Bible.

INTERVIEWER *(removes and holds up clean side of sinner's heart bookmark)*: God doesn't see a sinner's heart like this is— beautiful on the outside. *(Turns heart over.)* He sees the darkness and stains. Like this, we can't go to heaven. What can we do to get our hearts clean?

BIBLE: "**The blood of Jesus, God's Son, is making us clean from every sin**"— 1 John 1:7.

INTERVIEWER *(lays down heart bookmark and removes and holds up cross bookmark)*: The cross reminds us of the death of Christ, when He shed His blood for our sins.

BIBLE: "**Christ died for our sins as the Scriptures say**"—1 Corinthians 15:3.

INTERVIEWER: Is Jesus dead now?

BIBLE: "**He was buried and was raised to life on the third day as the Scriptures say**"—1 Corinthians 15:4.

INTERVIEWER: Had Christ ever done anything wrong that He should die such a death?

BIBLE: "**Christ had no sin**"— 2 Corinthians 5:21.

INTERVIEWER: How can Jesus help our hearts stained with sin?

BIBLE: Jesus "**is the One who made us free from our sins with the blood of his death**"—Revelation 1:5.

INTERVIEWER: What a wonderful Savior! We're so glad God gave us the Bible so we can know about Him and His death for us on the Cross.

SALVATION

Scripture References: Psalm 38:18; 51:7; Mark 1:15; John 1:12; 1 John 1:7; 5:12

Lesson Theme: Because Jesus died on the Cross for our sins, we can be forgiven and have our stained hearts cleansed.

Preparation: Put the sinner's heart bookmark and the believer's clean heart bookmark in the middle of a Bible.

INTERVIEWER *(removes and holds up the sinner's heart, showing the clean side)*: Our Bible has taught us about our hearts. We would like to think that God sees them like this. But really He sees a sinner's heart like this *(turns heart around)*. God sees every stain from sin. What does the Bible say about how we can get the sins removed?

BIBLE: "**The blood of the death of Jesus, God's Son, is making us clean from every sin**"— 1 John 1:7.

INTERVIEWER: What must we do to have Jesus' blood clean our hearts?

BIBLE: "**Change your hearts and lives and believe the Good News!**"—Mark 1:15.

INTERVIEWER: How should we feel about our sins?

BIBLE: "**I am troubled by my sin**"— Psalm 38:18.

INTERVIEWER: So we must be very sorry we have sinned— sorry enough to turn away from it to God. What happens when we accept the forgiveness of Jesus?

BIBLE: "**Some people did accept him. They believed in him. To them he gave the right to become children of God**"—John 1:12.

INTERVIEWER: What will our hearts be like after we receive Him?

BIBLE: "**Take away my sin, and I will be clean. Wash me, and I will be whiter than snow**"—Psalm 51:7.

INTERVIEWER *(removes and holds up the clean heart bookmark)*: So it all depends on how we respond to Jesus.

BIBLE: "**Whoever has the Son has life. But the person who does not have the Son of God does not have life**"—1 John 5:12.

INTERVIEWER: Isn't it wonderful that God gave us His Word so that we can know how to have our sins forgiven? If we accept Jesus, as the Bible tells us to do, we know we'll be in heaven some day.

CHASING GLOOM AWAY

Scripture References: Philippians 4:8; 1 Thessalonians 4:16-18

Lesson Theme: We can change negative attitudes by being thankful and praising God for the gifts He gives us.

Puppets Used: Either mouth or hardhead puppets will work for this play.

Characters:
Chris (a boy or girl)
Parent (father or mother)
Doom and Gloom (any puppet)
Joy and Cheer (any puppet)
Jerry (a boy; could be a girl with a name change)
Maggie (a girl; could be a boy with a name change)

Costumes:
Doom and Gloom: a black mask across the eyes and dark gray or black cloth draped over the head and body
Joy and Cheer: bright yellow cloth draped over the head and body

Backdrops:
Inside house scene and an outdoor scene. (These are not absolutely necessary. See Part 2, chapter 7, for instructions for making them.)

Scene I: As the curtain opens we see the inside of the house. Parent is on stage.

PARENT *(calls):* Chris! Chris! Come here. You must take the garbage outside before the garbage truck comes. Chris!

CHRIS *(enters and speaks in a very grouchy tone):* **I'm missing my favorite TV show. Why do I ALWAYS have to be the one to take the garbage out? I HATE taking out the garbage.**

PARENT: It's one way you can help around here. You don't do that much, you know.

CHRIS: **But I do the dirtiest job there is—taking out the STINKING garbage.**

PARENT: My, aren't you the grouch this morning? Now get busy and take out the garbage.

CHRIS: **Oh, all right. I guess I have to. Stupid old stinking garbage.** *(He makes a move as though kicking the garbage can. For the sound effect, hit metal against metal.)* **OW! OW! Now that STUPID OLD CAN hurt my foot.** *(He hops around as though in pain.)* **OW!**

PARENT: I'm sorry you hurt your foot, Chris. But it's your fault. You kicked the can. I'm sure you're not hurt too much. I'll help you this time. Come on, let's hurry. *(They exit, leaning over as though carrying the can. Soon they return.)* Chris, you've been grumpy and grouchy too much lately. You're full of doom and gloom all the time.

CHRIS: **Who wouldn't be if they had MY life? All the time I have to help around the house, everybody picks on me, and nobody wants to play with me. STUPID old house to live in, STUPID old school to go to, STUPID old town** *(he exits, muttering to himself)***, stupid old kids that live here, stupid . . .**

(Curtain closes)

Scene II: The curtain opens to an outdoor scene. Chris enters, followed closely by Doom and Gloom.

CHRIS: **What a ROTTEN day! It looks like it's gonna rain, and there's NOTHIN' to do, and my FOOT hurts.**

DOOM AND GLOOM: Doom and Gloom, Doom and Gloom; When I'm around, it's like a tomb.

CHRIS *(Whirls around and sees Doom and Gloom for the first time.)* **YIKES! Who are YOU?**

DOOM AND GLOOM: I'm Doom and Gloom, at your service.

CHRIS: **You got the wrong guy. I didn't ask for your service. I got ENOUGH troubles without YOU hanging around.**

DOOM AND GLOOM: But you called . . . or at least your whining and complaining invited me.

CHRIS: **Hey, it's not MY fault I'm grouchy. You just oughta see how I get treated. NOBODY loves me. EVERYBODY hates me.**

DOOM AND GLOOM *(in a mocking tone):* Oh, goody, I know that song: Nobody loves me. Everybody hates me. I think I'll go eat worms.

CHRIS: **Yeah, well, why DON'T you! . . . Now BEAT it! Here comes Jerry. Maybe he'll play with me.**

JERRY *(enters and walks toward Chris):* Hi, Chris! Where are you going?

CHRIS: **No place. There's NO place to go and NOTHIN' to do in this STUPID old town.**

JERRY: Hey, there's nothing wrong with this town that shootin' a few baskets won't fix up. How about going to my house and shootin' some?

CHRIS: **No. You can shoot better than me. You'd make fun of me.**

JERRY: No, I wouldn't. Come on.

CHRIS: **I don't want to play basketball.**

JERRY: Well, let's go down to the park.

CHRIS: **Naw, it looks like rain.**

JERRY: How about riding bikes?

CHRIS: **No. Your bike's faster than my bike. You'd go off and leave me. There's NOTHING to do. NOTHING'S any fun.**

JERRY: Well, maybe you're right. But I think I'll go see Mike. He likes shootin' baskets, or goin' to the park, or ridin' bikes. *(He exits.)*

DOOM AND GLOOM: Doom and Gloom, Doom and Gloom; When I'm around, it's like a tomb.

CHASING GLOOM AWAY *(continued)*

CHRIS: **You're back!**

DOOM AND GLOOM: Ah, but I never left.

CHRIS: **You can leave now. You have my permission.**

DOOM AND GLOOM: But then you really would have no company.

CHRIS: **Oh, shut up! Hey, here comes Maggie. Maybe SHE'LL play with me.**

MAGGIE *(enters)*: Hi, Chris. Isn't it a pretty day?

CHRIS: **What's pretty about it? It looks like rain.**

MAGGIE: Well, my dad says we could use some rain. Oh, I think it's a happy, happy day. Jody's cat had kittens and I'm going to see them. Wanna come?

CHRIS: **Naw. I hurt my foot, and I had to take out the stupid garbage, and Jerry won't play with me, and I HATE a cloudy day. I HATE this stupid town, too.**

MAGGIE: Well, you probably wouldn't like to see the kittens, after all. See ya. *(She exits.)*

CHRIS *(yells)*: **Wait, Maggie. I want you to play with me.**

MAGGIE *(yells from offstage)*: No, thank you. I don't like the grouch game.

DOOM AND GLOOM: Oh, I do, I do, I do. See: Doom and Gloom, Doom and Gloom; When I'm around, it's like a tomb.

CHRIS: Hey, I'm TIRED of having you around me, Doom and Gloom. I think I'll ask my mother/father how I can get rid of you. *(They exit. Curtain closes.)*

Scene III: As the curtain opens we see the inside of the house. Parent is on stage.

CHRIS *(enters)*: **Mom/Dad, this is the AWFULLEST day. I had to take out the stupid garbage, and I hurt my foot, and NOBODY will play with me, and I think it's going to rain. And now I've got this Doom and Gloom character that follows me EVERYWHERE I go.**

PARENT: I told you that. Anybody that is as grouchy as you will soon have nothing but doom and gloom.

CHRIS: **Well, how can I get rid of him?**

PARENT: Try changing your attitude. Think about all the good things in your life and where all those good things come from. You can't be grateful and have doom and gloom at the same time.

CHRIS: **ME? Be grateful? For what? I've got nothing but misery in my life.**

PARENT: Think back to the beginning of your day. What happened first to make you so miserable?

CHRIS: **I had to take out the stupid garbage.**

PARENT: Thank God for garbage.

CHRIS: **WHAT! What's good about garbage?**

PARENT: Much of it comes from the scraps or the packaging of food that we eat. Did you know that some people have very little garbage like that?

CHRIS: **Oh, yeah? Well, let's go live there.**

PARENT: You wouldn't like it. You see, the people that have no food garbage are ones that have little or no food. They're starving. As a matter of fact, they could probably live fairly well on garbage like ours.

CHRIS: **Ohhh. . . so I should be thankful for garbage because it means God has given us food to eat?**

PARENT: Yes. And what about your hurt foot? You caused that yourself, but can you think of a reason to praise God for a hurt foot?

CHRIS: **I guess so. At least I got a foot.**

PARENT: That's right. And you could have hurt it worse than you did. And what about the rain you've been complaining about?

CHRIS: **Maggie's dad said we could use it. I think I'm catching on. I thank the Lord I've got a mom and dad that love me, and a house to live in, and good friends to play with, and** *(Doom and Gloom sneaks away and exits)* **I'm thankful for the rain because—**(he turns around) **hey, where's Doom and Gloom?**

PARENT: Doesn't like your company, I guess. And look who just walked in the door. *(Joy and Cheer enters.)*

CHRIS: **Now THIS is an improvement! Who are you?**

JOY AND CHEER: I'm Joy and Cheer. Joy and Cheer, Joy and Cheer; Just praise the Lord, and I'll appear.

PARENT: Of course, you can have Doom and Gloom back any time, Chris.

CHRIS: **Uh, I don't think so, Mom/Dad. He get's pretty boring after a while. I think I'll go over to Jerry's and see if he still wants to shoot some baskets.**

PARENT: With your hurt foot?

CHRIS: **It's feeling better all the time.**

JOY AND CHEER *(follows him off stage, chanting)*: Joy and Cheer, Joy and Cheer; Just praise the Lord, and I'll appear.

BABY MOSES

Scripture References: Exodus 2:1-10; Numbers 26:59; Hebrews 11:23

Lesson Theme: God protected the baby Moses from death and used him when he was a grown man to lead God's people to the Promised Land.

Puppets: Either mouth or hardhead puppets will work for this play.

Characters:
Amram (Moses' father)
Jochebed (Moses' mother)
Miriam (Moses' sister)
Princess (Pharoah's daughter)
Slave (a girl or woman)

Costumes:
Amram: a long tunic and turban-like hat
Jochebed and Miriam: a long tunic and a cloth draped over their heads and falling over their shoulders and backs
Princess: A wig of black yarn hair cut evenly to about chin-length (ancient Egyptian style), colorful robe, jewelry
Slave: a robe

Prop: A basket with a cloth draped over the sides. (Baby Moses is not seen.) Push the end of a small stick into the bottom center of the basket. When a puppet "carries" the basket, place it over her arm and hold the stick from beneath, keeping the bottom of the basket out of sight of the audience.

Backdrops: Inside the home of Moses' parents; outdoor scene of water and sky. (These are not absolutely necessary. See Part 2, chapter 7, for instructions for making them.)

Sound Effects: A baby's cry (can be recorded on a cassette tape)

NARRATOR: Let's go back in time—way back to when the people of Israel were living in Egypt. It was a very hard time for them because the king who had treated them well had died and a new king had arisen. This king, called Pharaoh, made slaves of the Israelites (or Hebrews). He worked them very hard and treated them cruelly. He was afraid the Hebrews would grow great in number and join his enemies in a war. So he made a law that all the baby boys who were born to the Hebrews must be thrown into the river. We'll see what it was like in those days as we look in on a Hebrew family.

Scene I: As the curtain opens we see the inside of a house. Jochebed and Miriam are on stage.

JOCHEBED: **Miriam, I must prepare our evening meal. If you hear the baby start to cry, let me know at once. We can't take a chance that an Egyptian soldier hears him.**

MIRIAM: All right, Mother. I will go and stay near the baby. *(She turns to exit but stops; she turns back.)* Oh, Mother, my little brother is such a dear, sweet baby. I am so glad you and Father did not throw him in the river as Pharaoh said to do.

JOCHEBED: **Throw him in the river? I could never have done that. But we must be very watchful, or the Egyptian soldiers will do it for us.** *(Miriam exits. Jochebed moves about stage as though cooking, when Amram enters.)*

AMRAM: Jochebed, how has it gone today? Is the baby safe?

JOCHEBED: **Yes, so far, Amram. But he is almost three months old now, and his cries are getting louder. I fear I cannot hide him much longer. Oh, what are we going to do?**

AMRAM: I am praying to God to show us. If only there was some way to make Pharaoh himself want to keep the babies alive.

JOCHEBED: **If only he could see our fine child—Oh, I just thought of something. The princess, Pharaoh's daughter, comes down to the river to bathe. I could put our baby in a little basket, and put him in the shallow water near the river bank, and—**

AMRAM: She'd see the baby. Yes, yes! I think you have it! Why, our little boy would touch her heart, and she wouldn't allow him to be killed.

JOCHEBED: **I must find the best papyrus basket and make it waterproof.**

AMRAM: Make sure it's sealed tight. No water must enter the basket.

JOCHEBED: **I will. And Miriam could hide and watch to see what will happen. Oh, I believe God is answering our prayers!** *(They exit.)*

(Curtain closes.)

Scene II: The curtain opens to an outdoor scene of a river. Jochebed and Miriam enter from the right. Miriam is carrying the basket.

JOCHEBED: **This looks like a good place. I will put the basket there among the reeds.** *(She turns, faces the river, and puts the basket down near the left rear.)* **You watch carefully, Miriam; I will return home to pray for God's protection for our baby Moses. Don't be afraid.**

MIRIAM: I'm not afraid. God will take care of me, too. *(Jochebed exits, right. Miriam follows, standing just in front of the right exit. After a moment the princess and her slave girl enter at left and go to center front. Miriam quickly exits right, and peers into stage. Then the baby cries.)*

PRINCESS: Why, what is that? It sounds like a baby crying.

SLAVE: I think it's coming from the river.

 (continued)

PRINCESS (*turns toward river*): Look! I see a basket. Hurry quickly and get it. (*Slave goes to the basket, stoops down, and picks it up. She brings it to the princess, who peers inside. The baby's cry continues through her speech.*) Oh, look—it's a beautiful baby! Poor little baby, don't cry. (*She looks up.*) This is one of the Hebrew babies.

SLAVE: What are you going to do with it?

PRINCESS: I'm going to keep it. No one shall kill this baby.

MIRIAM (*enters and goes to the princess*): Shall I go and get one of the Hebrew women to nurse him for you?

PRINCESS: Yes, go. (*Miriam exits right, and soon returns with her mother.*)

JOCHEBED: You wish someone to nurse this baby?

PRINCESS: Yes. Will you do it?

JOCHEBED: I will be happy to take care of him.

PRINCESS: Then take him and nurse him, and I will pay you. (*Jochebed takes the basket. She and Miriam exit right and the princess and slave girl exit left.*)

(*Curtain closes.*)

NARRATOR: And so it was that not only was the baby safe, but his very own mother was allowed to care for him—and was paid to do the job! When the child grew older, Jochebed took him to Pharaoh's daughter, who named him Moses, saying, "I drew him out of the water." Moses grew up as the grandson of the very king who had wanted to destroy him. Later he became the great leader of Israel who led them out of Egypt, through the desert, and to the very borders of their homeland, Canaan. Just before his death, Moses told the Israelites: "The everlasting God is your place of safety. His arms will hold you up forever" —Deuteronomy 33:27. Those everlasting arms carried Moses all the way from the basket in the bulrushes, throughout his great life, and into God's presence at death.

SIR STUMPY

Scripture References: Genesis 3:1-6; Luke 15:11-32; 1 John 1:9

Lesson Theme: We should confess our sins to God and He will freely forgive us, just as the father forgave his prodigal son.

Puppets Used: Either mouth or hardhead puppets will work for this play.

Characters:
King (a man)
Prince Downfall (a boy)
Fruit Lady (an old woman or old man)
Impy (a villainous man or woman)
Princess Lawkeeper (a young woman)
Queen Goodygood (a woman)
King's Messenger (a boy or a girl)
Sir Stumpy (a scarecrow; see Part 2, chapter 11, for instructions for making a scarecrow)

Costumes: English royalty, eighteenth century

Props:
golden fruit
two small bottles
a small open book
a recording of horses hoofs

Backdrop: an outdoor scene or a plain backdrop (These are not absolutely necessary. See Part 2, chapter 7, for instructions for making them.)

Scene I: The curtain opens on an outdoor scene. The king and prince enter from the right. The king stands at left front; prince at right.

KING: Here we are, my son—outside the palace walls. Are you sure you want to go alone?

PRINCE: **Yes, Father. You promised that some day you'd let me go by myself to meet the people in our realm.**

KING: That's right. But I'm not sure you're old enough yet.

PRINCE: **Oh, I'm getting very big and strong. I'm old enough.**

KING: Perhaps so. But there's one rule you must always obey if I let you go.

PRINCE: **Tell me what it is.**

KING: You must never, never eat the golden fruit. It's the one way you can be harmed by our enemy, Impy. No matter who offers it to you, do not eat the golden fruit.

PRINCE: **I'll have no trouble remembering that. No matter who offers it to me, I will not eat the golden fruit.**

KING: Then you have my blessings, Prince Downfall. Meet the people. Let them get to know their prince. And may you always act like the son of a king. *(King exits left.)*

PRINCE: **HOORAY! On my own at last! I want to tell everyone I meet that I'm their prince.** *(Looks toward left rear.)* **Oh, I see someone coming.**

FRUIT LADY *(enters, carrying fruit)*: Fruit for sale! Beautiful, beautiful fruit for sale! Who will buy an old lady's fruit? *(Walks toward prince.)* Will you buy my fruit, my fine young man?

PRINCE *(proudly)*: **I am Prince Downfall, ma'am. Let me see your fruit.** *(Looks at fruit.)* **Why, you have golden fruit. I must not eat that. But your prince will be kind to you. I'll pay for the fruit.** *(He pretends to hand her money.)*

FRUIT LADY: I'm not asking for charity, Prince Downfall. You must take the fruit you paid for. Here you are. *(Hands fruit to prince and quickly exits left.)*

PRINCE *(calls)*: **But I don't want. . . . Oh, she's gone. Now what shall I do with this fruit?** *(Looks down at the fruit, not seeing Impy sneaking in from left.)*

IMPY: My, what beautiful fruit! Do you know that's the most delicious fruit in the whole world?

PRINCE *(looks up startled)*: **Oh, you startled me. Say, do you want this fruit? I'm Prince Down—**

IMPY *(interrupts)*: I know who you are. But you must eat that fruit yourself. You're a lucky boy to have such beautiful fruit.

PRINCE: **It IS beautiful. But Father warned me not to eat the golden fruit.**

IMPY: Ah, my prince, you're indeed a splendid fellow for wanting to obey your father. But surely he would want you to have the fruit—if he loves you, that is. Just take a little taste. You'll see it's all right.

PRINCE: **Well . . . uh. Are you sure it's all right?**

IMPY: Why, I'm your good friend. Would I mislead my prince?

PRINCE: **No, of course you wouldn't. I'll just take a little taste.** *(Tastes fruit and falls down. After pause scarecrow rises in his place.)*

SCARECROW *(Speaks in monotone throughout)*: What—has—happened? Who—am—I?

IMPY *(laughs gleefully)*: Hee, hee, hee! You've become a scarecrow, my prince. You'll never forget me, will you? *(Scarecrow hops around.)* I'll give you a name. Hmm—what shall it be? I know—Sir Stumpy will be your name, because of the way you stump along. Sir Stumpy it is! Hee, hee! Sir Stumpy! *(Exits left.)*

SIR STUMPY: **Oh—that—was—the—enemy—Impy. I—listened—to—him—and—ate—the—golden—fruit. Now—I'm—a—scarecrow. I'm—just—the—same—as—dead. What—shall—I—do? I—can't—go—back—to—my—father—like—this.** *(Hops back and forth across stage front. Sound of horse's hoofs is heard.)*

PRINCESS LAWKEEPER *(speaks offstage)*: Whoa, whoa! *(Horse's hoofs stop.)* Oh, I see someone in trouble. I'll get down off my horse and go to help him. *(Enters left after short pause carrying bottle.)*

SIR STUMPY: **Oh—kind—princess—can—you—help—me? I—am—Sir—Stumpy—the—Scarecrow—but—I—was—Prince—Downfall. Can—you—make—me—a—boy—again—so—I—can—go—back—to—my—father?**

SIR STUMPY *(continued)*

PRINCESS LAWKEEPER: Of course I can help you. My name is Princess Lawkeeper. I have a special drink for you. It will help you keep the law, and so you'll be changed. *(Puts bottle to Stumpy's lips.)* Drink it, Sir Stumpy. *(He drinks and she exits, left.)*

SIR STUMPY *(calls)*: **Wait—Princess—Lawkeeper—I— am—not—changed.** *(Sound of horse's hoofs fades away.)* **Oh—she's—gone. She—was—wrong. The—law— did—not—help—me.** *(Impy pops up from below.)*

IMPY: Hee, hee, hee! What's the matter, Sir Stumpy? Having trouble? Hee, hee, hee! *(Drops down. Sound of horse's hoofs.)*

QUEEN Goodygood *(calls offstage)*: Stop the carriage! Stop the carriage! *(Horse's hoofs stop.)* There's the poor fellow I've come to help.

SIR STUMPY: **Oh—maybe—this—person—can—help— me.**

QUEEN Goodygood *(enters at left, carrying a bottle)*: Ah, I've found you! I live in the land of the Do Goods. My name is Queen Goodygood. Here's something for you to drink that will help you be kind and good. Then you'll change to a boy again. *(Puts bottle to Stumpy's lips.)* Drink it all, Sir Stumpy. *(She exits left. Sound of horse's hoofs fading away.)*

SIR STUMPY *(calls)*: **Come—back—Queen—Goodygood. I'm—not—changing. Oh—she—was—wrong—too.** *(Impy pops up.)*

IMPY: You'll never change, Sir Stumpy. There's no use to try. You'll be Sir Stumpy forever. Hee, hee, hee *(drops down)*.

SIR STUMPY: **Oh—what—can—I—do? Can—no—one— help—me?** *(King's messenger enters from left carrying an open book.)*

MESSENGER: Would you like my help, Sir Stumpy? I'm the king's messenger.

SIR STUMPY: **Could—you—really—help? The—others— could—not.**

MESSENGER: Yes, if you'll do what my book says. It's never wrong. It was written by your father.

SIR STUMPY: **Please—tell—me—what—it—says.**

MESSENGER: The book says you must go back to your father as you are. Ask him to forgive you. He will change you.

SIR STUMPY: **I—can't—go—back—like—this. I'm—too— ashamed. I—must—change—first.**

MESSENGER: You can never change yourself. Go to your father now, as you are. Tell him you have done wrong by eating the fruit. Believe him to change you.

SIR STUMPY: **I'll—do—it. I'm—not—worthy—to—be— his—son—but maybe—I—could—be—his—servant.** *(They exit, right, with Stumpy hopping along.)*

(Curtain closes.)

Scene II: The curtain opens and the king enters from the left, looking toward right rear. Then Sir Stumpy hops in at right.

SIR STUMPY: **Oh—Your—Highness—I—was—coming— to—you.**

KING: I knew you were coming. I could not wait to see you, so I came to meet you.

SIR STUMPY: **I—ate—the—golden—fruit. I—have— sinned. Do—you—forgive—me?**

KING: I forgive you freely! And now I change you to a boy again and make you my son again. *(Scarecrow falls down and prince arises.)*

PRINCE: **Father, Father, thank you! I am alive again!**

KING: I'll tell the servants to get the best robe for you. They'll put a ring on your finger and shoes on your feet. We'll prepare a feast and be merry.

PRINCE: **Oh, how happy I am, Father!**

KING: My son, you were dead, and you're alive again. You were lost, and now you're found. I shall give you a new name, Prince New-Man, for you've been born again.

PRINCE: **Oh, I shall always try to obey you now, Father, for I shall never forget what it was like to be Sir Stumpy.** *(They exit.)*

Application

Who does the king in this story remind you of? He's a lot like the father in the story of the Prodigal Son, who makes us think of God.

When God created Adam and Eve and put them in the Garden of Eden, what one thing did he tell them they could not do? They were not to eat of the fruit of the tree of the knowledge of good and evil. But just like Prince Downfall, who disobeyed his father and ate the golden fruit, Adam and Eve ate the very fruit God told them not to. They sinned. Adam and Eve's sin affected the whole human race. We are all born sinners. And we all sin on our own too.

Who in the story we just saw tried to help Sir Stumpy turn back into a boy? Princess Lawkeeper and Queen Goodygood gave him something but it didn't help. We can't get rid of our sin by following rules or by being good.

How did Sir Stumpy become a prince again? He had to return to his father just the way he was and tell his father he disobeyed. What happened then? His father forgave him for disobeying. How do we get rid of our sin? We must go to God, our Heavenly Father, and tell him that we've done wrong. Then He forgives us and makes us as clean as new snow. *(Give a personal invitation to any children who would like to ask God to forgive their sins.)*

Resources for Puppetry and Ventriloquism

Detweiler, Clinton. *Ventriloquism in a Nutshell.* Littleton, Colo.: Maher Ventriloquist Studios, 1974.
The basics of ventriloquism with exercises and script segments.

Engler, Larry and Carol Fijan. *Making Puppets Come Alive: A Method of Learning and Teaching Hand Puppetry.* New York: Taplinger Publishing Co., Inc., 1980.

Gilbertson, Irvy. *More Practical Puppet Plays.* Springfield, Mo.: Gospel Publishing House, 1980.
Scripts based on biblical principles: eight skits for two- to six-year-olds and nine skits for six- to twelve-year-olds.

Gilbertson, Irvy. *Practical Puppet Plays.* Springfield, Mo.: Gospel Publishing House, 1977.
Scripts based on biblical principles and stories: six skits for two- to six-year-olds, eleven skits for six- to twelve-year-olds.

Gilbertson, Irvy. *Puppet Plays for Missionettes..* Springfield, Mo.: Gospel Publishing House, 1982.
Eighteen scripts based on biblical principles, specifically designed for girls (but easily adaptable for a mixed audience.)

Harp, Grace. *Handbook of Christian Puppetry.* Denver: Accent Books, 1984.
Making, staging, manipulating, coordinating, and using puppets effectively in the classroom.

Marsh, Fredda. *Putting It All Together in a Puppet Ministry.* Springfield, Mo.: Gospel Publishing House, 1978.
Basics of puppetry, instructions for making puppets and stages, twenty puppet skits based on biblical stories and principles.

Pearson, Mary Rose. *Fifty-two Children's Programs for Church Time.* Denver: Accent Books, 1985.
Fifty-two Bible lessons with fifteen puppet plays and twelve dialogues (for puppeteer or ventriloquist) to illustrate the lessons.

Pearson, Mary Rose. *More Children's Church Time.* Denver: Accent Books, 1982.
Twenty-six Bible lessons with fifty-two puppet plays to illustrate the lessons.

Schindler, George. *Ventriloquism: Magic with Your Voice.* New York: David McKay Co., Inc., 1986.
Details for becoming a ventriloquist.

VonSeggen, Dale and Liz VonSeggen. *Puppets: Ministry Magic.* Loveland, Colo.: Group Books, 1990.
Instructions for organizing and directing a teenage puppet team. Nine puppet scripts: some for children, some for teenagers and adults.

VonSeggen, Dale and Liz VonSeggen. *Reaching and Teaching with Puppets.* Videocassette. Order from One Way Street, Inc., Box 2398, Littleton, Colo. 80161.
Ninety-minute video covers training puppeteers and developing a puppet ministry. Has several performance segments.

Warner, Diane. *Puppets Help Teach.* Denver: Accent Books, 1975.
Twenty-six scripts for younger children based on Bible stories, biblical principles, special occasions, and holidays.

Zabriskie, Pat. *Pointing the Way with Puppets.* Springfield, Mo.: Gospel Publishing House, 1981.
Twelve scripts teaching the importance and principles of the Bible, and a feature-length Christmas script.

Zabriskie, Pat. *The Puppet People.* Springfield, Mo.: Gospel Publishing House, 1979.
Seventeen puppet scripts based on biblical principles.

Patterns and Ready-made Puppets

Puppets (many come with audiocassettes of skits and script books)
Gospel Publishing House
1445 Boonville Avenue
Springfield, Mo. 65802-1894
(request a general catalog)

Puppets and Scripts
Bible True Audio Visuals
1441 S. Busse Road
Mt. Prospect, Ill. 60056

PVC Pipe Stage Patterns:
The Son Shine Puppet Co.
P.O. Box 6203
Rockford, Ill. 61111
("Pipe & Curtain Puppet Stage Plans" by Glenda Hoyle)

Organizations for Puppeteers and Ventriloquists

Fellowship of Christian Magicians
Box 1027
Wheaton, Ill. 60189-1027

Fellowship of Christian Puppeteers
F.C.P. Mail Center
P.O. Box 4361
Englewood, Colo. 80155

North American Association of Ventriloquists
Box 420
Littleton, Colo. 80160

Scripture References for Part Three

OLD TESTAMENT

NEW TESTAMENT

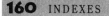

Lesson Themes for Part Three

Subject Index